IMAGES of America
THE PORTLAND COMPANY
1846–1982

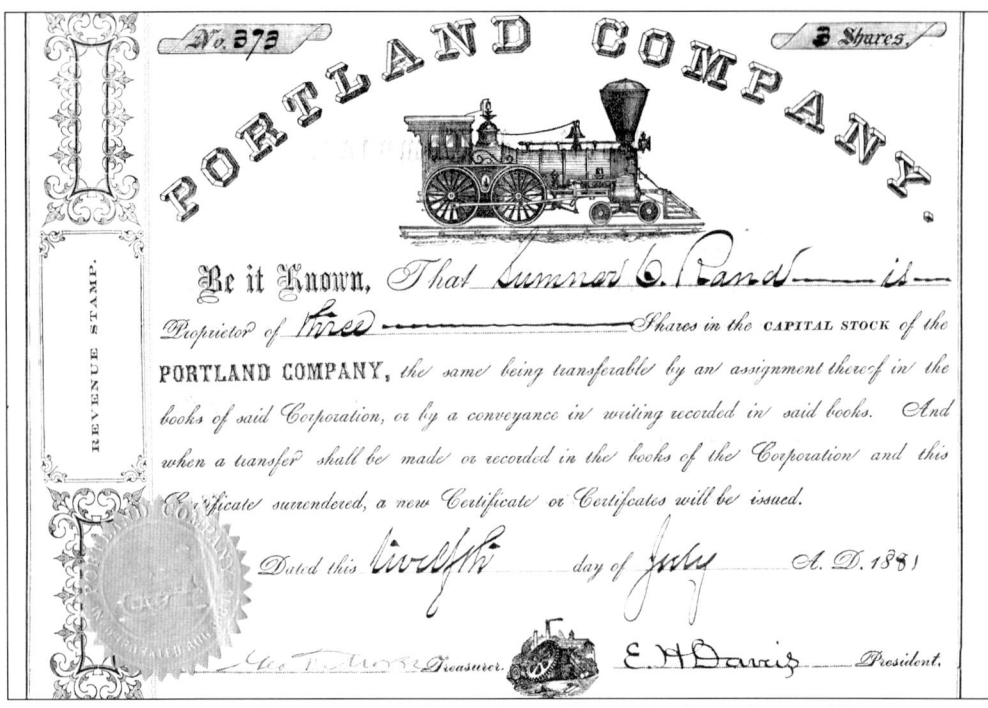

Shown here is a Portland Company stock certificate of 1881 for three shares sold to Sumner C. Rand. The certificate is signed by George F. Morse, the treasurer, and by E.H. Davis, who was the president of the Portland Company at the time. These stock sales were to raise badly needed capital for expansion and equipping the complex to keep up with the growing manufacturing needs.

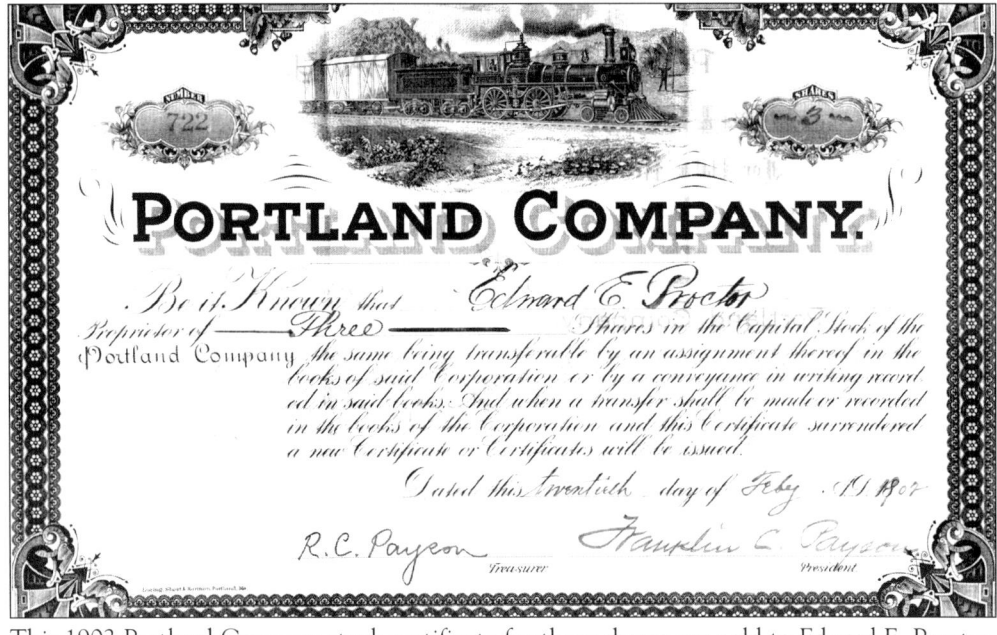

This 1902 Portland Company stock certificate for three shares was sold to Edward E. Proctor. The certificate is signed by Richard Payson, the company treasurer, and by Franklin C. Payson, who was the president of the Portland Company.

IMAGES of America
THE PORTLAND COMPANY
1846–1982

David H. Fletcher

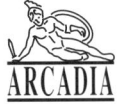

Copyright © 2002 by David H. Fletcher.
ISBN 0-7385-1140-4

First printed in 2002.

Published by Arcadia Publishing,
an imprint of Tempus Publishing, Inc.
2A Cumberland Street
Charleston, SC 29401

Printed in Great Britain.

Library of Congress Catalog Card Number: 2002111015

For all general information contact Arcadia Publishing at:
Telephone 843-853-2070
Fax 843-853-0044
E-Mail sales@arcadiapublishing.com

For customer service and orders:
Toll-Free 1-888-313-2665

Visit us on the internet at http://www.arcadiapublishing.com

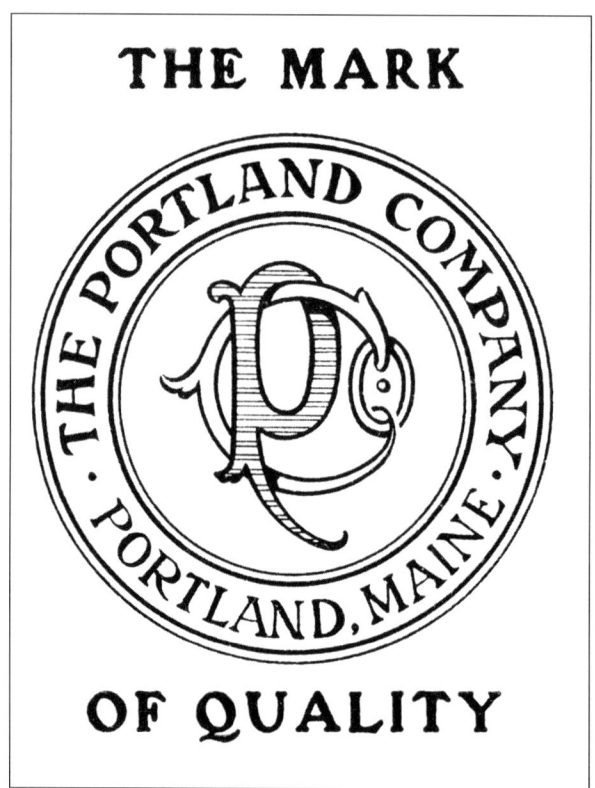

This photograph illustrates only one of the many Portland Company logos used on cast products and in company advertisements. The logos varied over the years and differed for various products and uses. The "PCo." logo was also cast in iron and graced the doors of large industrial boilers.

Contents

Acknowledgments 6

Introduction 7

1. Portland Company Facilities and Employees 9

2. Railroad Locomotives, Rolling Stock, and Parts 23

3. Vessels, Marine Engines, and Boilers 45

4. Automobiles and Trucks 75

5. Elevators 87

6. Fire Engines 91

7. Paper Mill Equipment 97

8. Lighthouses, Snowplows, and Other Products 103

ACKNOWLEDGMENTS

I would like to thank all of the dedicated staff at the Maine Historical Society for running boxes of documents back and forth for me hundreds of times, for helping me with images, and for their overwhelming encouragement to take on this project and see it accomplished.

Also, I would like to thank the Portland Fire Department for use of its Portland Company fire engine photographs for the chapter on fire engines and especially Michael A. Daicy, the department's fire historian.

This work is dedicated to the many hardworking Portland Company employees who labored long hours to produce sometimes things of beauty, as well as useful things, such as the steam-powered locomotives that live and breathe steam and fire and instill wonder in the hearts of all children from ages 1 to 101. Most of them were from the 1800s and have long since departed this earth, but I especially want to thank the draftsmen, whom I have come to know intimately although only through their wonderful, and many times very artful, engineering drawings with their abundant fingerprints on all manner of Portland Company paper documents in this collection at the Maine Historical Society. Sometimes I get to glimpse a face but sorrowfully will never be privileged to attach a name to it.

I also want to dedicate this volume to my only son, Jason D. Fletcher, for all the years of traveling with me to railroad "anythings" and letting me share with him my love of steam-powered trains.

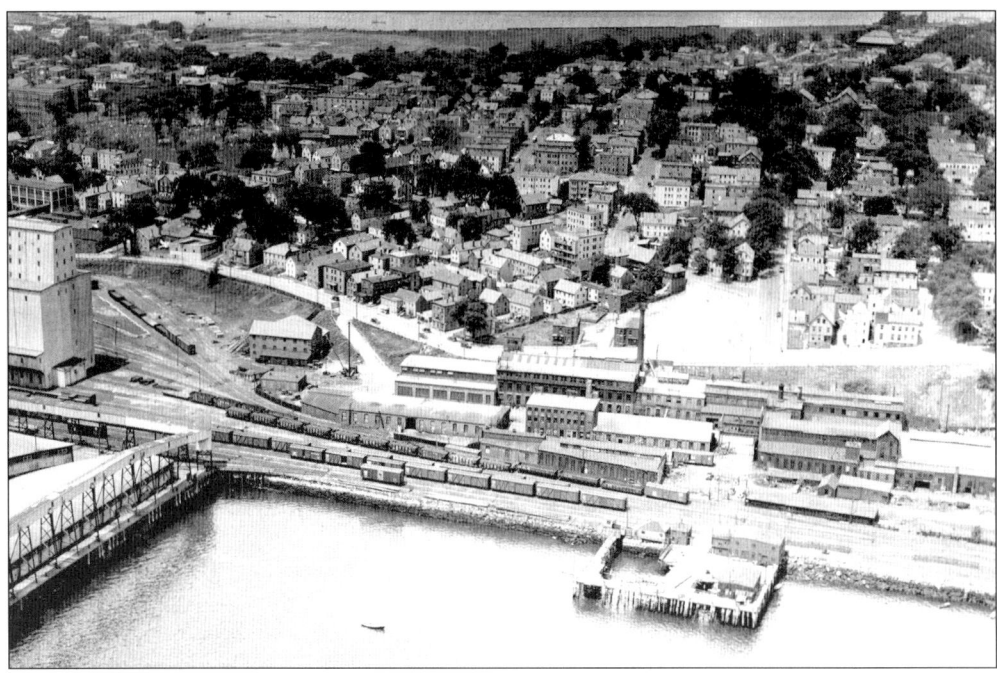

This superb aerial photograph of the Portland Company complex was taken from over Portland Harbor c. 1938. In the foreground we can see the company pier, where equipment was installed in over 400 vessels. The Grand Trunk Railroad went though the company property to its stations, yard, and grain elevators, seen here on the left. Also there were several piers for freighters to dock alongside to load and unload cargo to and from the freight cars that were pushed out onto the various piers.

Introduction

The Portland Company was founded in 1845 at 58 Fore Street, on 10 acres of filled land on the waterfront, as the Portland Iron Manufacturing Company under the leadership of the first president, John A. Poor. Later, in 1846, the name was changed to the Portland Company, and it remained under that name until the operation ceased in 1982.

The company was founded primarily to meet the needs of the industrial age and to build steam railroad locomotives for the newly formed Atlantic & St. Lawrence Railroad. The company was convenient to the railroad, as the main line of this railroad ran between the shop buildings and the waterfront and down Commercial Street. The railroads right-of-way was also on filled land from the foot of Eastern Promenade, where it came off a trestle from the northeast and down along the piers to the south end of Portland.

The first locomotive, the *Augusta*, came from the new shops in 1848 and was manufactured for the Portland, Saco & Portsmouth Railroad. For the next 60 years, the shops turned out a total of 630 steam locomotives in at least five different gauges, the bulk of which were built before 1900. The company built locomotives for Boston & Maine, Maine Central, Northern Pacific, Panama Railroad, Mexican Central, Sandy River, Wiscasset and Quebec, Portland & Rochester, the Intercolonial in Canada, and many others. The Portland Company was the only locomotive works in the country to be founded primarily to produce locomotives, as most of the other builders started off as machine shops. Besides locomotives, the company built hundreds of freight and passenger cars, heavy snowplows, and even Leslie rotary snowplows under contract from that company.

One oddity produced in 1889 was a pair of monorail steam engines for the Boynton Bicycle Railway in New York. The Portland Company's first engine was an 0-1-1-1, having a 93-inch-diameter double-flanged driver and a double-decked cab, with the engineer standing above the fireman. The engine was only 4 feet wide so it could pass another similar train on already existing two-rail tracks. The passenger car built at the Portland Company to be pulled behind held 108 persons and was 14 feet high and 4 feet wide, with seats entered from the outside doors of each compartment. This railroad equipment was planned to be used all over the world but never gained much acceptance.

Just about everything needed to manufacture a locomotive, including boilers, valves, wheels, frames, and wood cabs, was built in the company shops. The Maine Narrow Gauge Railroad & Museum operates currently out of the old electrical shop and is operating two-foot-gauge steam locomotives along one mile of the waterfront of Casco Bay.

The Portland Company had a full complement of the necessary shops as well as two foundries to pour both iron and bronze castings. About every 20 years, as its needs grew, the company built new shops and redesigned and reequipped the old shops. The company was one of the largest employers in the state of Maine, employing several hundred workers, therefore significantly impacting the local and state economies.

The earliest steam locomotives were built to burn wood, as can be seen by their large bulbous stacks for trapping live cinders to keep from setting the landscape ablaze as they went speeding along at alarming speeds of sometimes over 100 miles per hour. This would have been a most terrifying speed in the mid-to-late 1800s, when people were used to traveling by horse. Many locomotives were shipped overland on the rails, but a large number of them were lashed to the decks of ships and went around the Horn to the West Coast. Before 1880, most locomotives and cars were very highly decorated on the outside with bright colors and gold and silver designs. Some even had vignettes painted on them. However, after coal was introduced as the primary engine fuel, with all its oily soot, the colors used became darker and more subdued, and the designs faded into artful line decorations.

Along with locomotive construction, the company built steam engines for industrial and marine uses. It built boilers and engines for over 350 vessels. The Portland Company even built some vessels from the keel up at its boatyards just across the harbor in South Portland. When a vessel was launched, it would be towed to the Portland Company pier for outfitting and the installation of all of the necessary equipment. The types of vessels outfitted included towboats (tugs), fishing vessels, yachts, dredges, freighters, fireboats, and ferries. Among the more notable vessels equipped were the great side-wheeled passenger steamers, built in the late 1800s in Bath, Maine, such as the *Portland, State of Maine, Cumberland,* and *Bay State*.

Two notable vessels built in Portland for the government's use in the Civil War were the gunboats *Agawam* and *Pontoosic,* and several locomotives and some cannon were also manufactured for the Union's effort in the war. During both world wars, the company produced munitions and aircraft parts, with women working in most of the shops when the men were called away to serve.

In 1859, J.B. Johnson came from Boston to build steam-powered horse-drawn fire engines. The first engine (produced in 1859) was the *Greyhound*. The Portland Fire Department over the years purchased several fire engines from the firm, and the Portland Company engines served the firefighters well during the Great Fire in Portland on July 4, 1866.

Elevators of both passenger and freight designs were manufactured and installed in multistory buildings all across America. The first elevators were hydraulically powered, and electrically powered elevators were produced a few years later. There are still some Portland Company–manufactured elevators in use today in Portland and other cities. Most of the elevator cars were built of solid oak with an iron-and-steel reinforcing framework.

The Portland Company built all manner of special equipment for the paper industry, including pulp digesters, boilers, tanks, steam accumulators, chippers and debarkers, vomit stacks, turbines, penstocks, water-control gates, and gate-hoisting equipment. Several of these mills equipped a century ago are still in operation in Maine today.

In 1908, the Portland Company started selling new Knox automobiles and trucks and became the exclusive distributor of this expensive automobile that was manufactured in Springfield, Massachusetts, and driven to Portland even during the winter months. Knox fire trucks were a favorite with many fire departments in the United States and abroad, and the Knox-Martin three-wheeled tractor was one of the first tractors to pull a trailer. It was popular to replace the horses on the large heavy fire engines of the late 19th century. In 1910, the Portland Company took on the Brush, Cole, and Thomas automobile lines to appeal to the middle and lower income buyers. The company was a very active participant in the Portland automobile show each February. It also operated an automobile and truck repair garage on the company premises. The garage also fitted Sargent snowplows on heavy trucks and tracked vehicles.

An inventor by the name of Chapman patented a device called an "electric neutralizing machine," which neutralizes the heavy static charges that can be produced in paper and textile mills, causing problems with production.

Another invention was the Thomes core box machine by Frank E. Thomes to saw and shape the wooden patterns and pattern core boxes for the castings. Before this ingenious machine was developed, most pattern work was done by hand sawing and carving. The various models of this machine were sold all over the world.

In later years, the company produced barrel-washing machines, inside rotary welders, and plastic bottle extruding and forming machines under the Portco name. Also, the company produced a neutron reactor shell for the Rowe, Massachusetts atomic electric generating plant. Decorative and architectural castings were made for buildings, including lighthouse parts, streetlights, gates, and grates. Overall, the Portland Company produced about any metal article needed in the fast-growing industrial age.

The Portland Company Collection of more than 25,000 documents held by the Maine Historical Society is certainly a clear window into the state's industrial past. The thousands of original engineering drawings and the more than 2,500 period photographs from which this book was illustrated are most fascinating. Most of the artifacts can be reproduced, for purchase by the public, for a fee by contacting the society at 489 Congress Street in Portland, Maine, 04101. The society can also be reached at 207-774-1822 or at rdesk@mainehistory.org.

One
PORTLAND COMPANY
FACILITIES AND EMPLOYEES

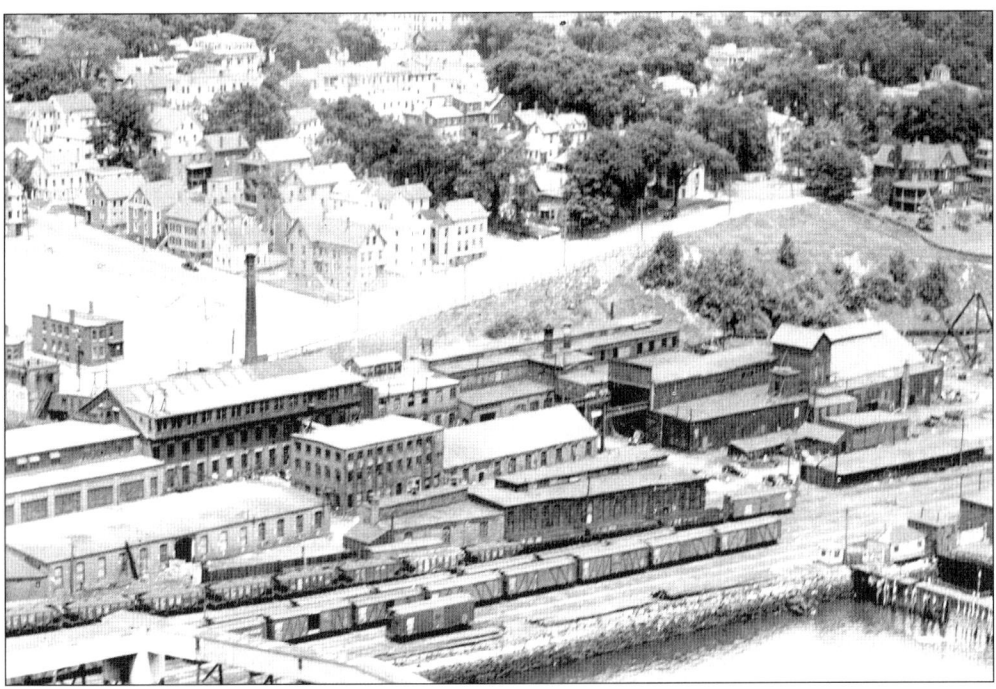

A closer look at the Portland Company complex shows all the freight cars that passed by the company complex each day c. 1938, when this photograph was taken. Also passenger trains passed through the property, going into the city of Portland. The buildings of the Portland Company shops evolved over the 136-year life of the company, as about every 20 years there was some major reorganization of the shops and new buildings and additions added. The Maine Historical Society, where the Portland Company Collection is housed, has many plans of the layout of this large complex available to the public for reproduction.

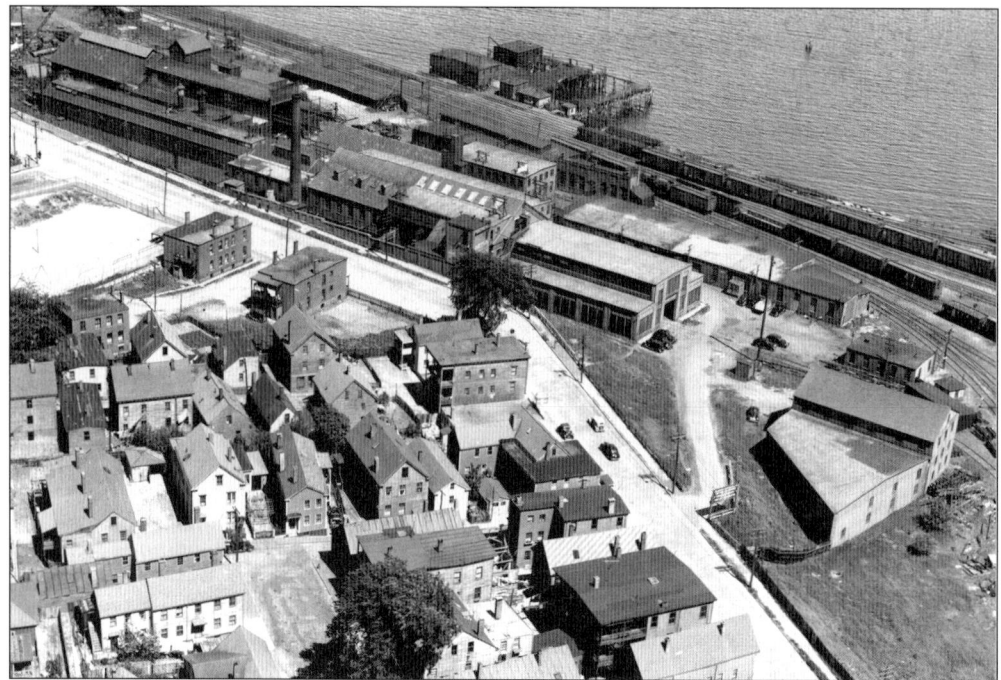

Pictured is another c. 1938 aerial photograph, taken from over the land to show the opposite side of the company complex, which covered about 10 acres of man-made land. The foundry is to the left and continues into the machine and erecting shops. The pattern building, with its two additions, can be seen on the right side of the entrance driveway.

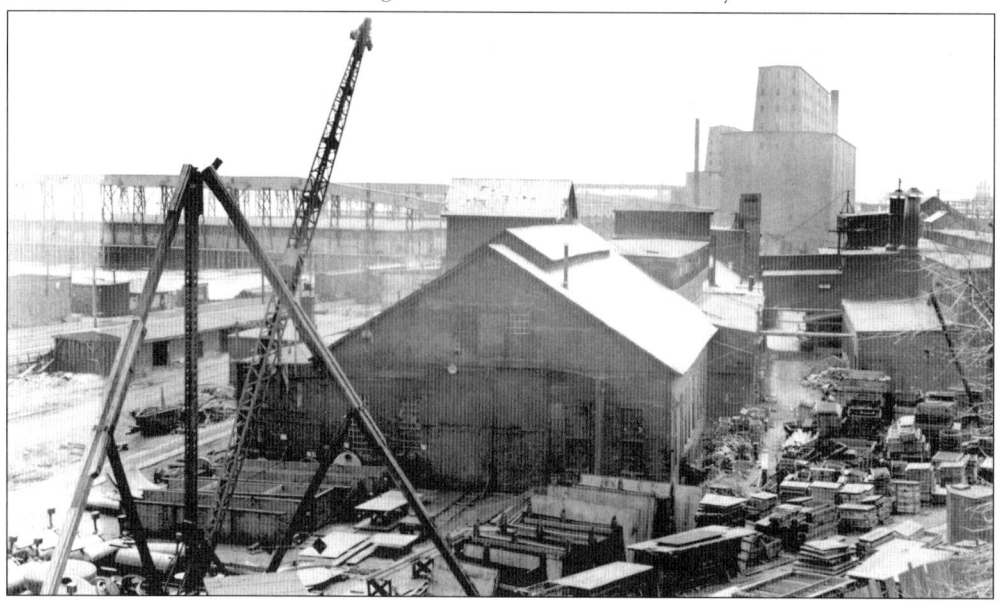

In the foreground, we see the Portland Company foundry building surrounded by casting flasks. Beyond the complex, and toward the south, we can see the two large Grand Trunk Railroad's grain elevators and the conveyors going out onto the piers for loading ships to send the millions of bushels of grain brought in from Canada to distant points in the United States as well as to foreign markets in Europe and Central and South America.

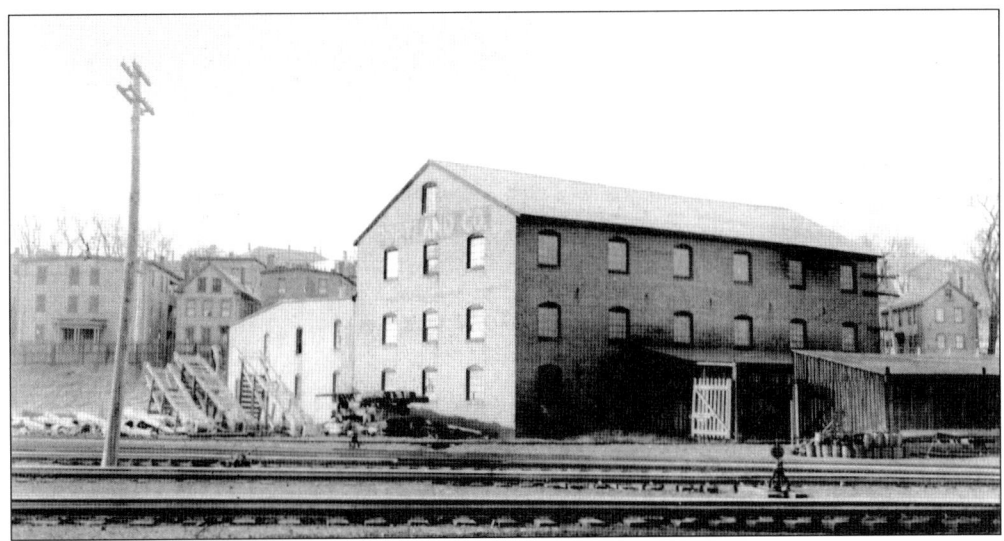

Here is another view of the large brick pattern storage buildings of the Portland Company, where the thousands of wooden patterns used in the two foundries over the 136 years of operation were stored. The company also had a separate brass and bronze foundry in the complex besides the iron foundry.

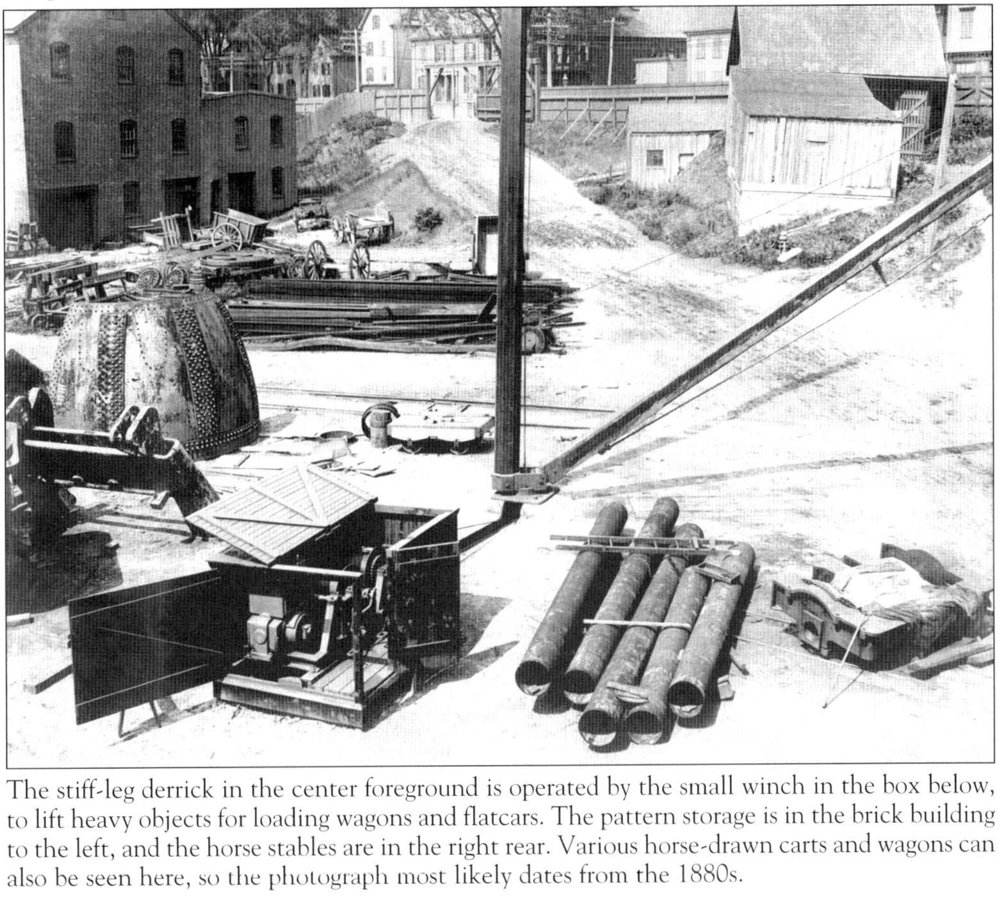

The stiff-leg derrick in the center foreground is operated by the small winch in the box below, to lift heavy objects for loading wagons and flatcars. The pattern storage is in the brick building to the left, and the horse stables are in the right rear. Various horse-drawn carts and wagons can also be seen here, so the photograph most likely dates from the 1880s.

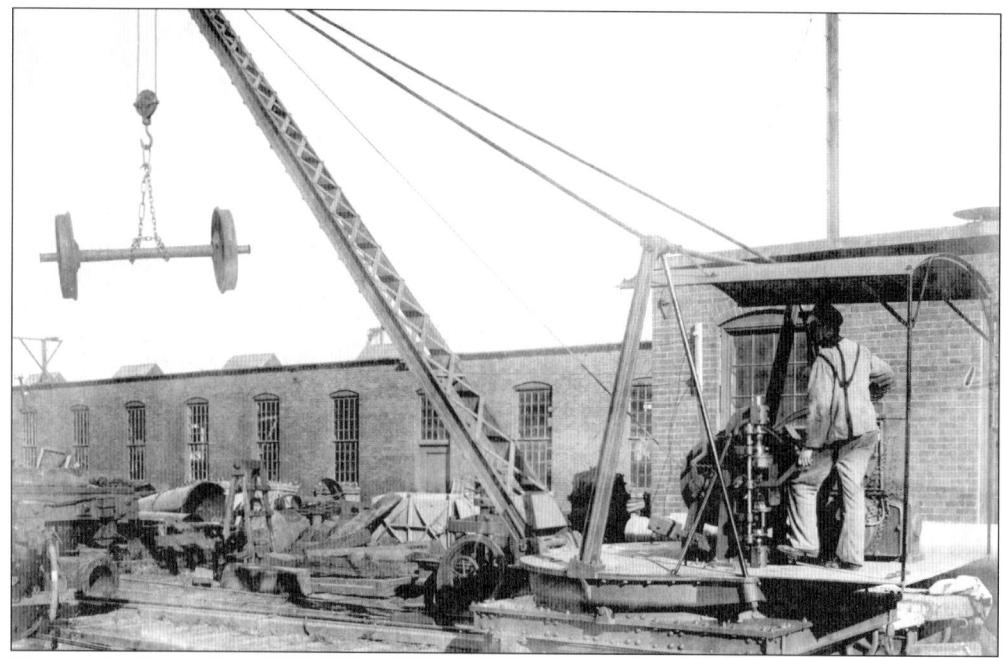

The Portland Company electric traveling rail crane is pictured outside the shops, lifting items to be loaded or unloaded onto rail cars or wagons for shipment to customers.

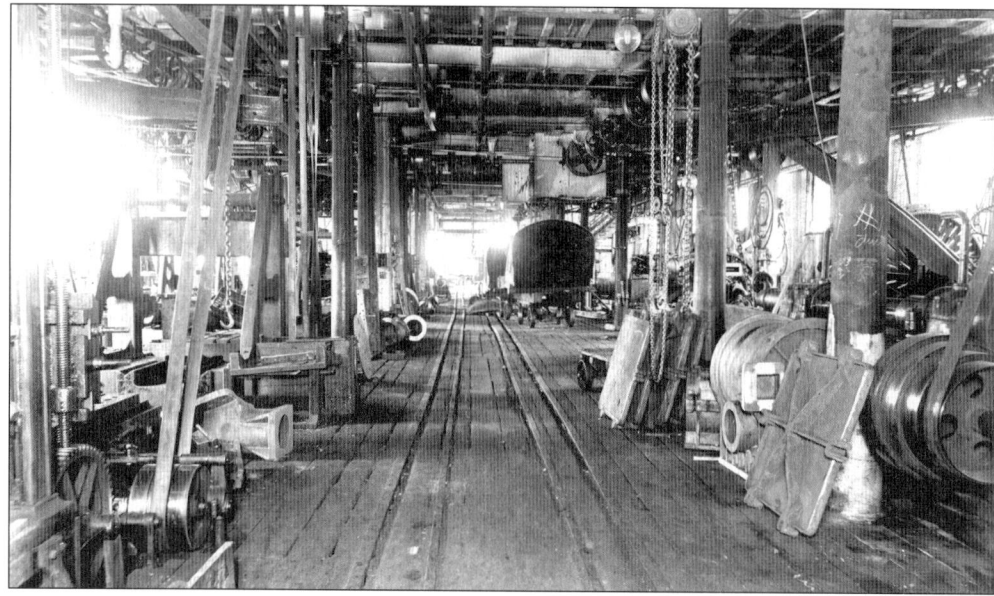

Here in the company machine shop, we can see the various lathes and milling machines used to shape the cast and forged parts for the larger railroad and marine products. Note the dual-gauge railroad tracks in the shop. The Portland Company built and worked on cars and locomotives of five or six different track gauges in the 19th century. Railroad track gauges in the country are now standardized at four feet eight and one-half inches between the railheads, but this standardization was not achieved until the 1870s. The Grand Trunk Railroad started as the 66-inch "Empire" gauge and went to standard gauge on September 25, 1870. All 300 miles of track were regauged between midnight and 7:00 a.m.

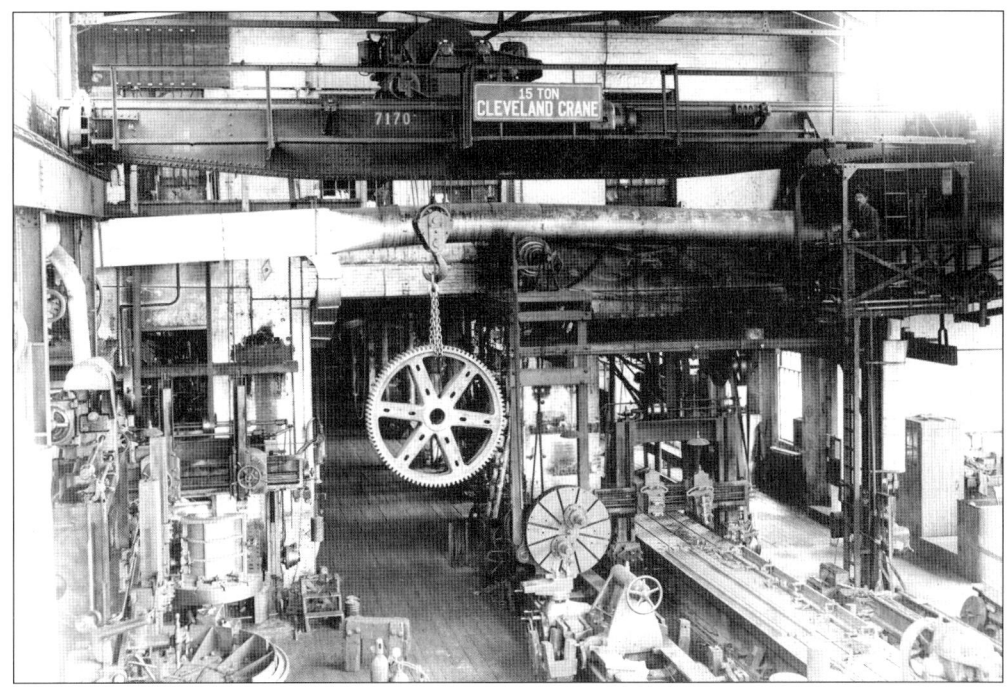

This photograph offers an interesting view of the company machine shop with its 15-ton overhead Cleveland traveling crane. These large traveling cranes moved the length of the shops and could lift any item from side to side or carry it along the shop from one end to the other to be machined and then load the item on rail a car if necessary.

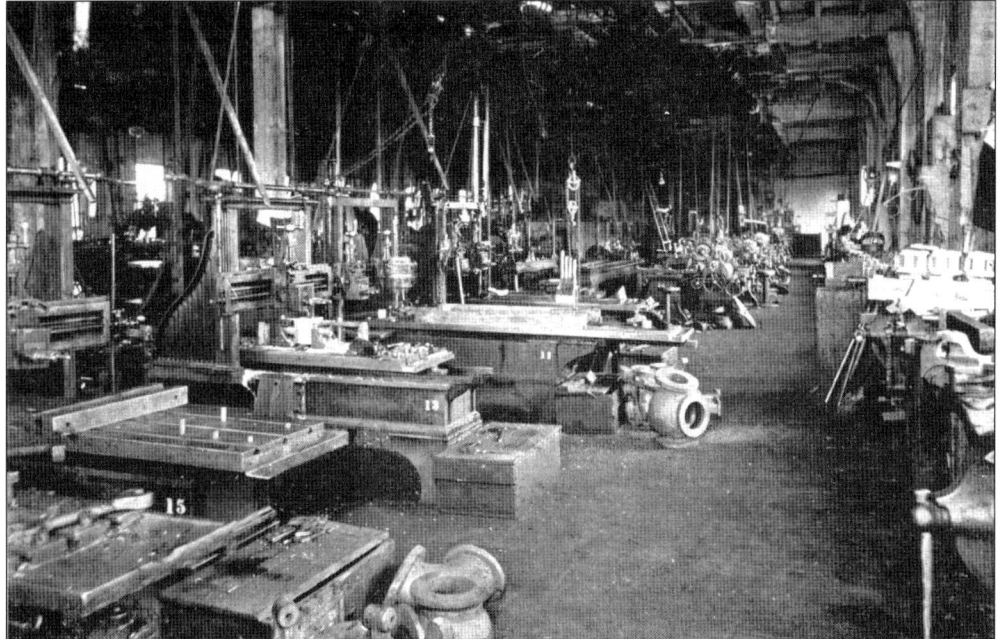

Many large milling machines were needed in this well-equipped company machine shop to machine the rough castings to the close tolerances needed on many of the large cast parts when fitting them together.

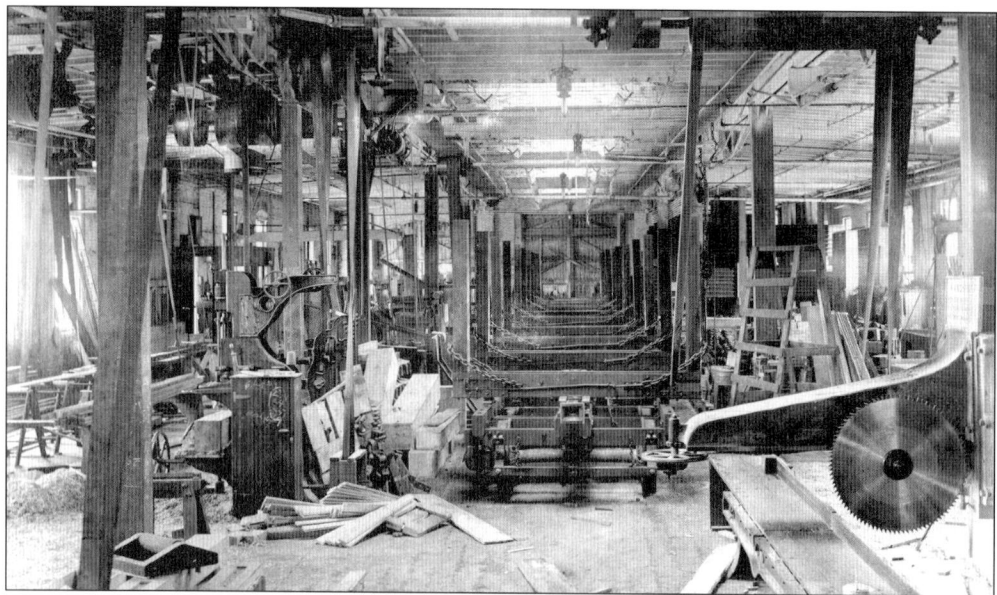

The interior of the car shop reveals some of the hundreds of log bunks manufactured for various Maine railroads. These log bunks were being built for the Somerset Railroad. We also can see the "link and pin" coupler style used on most railroad cars of that period. Later, they were banned because they were so dangerous to brakemen trying to couple and uncouple them, and they were replaced by the knuckle-style couplers used today.

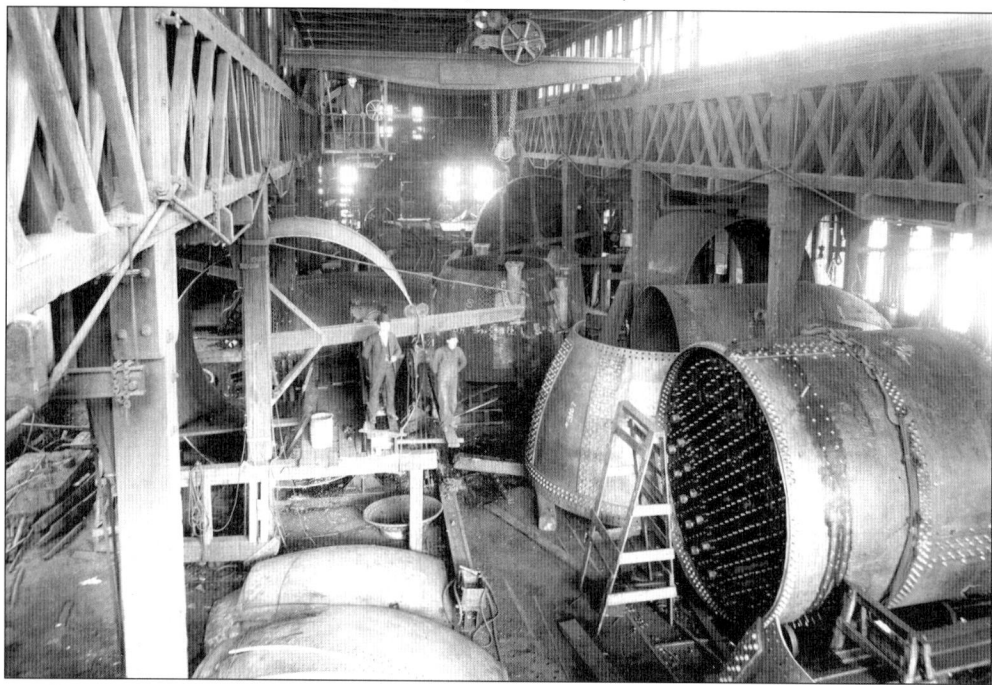

To the right, this photograph shows the construction of the Scotch-type boiler for the Peary Arctic Club, for the explorer steamer *Roosevelt* and three other steamer boilers in the company boiler shop. Note the Cleveland traveling crane used to lift the heavy sections of boiler plate and to load the large units onto dollies or railroad cars for transporting to the installation site.

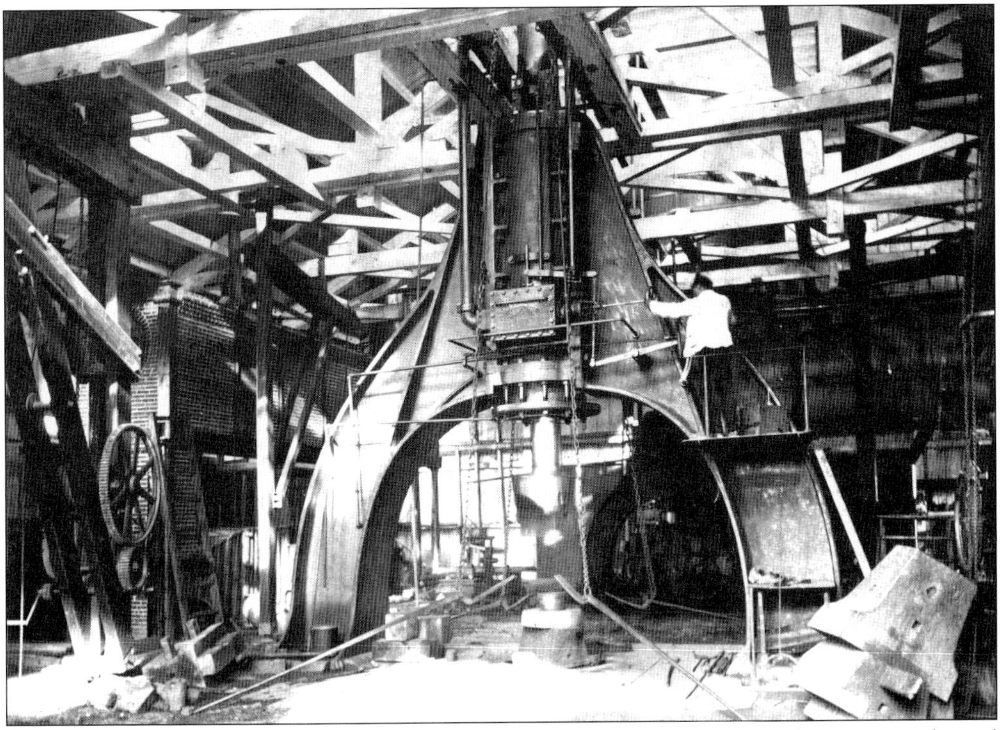

This giant press in the Portland Company shops was used to form metal parts into desired shapes for the fabrication of large products.

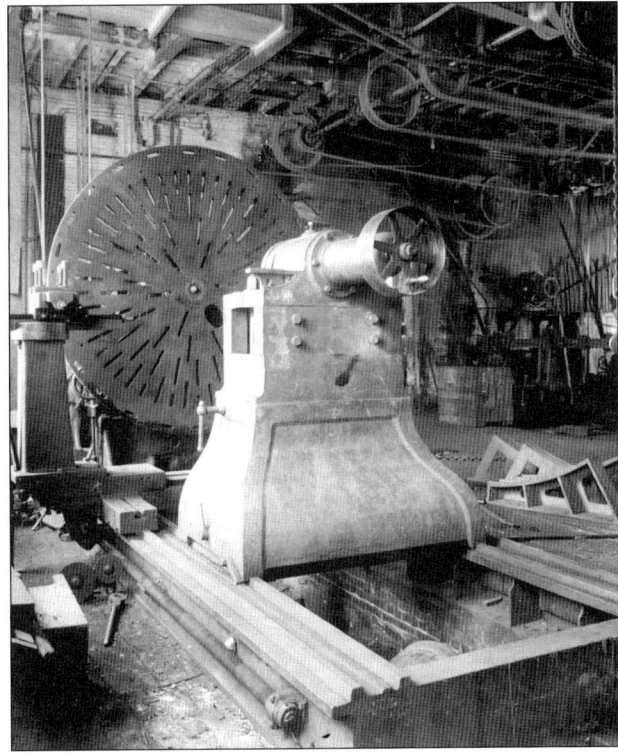

Pictured is a heavy lathe used to turn large wheels, drums, and rings in the company machine shop. It could also be used to turn most of the largest locomotive tires.

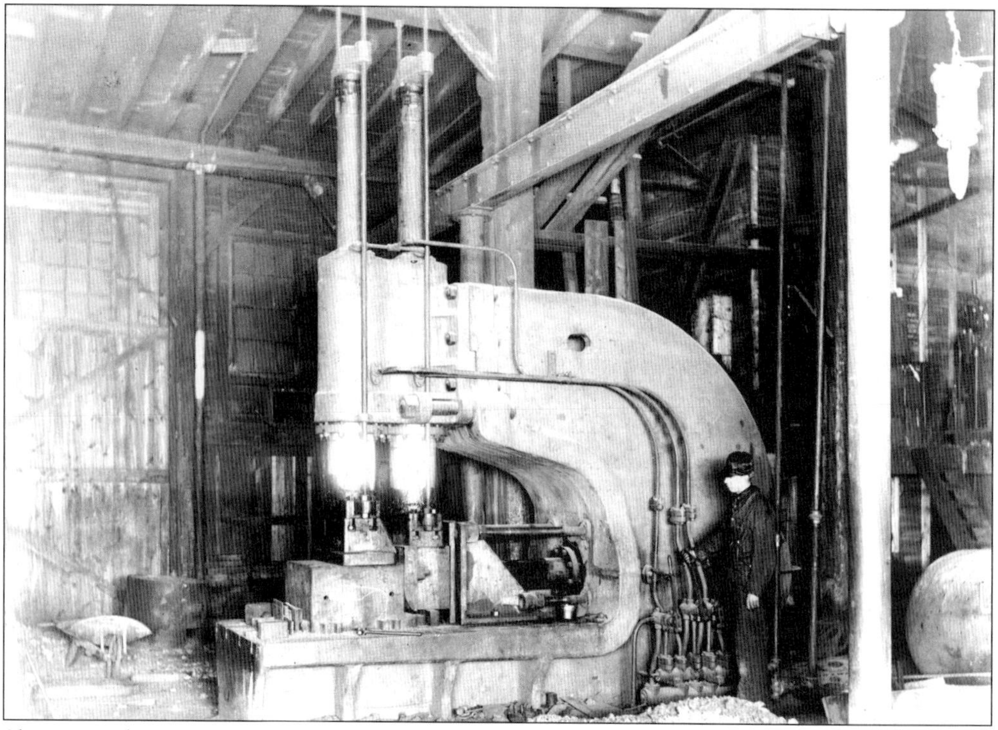

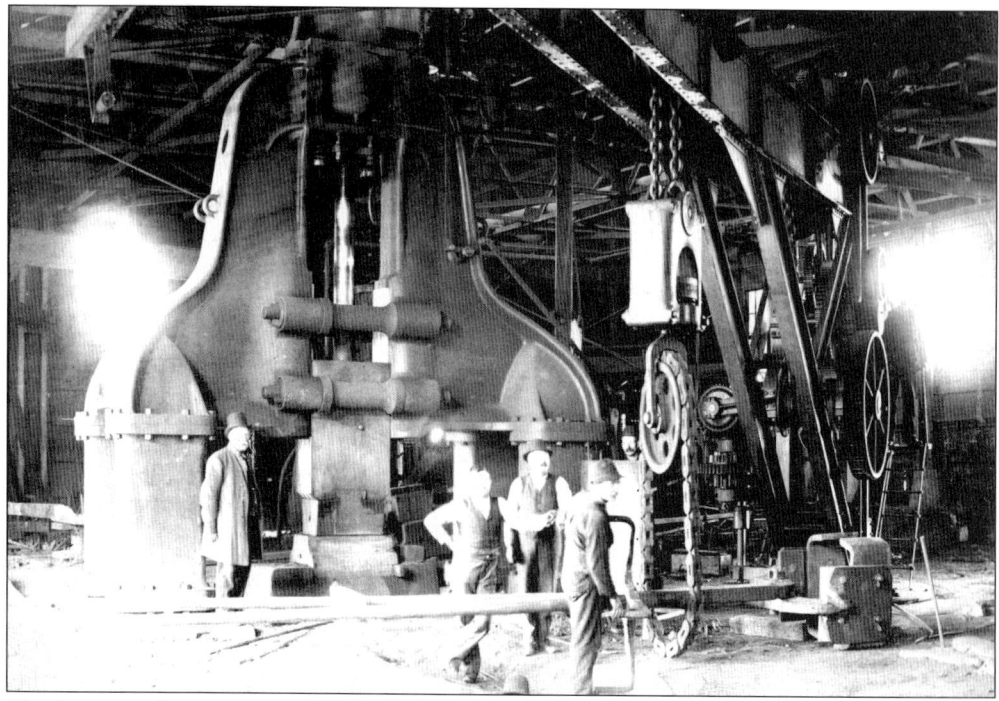

Shown in this view is a 200-ton flanging machine in the company shop, used to make the flanges on boiler plates so they will bolt or rivet together.

The large trip hammer was used in the company blacksmith shop to forge large billets of iron into useable shapes for machining and the fabrication of various products.

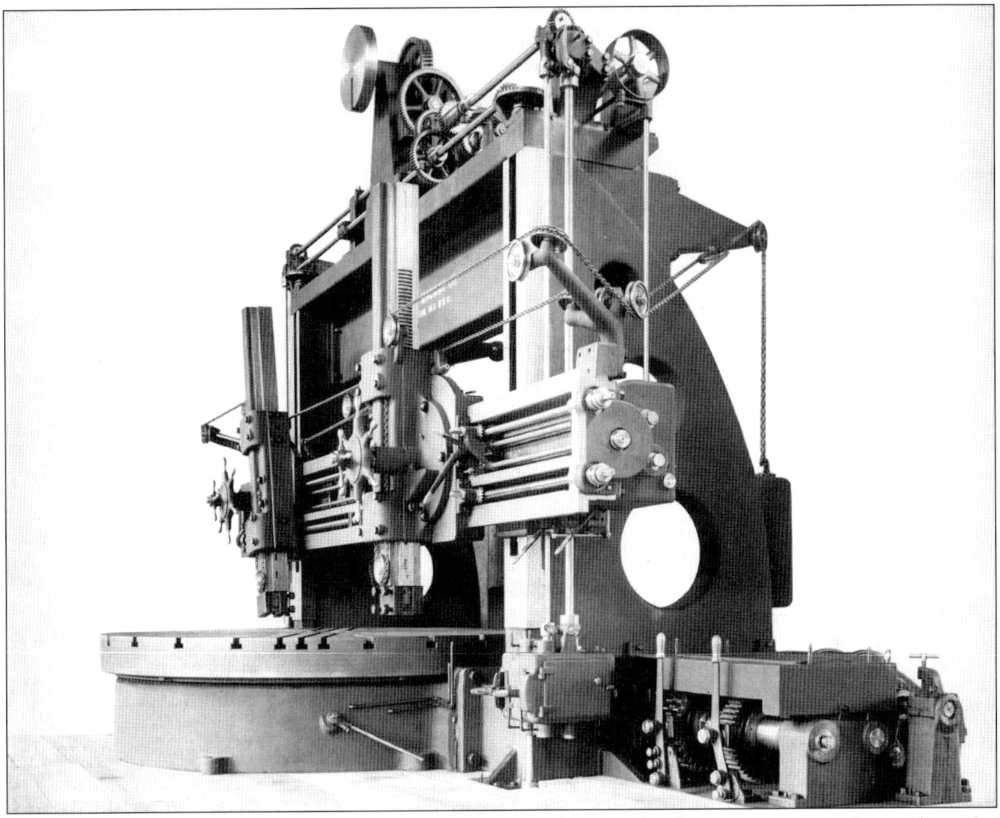

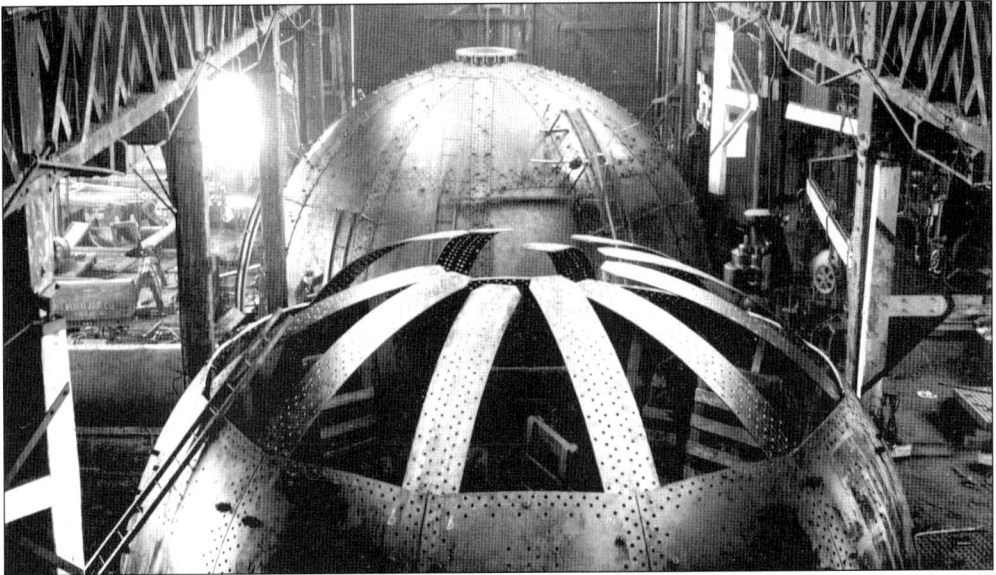

This very large milling machine was essential to the Portland Company machine shop for milling the large castings that were produced in substantial numbers.

Two large steam accumulators are nearly completed in the boiler shop. The curved sections were predrilled for the rivets binding them together. These vessels have to sustain high pressures in paper mills just as boilers must.

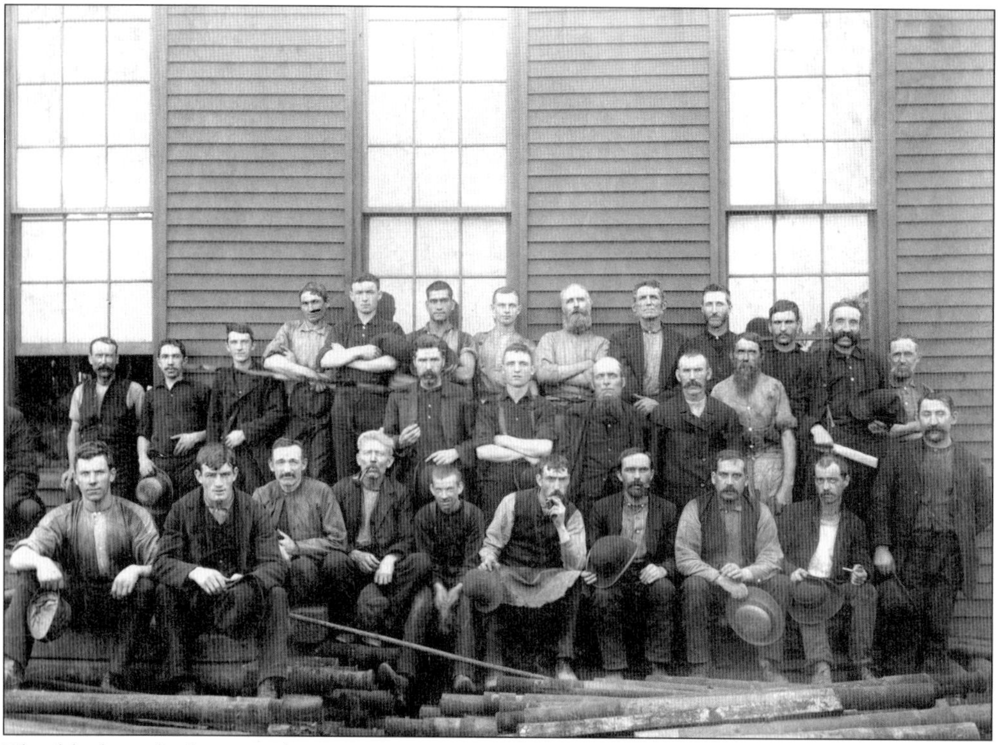

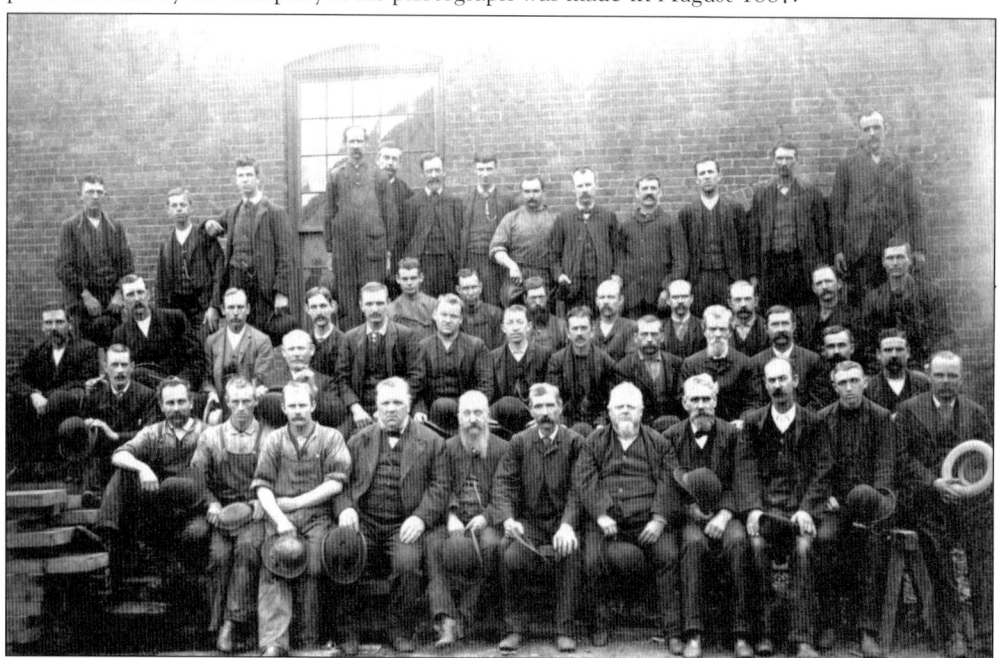

The blacksmith shop employees were responsible for the forging and fabrication of various products built by the company. This photograph was made in August 1887.

The machine shop employees pose for a photograph in August 1887. They made up the largest group of workers employed by the Portland Company. Many of them can be seen in other photographs of the machine shop.

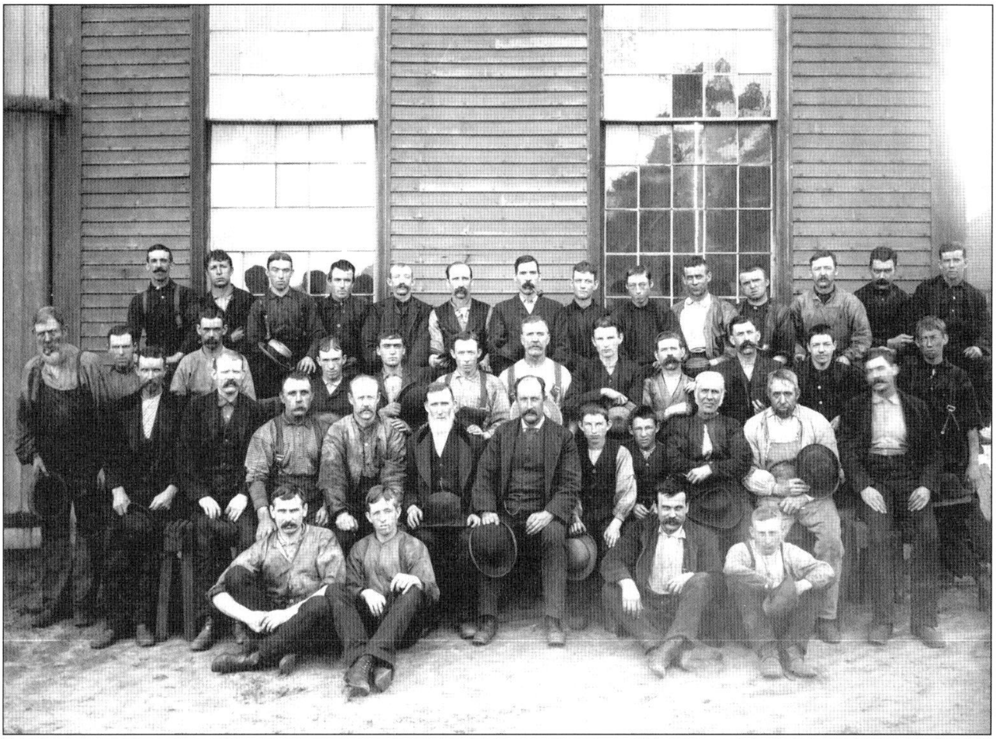

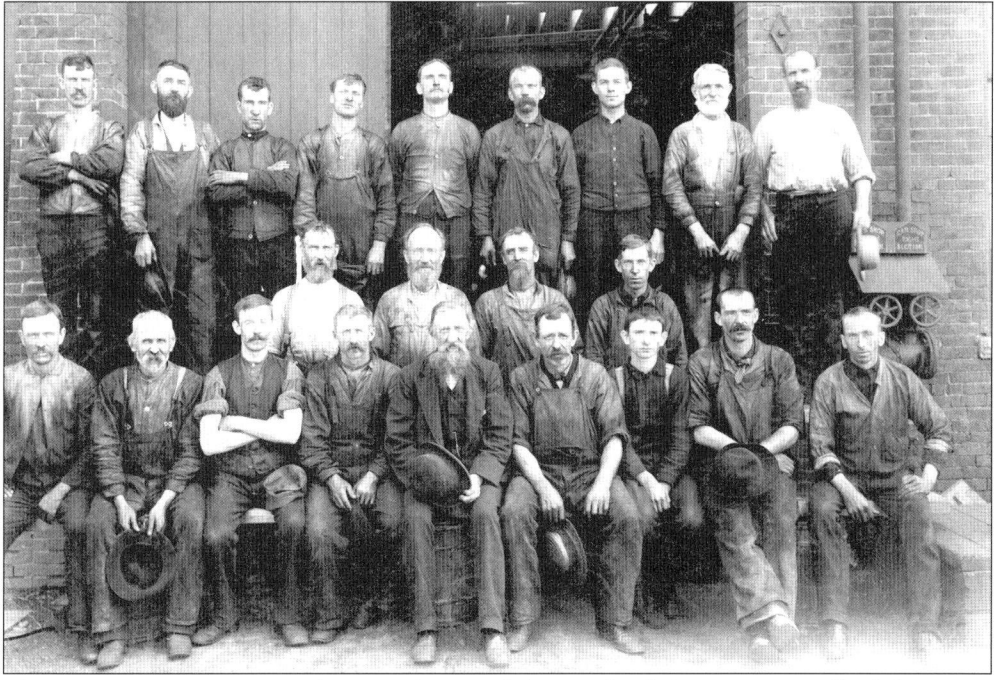

The boiler shop employees were vital for the production of the 630 steam locomotive and hundreds of marine and industrial boilers built by the Portland Company during the 19th century.

The setting-up, or erecting, shop employees of the Portland Company put all of the pieces together to make the final product complete. The men were all photographed in 1887.

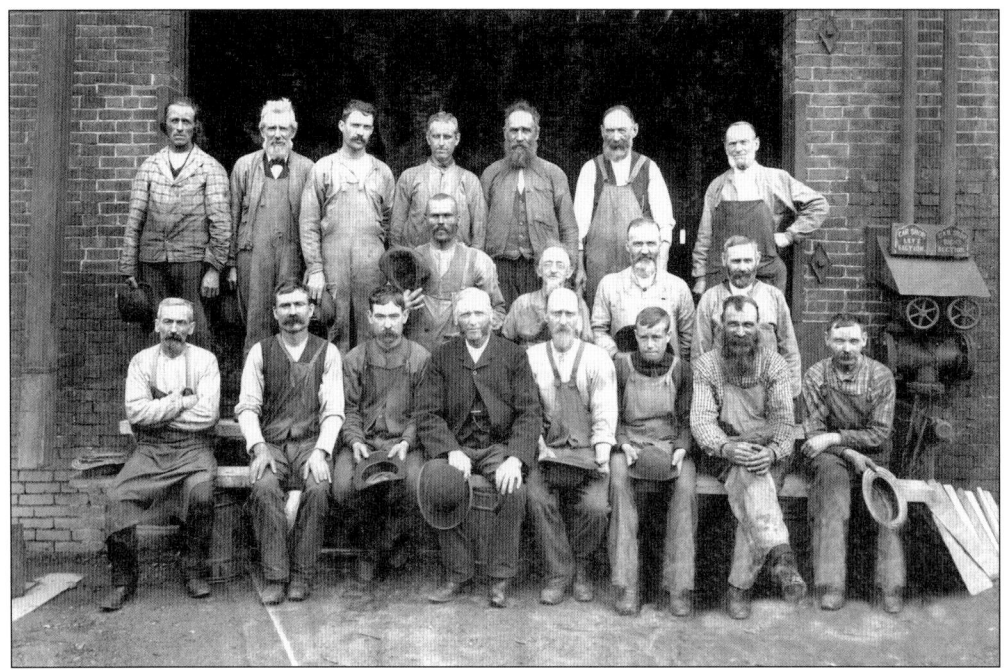

The carpentry shop employees pictured here built cabs for the railroad locomotives and were responsible for all the woodworking done in building the thousands of railroad cars built in their shop.

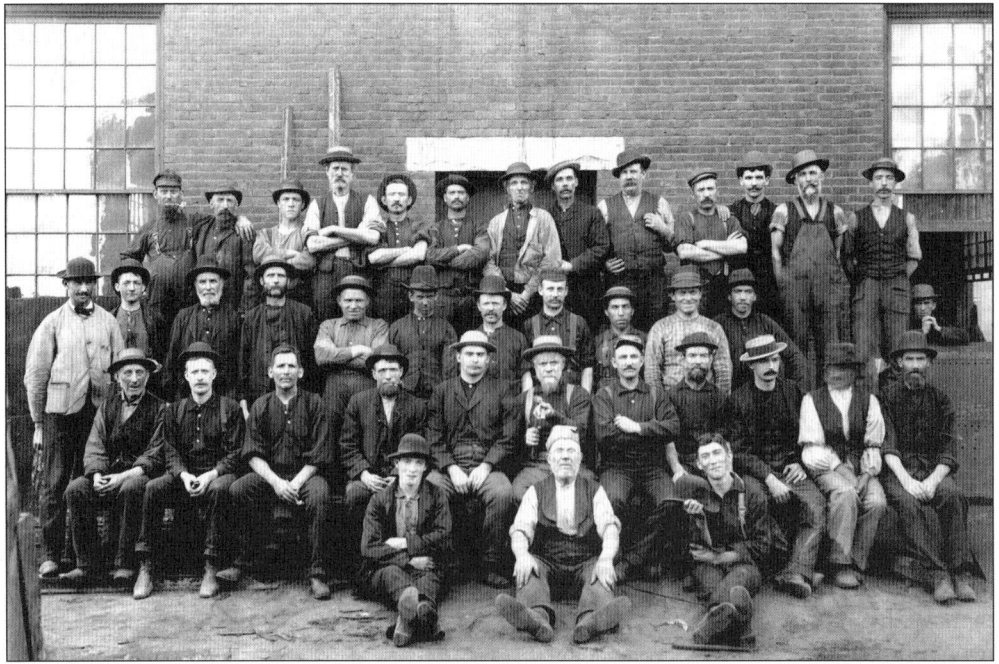

During August 1887, the Portland Company had a photograph made of each shop's employees. Here are the men who worked in the foundry, casting all the major parts for the many locomotives and marine engines built during the latter part of the 19th century. The foundry was most certainly a very hot place to work in August.

Two
Railroad Locomotives, Rolling Stock, and Parts

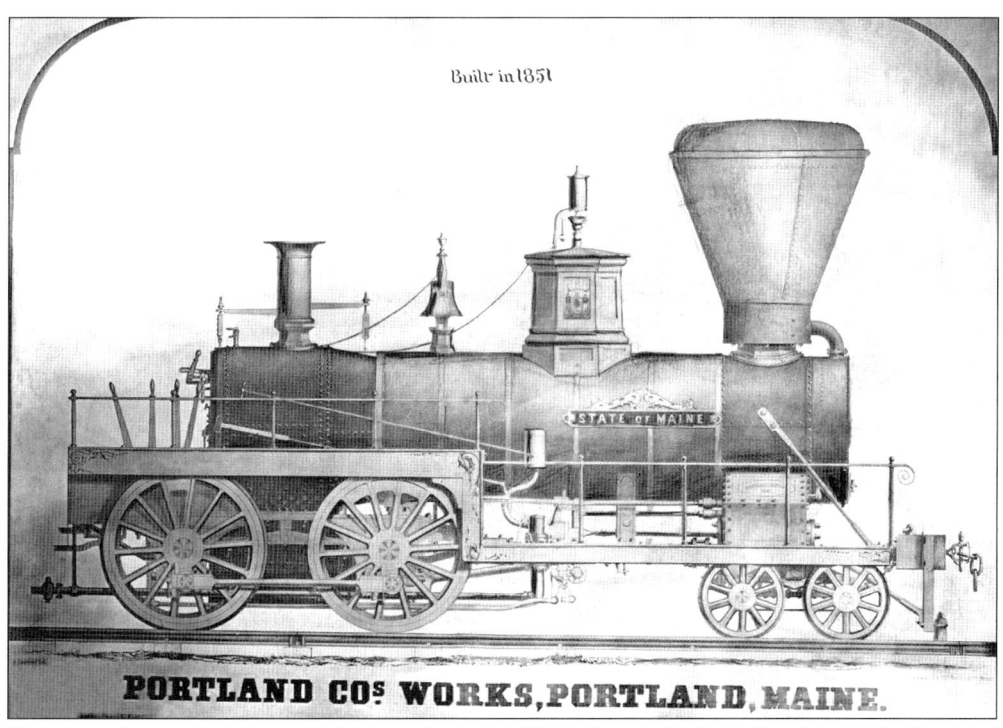

The steam locomotive *State of Maine* was built in 1851 in Boston by John Souther for the Portland & Kennebec Railroad. This is a photograph of it after the Portland Company rebuilt it in 1869 and it ended its useful life as a Maine Central Railroad switcher, later sold to and scrapped by the Portland Company. It had 60-inch wheel centers and was always a wood-fired locomotive.

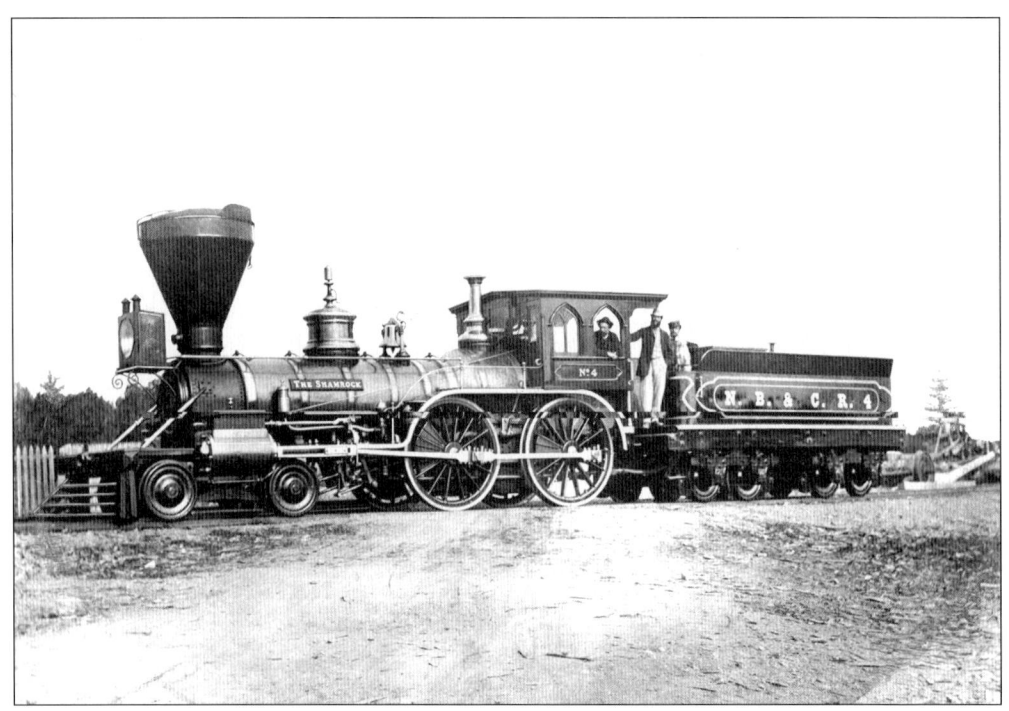

This grand locomotive, the *Shamrock*, No. 4, was built for the New Brunswick & Canada Railroad in 1858 as shop No. 108. Nine similar locomotives, all 66-inch gauge, were constructed for this railroad.

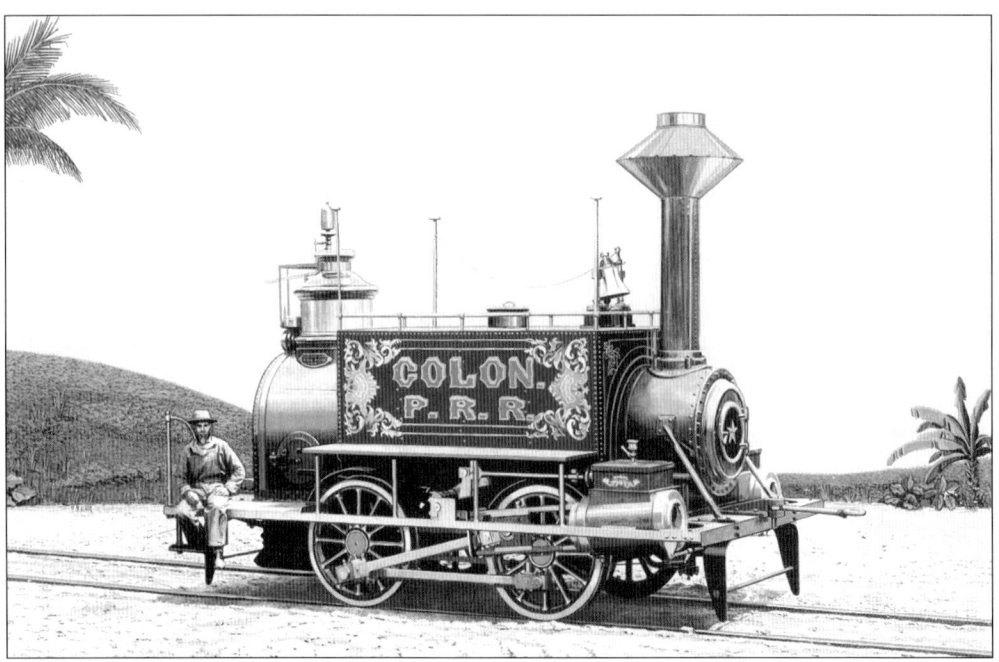

The *Colon* was built by the Portland Company in 1865 as a 0-4-0T tank engine for the Panama Railroad. It did not have a cab as did most engines used in North America at that time. This was probably in consideration of the heat factor for the crew.

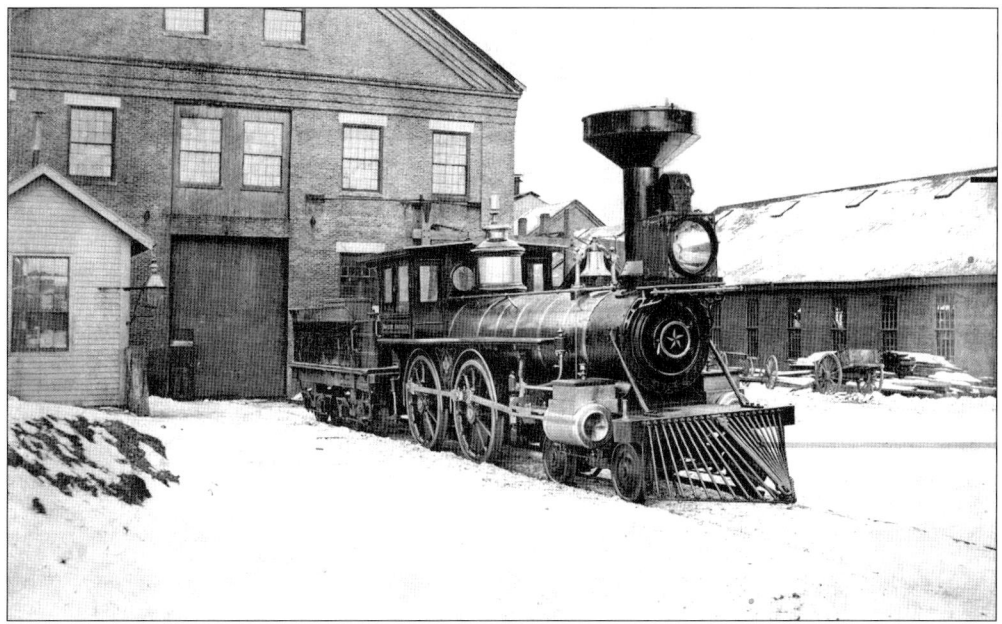

This 60-inch-gauge 1868 locomotive built for the Panama Railroad was called *North America*. It was one of 20 engines built for this road between 1865 and 1873 and was shop No. 151. It is sitting in front of the erecting shops, awaiting shipment to South America by sea. The tiny building at the left is the timekeeper's shack.

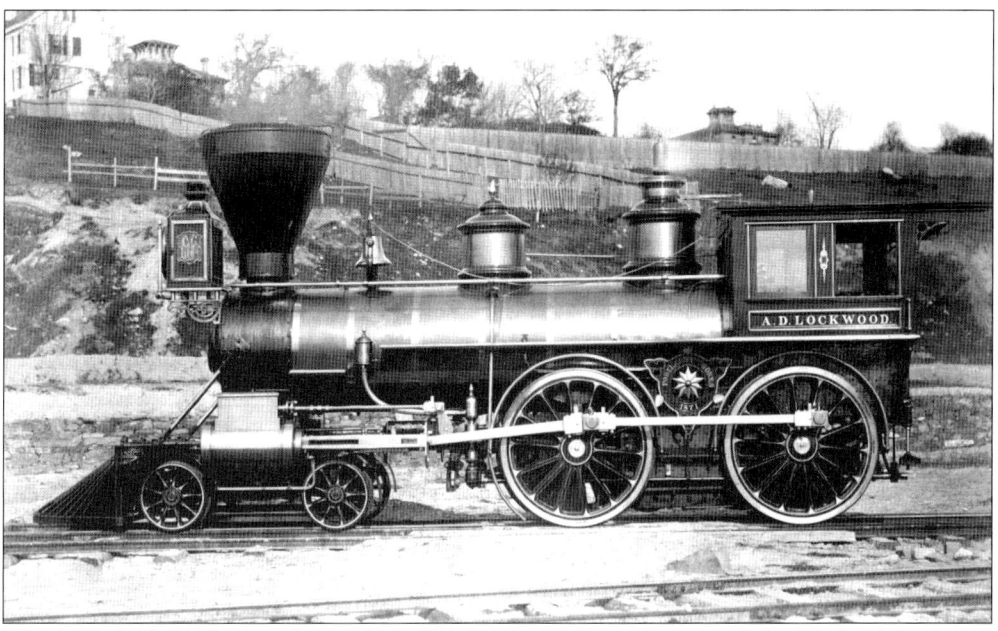

The *A.D. Lockwood*, No. 15, was the 156th locomotive to come out of the Portland Company shops. It was standard gauge and erected in 1869 for the Grand Trunk Railroad. It had large-diameter drivers, making it a fast passenger train engine. Here again, we can see the attractive company logo on the frame between the driving wheels. Often, official builders' photographs show the engine with no tender, which carried the engine's fuel and water.

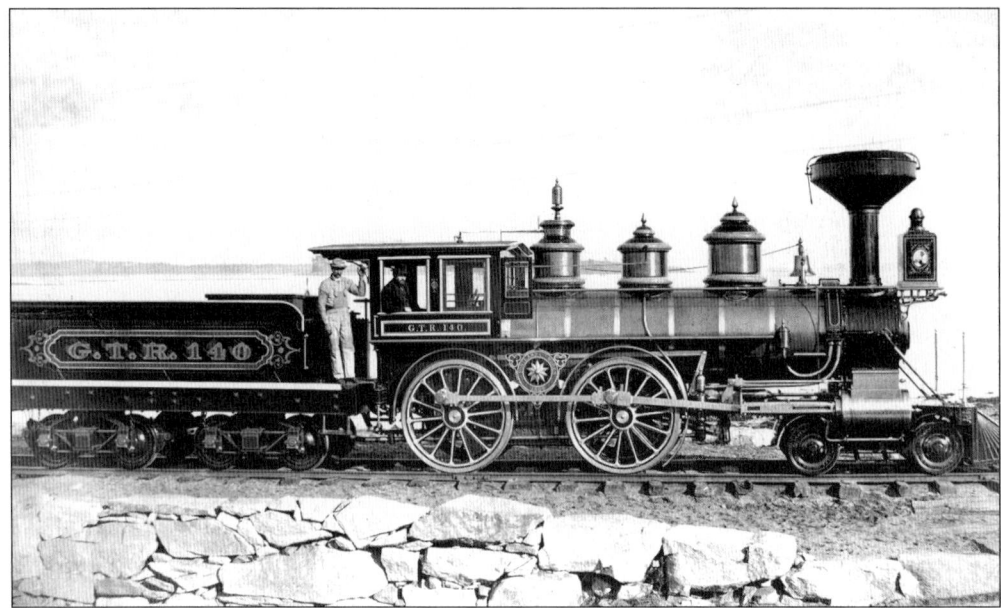

This is a very nice photograph of the Grand Trunk locomotive No. 140 on the mainline track outside of the Portland Company. Built in 1869 as a 66-inch-gauge locomotive, it was later converted to standard-gauge width in 1870. Note the dress of the engineer in his cab seat and the fenders on the large driving wheels. The large oil headlight has a picture of flowers painted on the sides, and the cabbage stack denotes an early wood-burning engine.

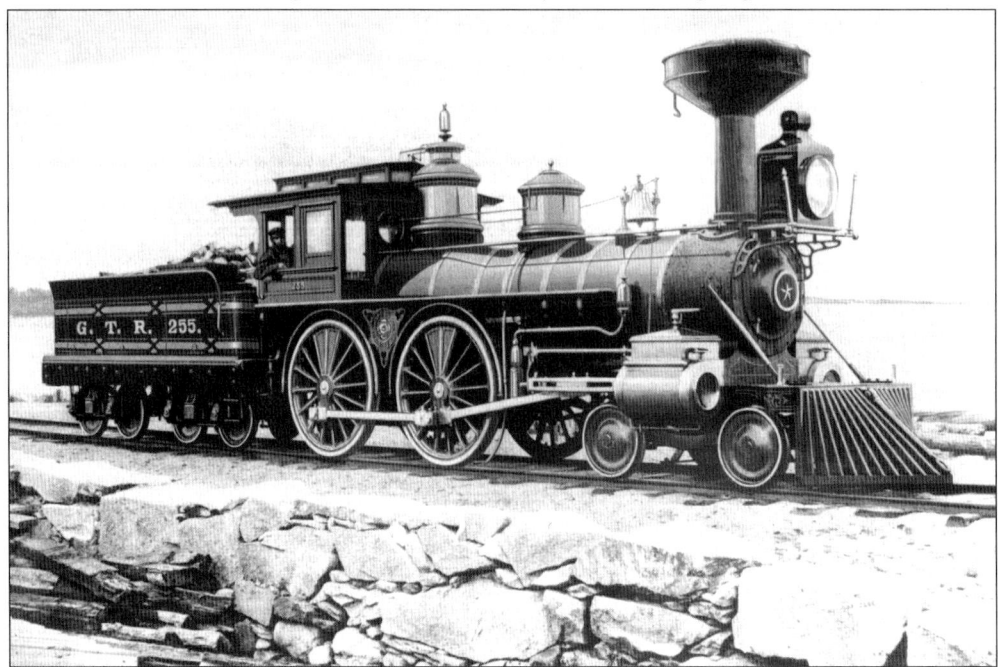

Pictured here is a very handsome locomotive, No. 255, built for the Grand Trunk Railroad in 1873 with an unusual clerestory cab. The engine rests in front of the company shops on Portland Harbor. It has 61-inch drivers and made to fit standard-gauge track with 56 1/2 inches between railheads. Note the large triangular company logo between the driving wheels.

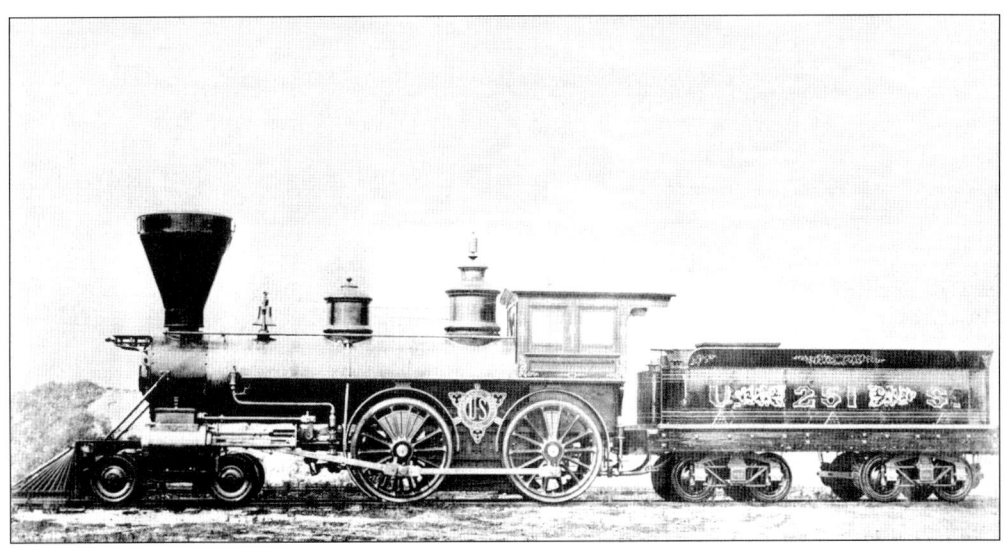

The Portland Company built to order several 60-inch-gauge locomotives during the Civil War for the U.S. government and delivered them in 1864. More engines, however, were procured from the company under less willing circumstances by the government, as the four other locomotives they wanted were under contracts from civilian railroads. The photograph above clearly shows from the builder's plate that this locomotive was built in 1863, and the "U.S." is cast right into that plate. Company records show that four engines were built for the government in 1864 and not delivered until September of that year, so was this one of the earlier built locomotives meant for a private road?

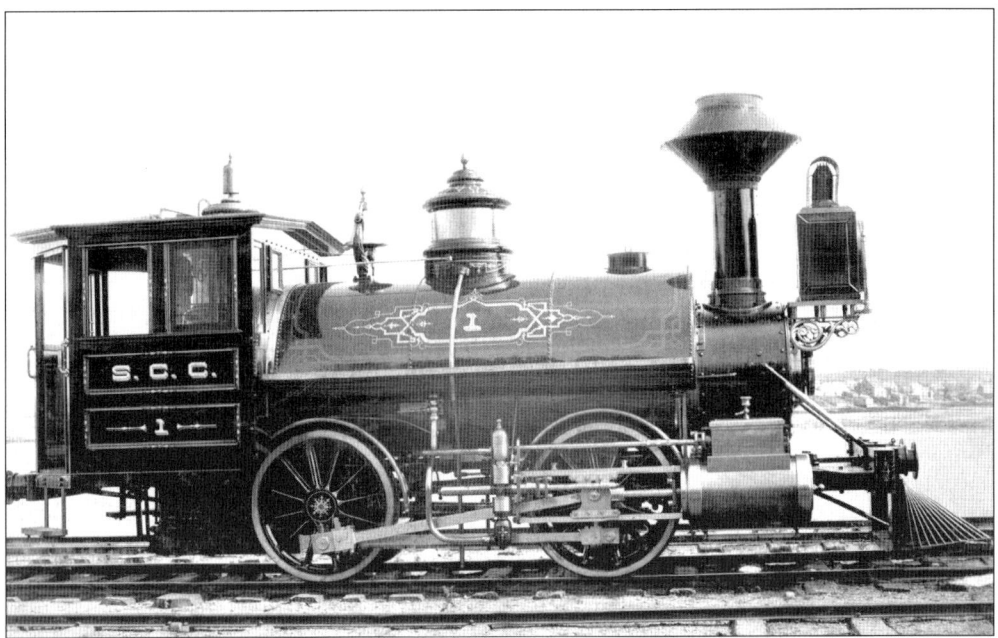

Pictured is an elaborately decorated 0-4-0T switcher locomotive built in 1876 for the Steel Company of Canada as a 36-inch-gauge tank engine. Tank engines had no tender, as they carried their own fuel and water in tanks on the engine and not trailing behind in a separate tender. Also note the very unusual corner cab doors cut on the diagonal.

27

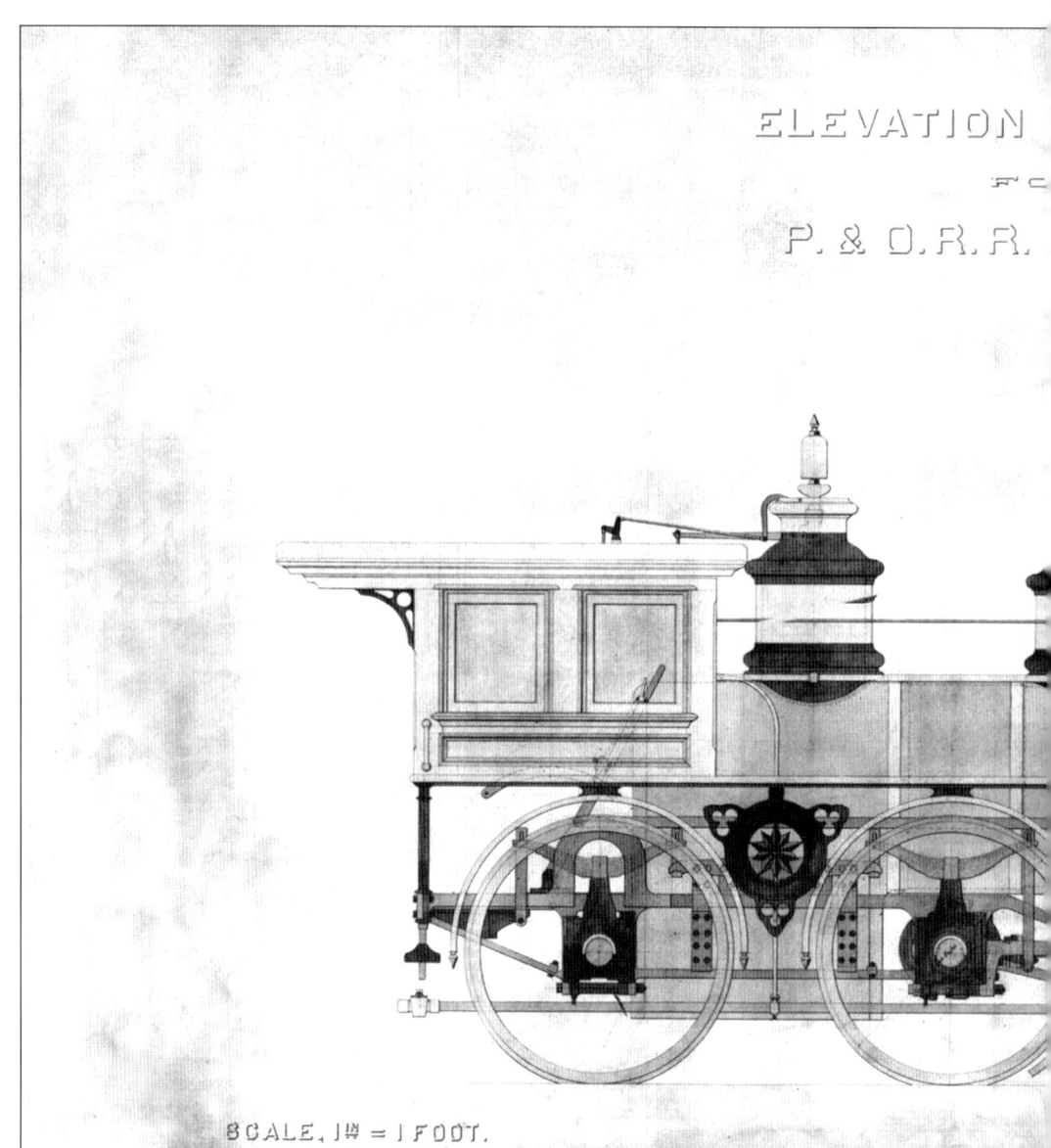

Shown here is an early general arrangement elevation engineering drawing of Portland & Ogdensburg Railroad locomotive *Lamoille*, No. 2. It was Portland Company shop No. 196, was built in 1871 for the Vermont Division, and went to the Lamoille Valley Railroad in Vermont.

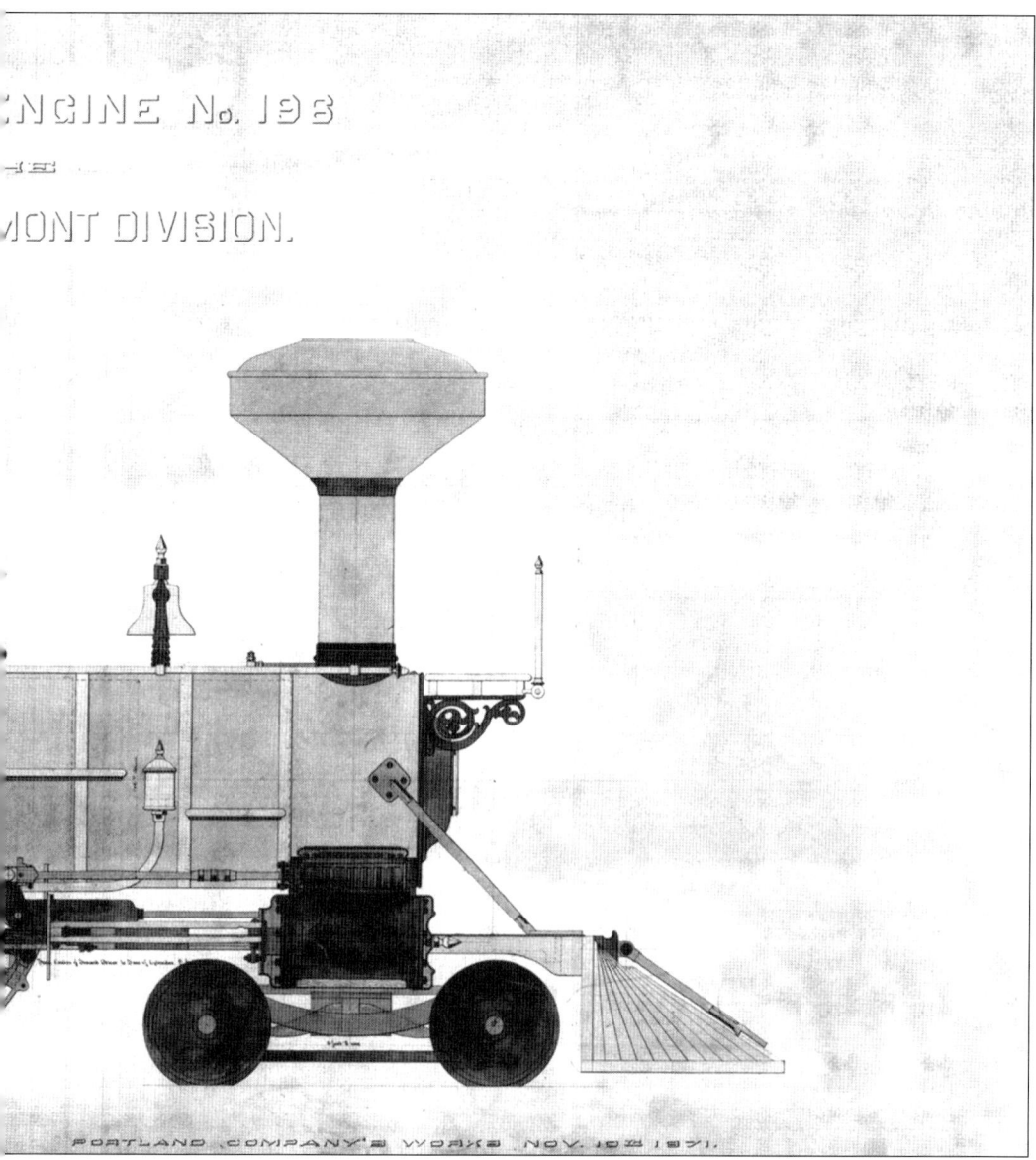

The 10,000-plus engineering drawings in the Portland Company Collection of all areas of production are available for copying from the Maine Historical Society in Portland, Maine.

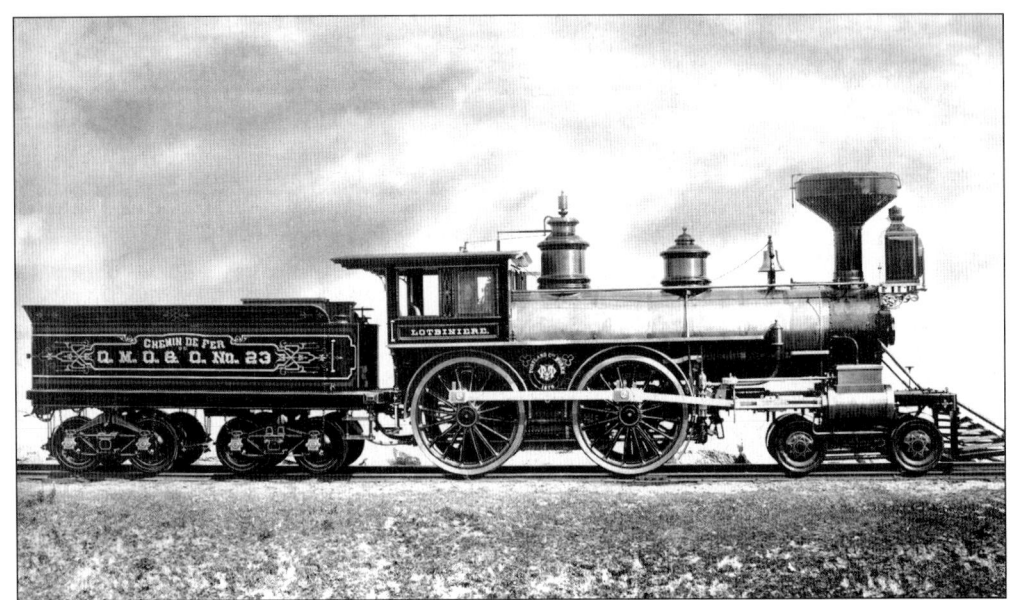

The Quebec, Montreal, Ottowa & Occidental Railroad locomotive No. 23, with 68-inch drivers for fast passenger service, waits in the sunshine along Portland Harbor. Built in 1878, this beautifully decorated machine sports an unusual Portland Company logo between the drivers. It was shop No. 350.

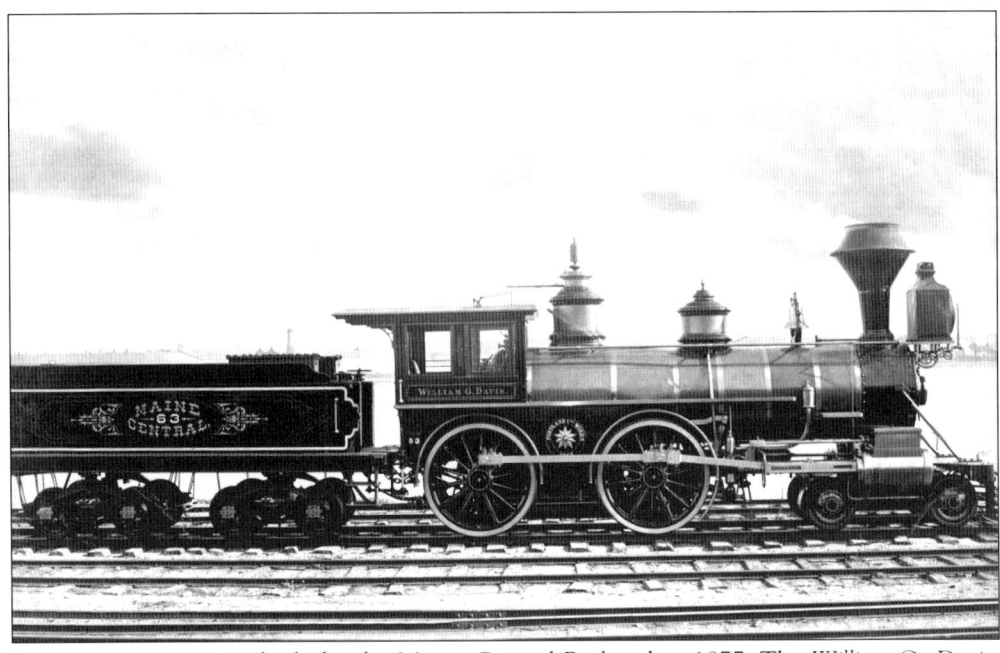

Here we see an engine built for the Maine Central Railroad in 1877. The *William G. Davis*, No. 63, was a standard-gauge engine. This official photograph was taken on Tuesday, April 24, 1877, at 4:00 p.m.

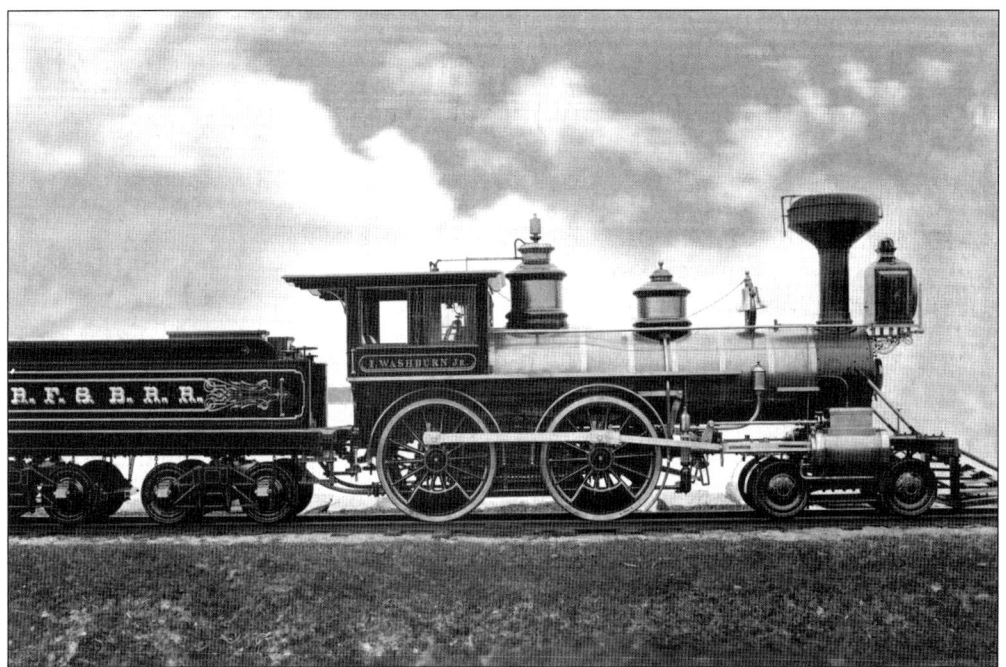

Two locomotives were built by the company in 1878 for the Rumford Falls & Buckfield Railroad. Here we see the *I. Washburn Jr.* outside the locomotive works, ready for delivery. The shop number was 356 on this engine, which was gauged for standard track.

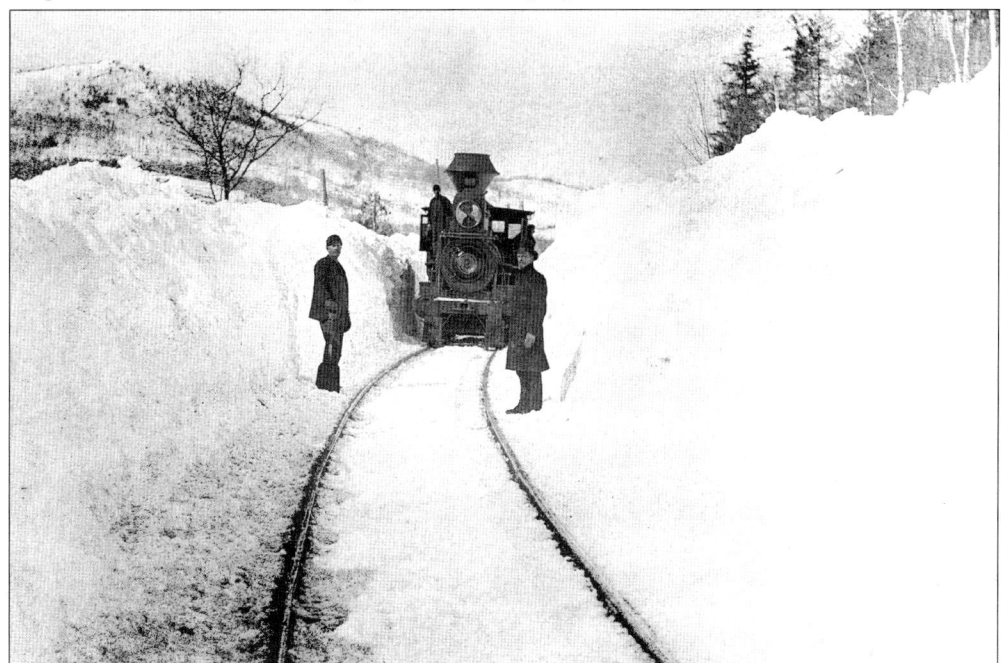

Heavy snows in Maine challenge this Rumford Falls & Buckfield Railroad locomotive in the 1880s. It was named the *S.C. Andrews*, No. 2, and was built in Portland in 1878 as shop No. 357. When the snowdrifts got too high and heavy for the rail snowplows to break through, the crew and sometimes the passengers had to get out and shovel.

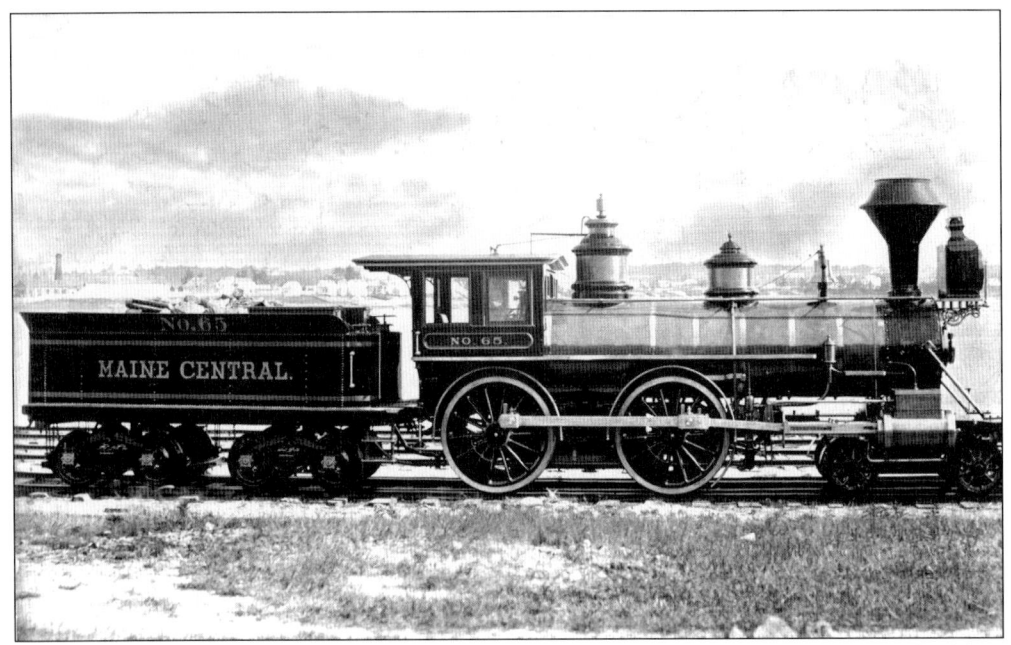

Maine Central Railroad engine No. 65, built in the shops in 1879, poses for a builder's photograph in the afternoon sun.

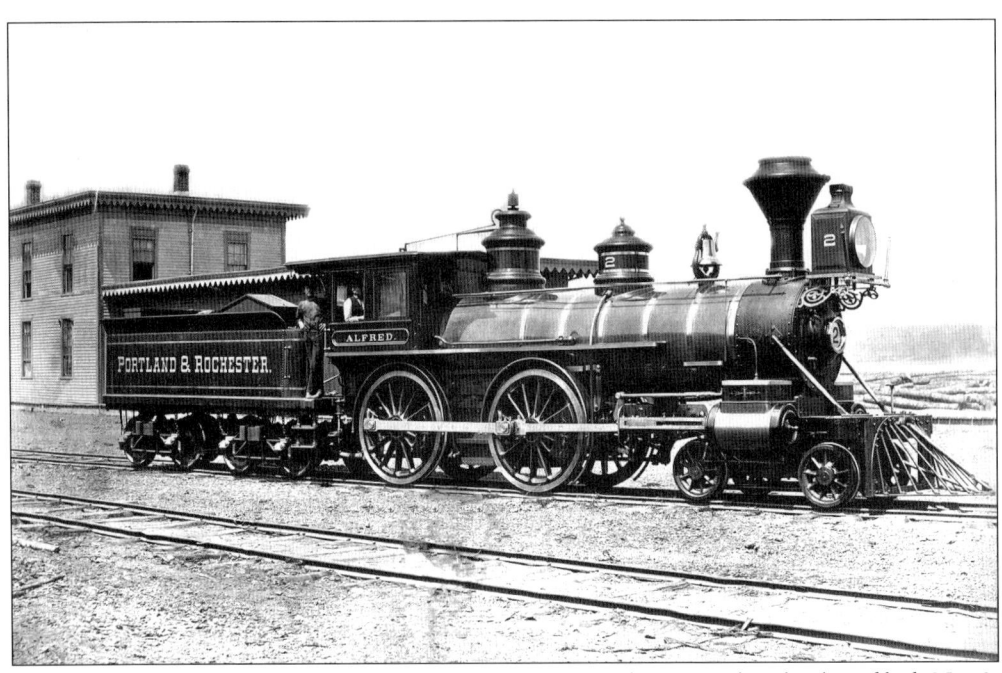

This locomotive was built in 1880 for the Portland & Rochester Railroad. The *Alfred*, No. 2, is of standard gauge, has 61-inch drivers, and is posed out on the main line.

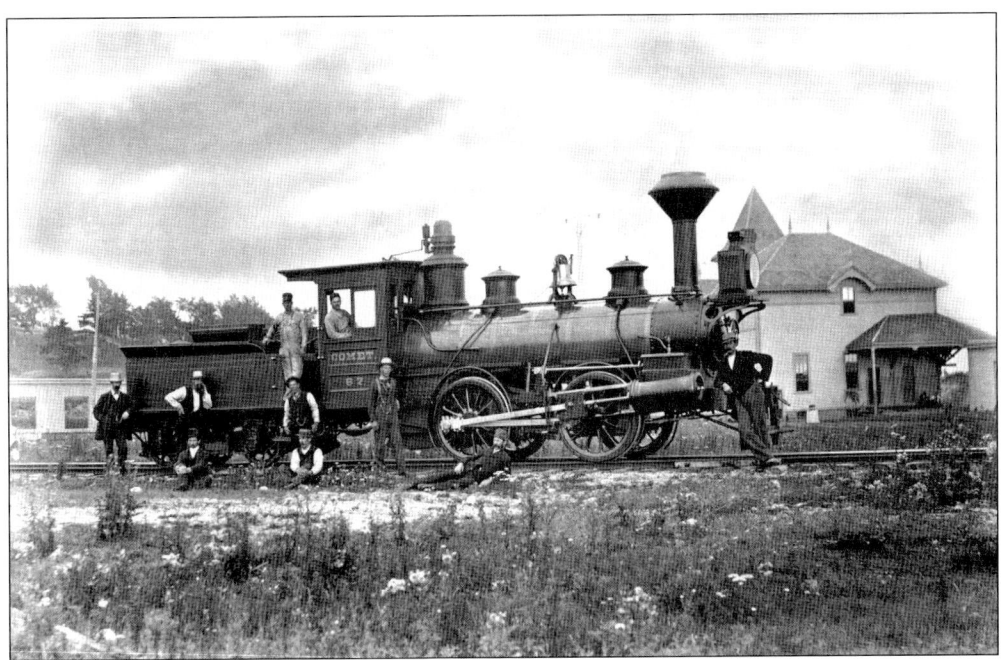

The *Comet*, No. 57, was built as a 4-4-0 in 1881 for the Maine Central Railroad. Here we see it as an 0-4-0 switch engine for standard-gauge operation.

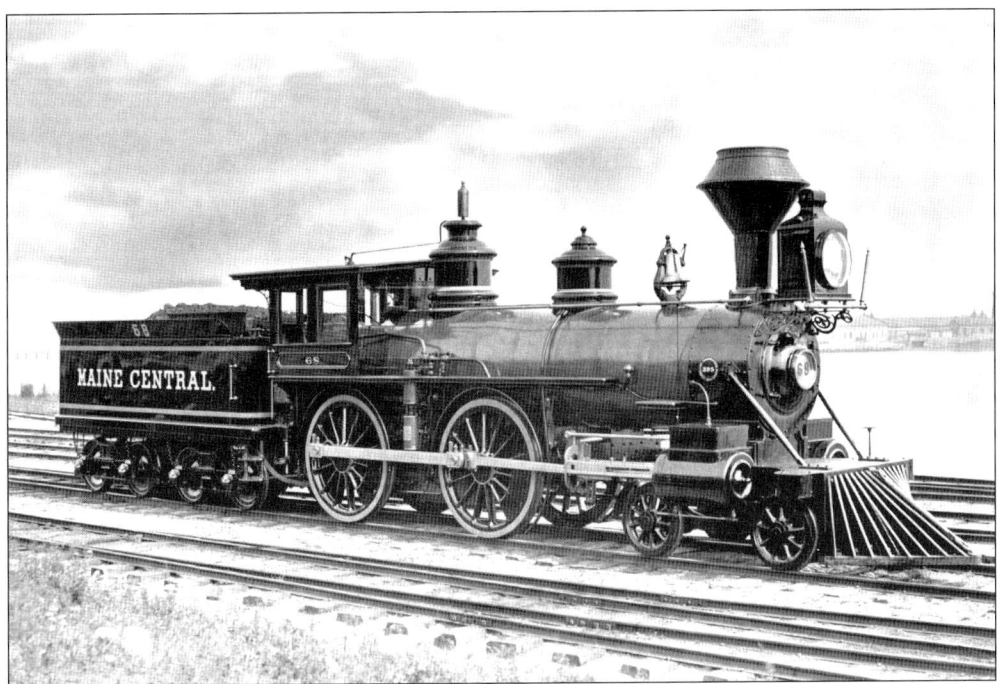

Many 4-4-0 steam locomotives were built for the Maine Central Railroad in Portland. No. 68, shown here on the rails, was outshopped in July 1881 and was of standard gauge. Shop No. 395 was one of over 70 locomotives built for the Maine Central Railroad by the company.

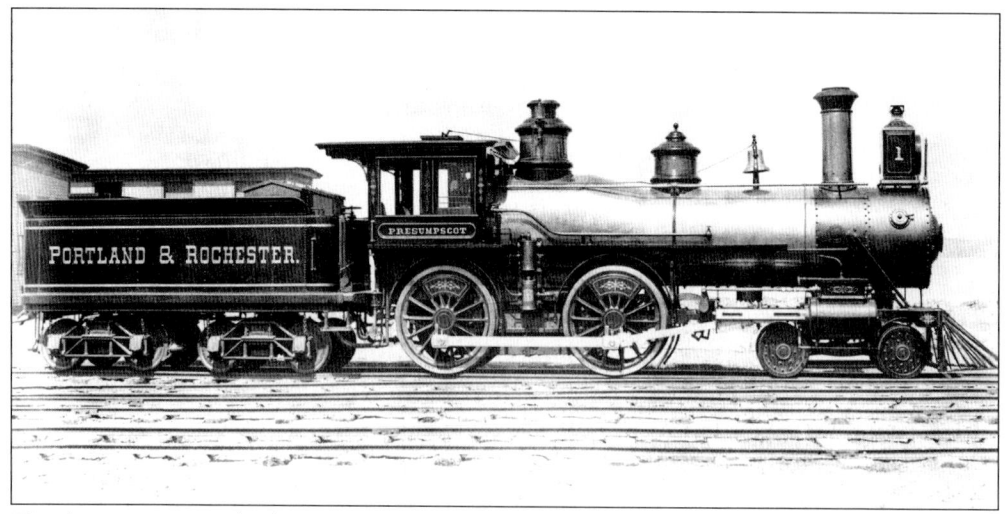

This locomotive was built in 1886 for the Portland & Rochester Railroad. The *Presumpscot*, No. 1, is of standard gauge and has 62-inch drivers for passenger train service. Here we have a great view of the sand pipes going down in front of the forward drivers from the sand dome to drop sandy grit onto slippery rails if extra traction was needed.

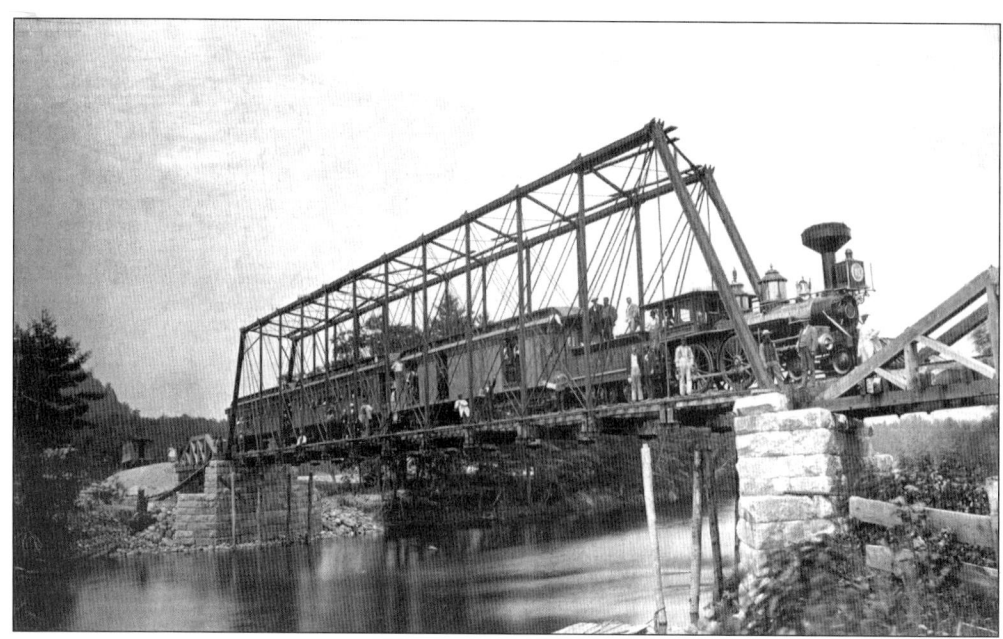

Portland & Rochester locomotive No. 8, *Ossippee*, poses on a steel truss bridge with its passenger train in the early 1880s. Portland Company shop No. 453 was built in 1883 and was of standard gauge, as were the other nine engines built for that road by the Portland Company.

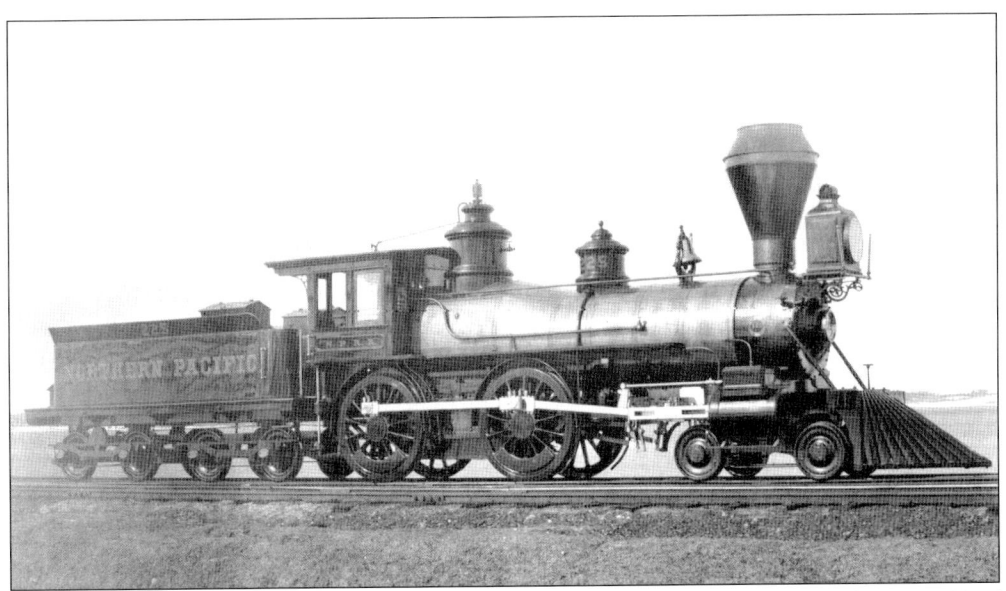

Locomotive No. 225 was constructed in 1883 for the Northern Pacific Railroad. Over 100 of the engines were sent to that railroad in the 1880s. The 4-4-0 engines, with their standard-gauge wheel sets, were sent both overland, and about half were lashed on ships and sent around the Horn to the West Coast.

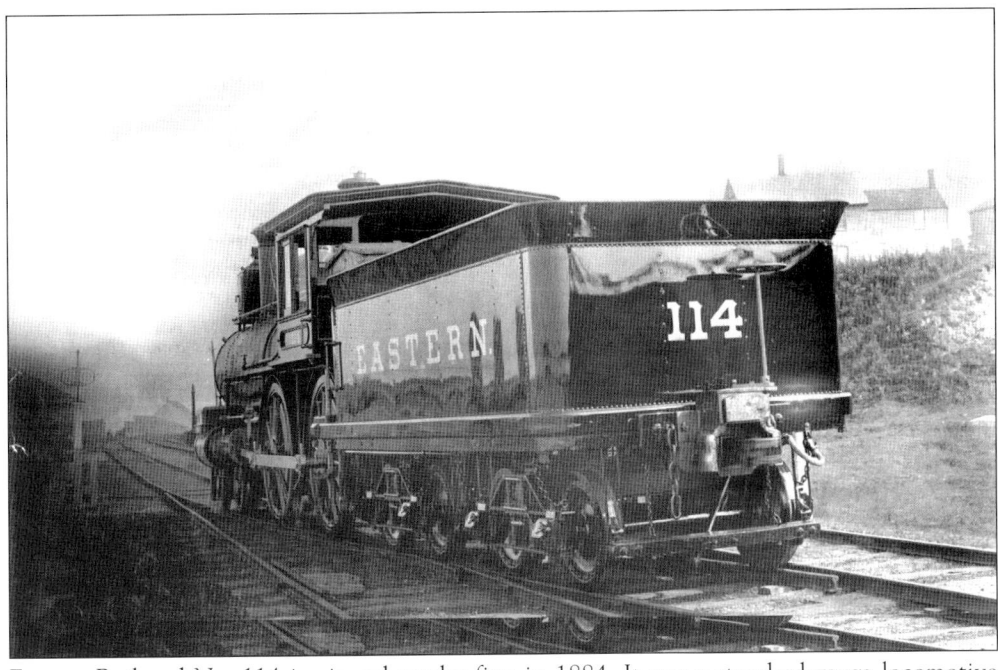

Eastern Railroad No. 114 is viewed tender first in 1884. It was a standard-gauge locomotive built in 1884 as shop No. 536. The Eastern Railroad ran along the coast from Boston to Portland as a competitor of the Boston & Maine Railroad but was eventually taken over as the Boston & Maine's Eastern Division.

35

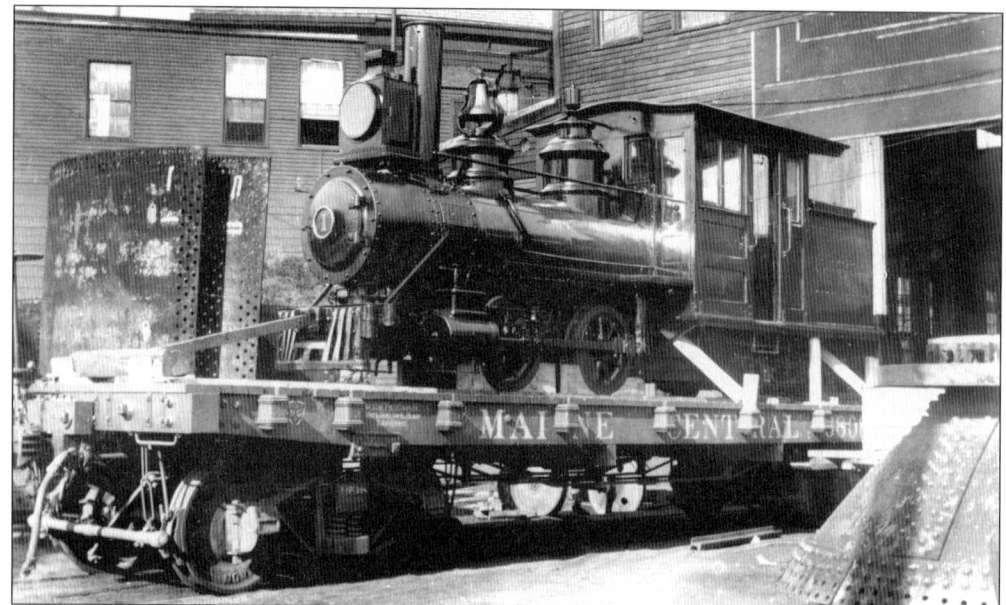

Monson, No. 1, was built by the Hinckley Locomotive Works in Boston in 1881 for the Monson Slate Company in Monson, Maine. It was a "two-footer" (24-inch gauge) and was used to haul slate the six miles to the Maine Central Railroad's main line. The railheads were only two feet apart, so this road was called the "2 by 6." Here we see the *Monson*, No. 1, loaded on a Maine Central flatcar in 1910 after being outshopped at the Portland Company and ready to be put back into service again.

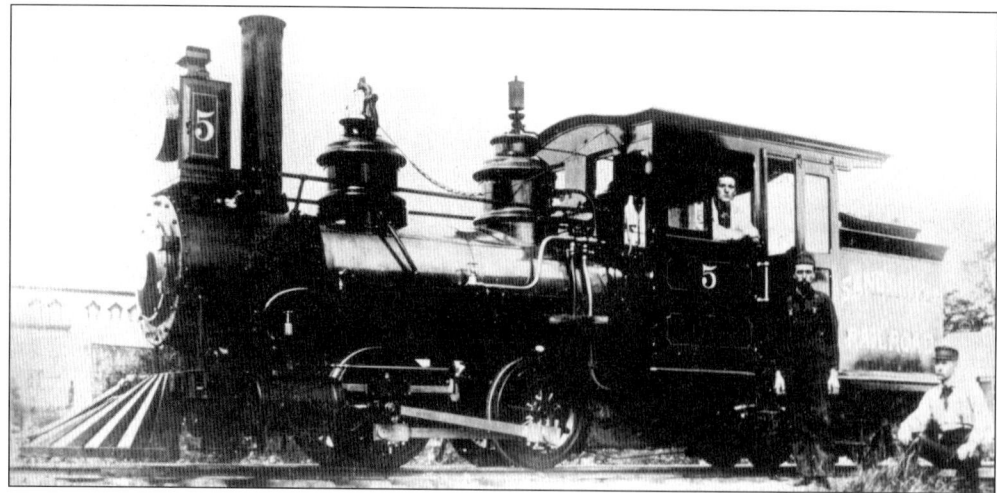

Here we see the newly Portland Company–built 1892 two-foot locomotive for the Sandy River Railroad in Phillips, Maine, as the *N.B. Beale*, No. 5. The Portland shop number is 622. It has 33-inch drivers and is always said to resemble the Hinkley engines from the shape of the cab roof predominately. This is, in fact, because Portland purchased a lot of the Hinkley engineering drawings and patterns from the Hinkley Works in Boston when Hinkley went out of business. Portland even hired some of the former Hinkley employees. This locomotive ran on several roads during its long life and is now back at the Wiscasset, Waterville & Farmington Railway Museum in Alna, Maine, where it will run again to the delight of rail fans the world over, on the original two-foot roadbed.

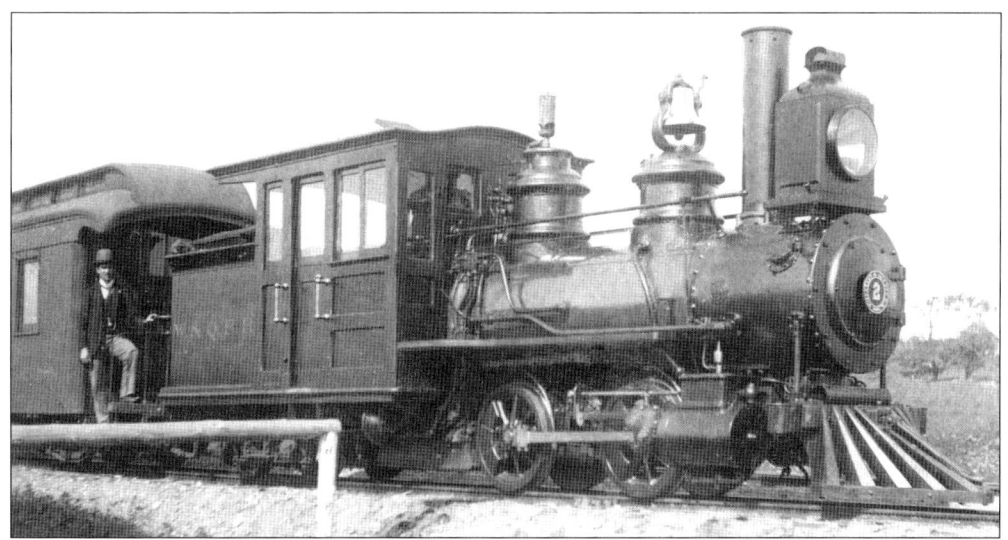

The Portland Company built a total of eight locomotives for the Maine two-foot railroads. The "two-foot" refers to the 24-inch distance between the railheads on the track versus the 56 1/2 inches of standard-gauge rails. This Wiscasset & Quebec Railroad locomotive was built in 1891 as the road's No. 2 engine. Today there is only one "two-footer" from the Portland Company remaining. It was built for the Sandy River Railroad in Phillips, Maine, and is now at the Wiscasset, Waterville & Farmington Railway Museum in Alna, Maine, being restored to ply the tiny rails once more, pulling the same 1894 Jackson & Sharp–built coach pictured above, from the old Wiscasset & Quebec Railroad and leased currently from the Maine Narrow Gauge Railroad & Museum.

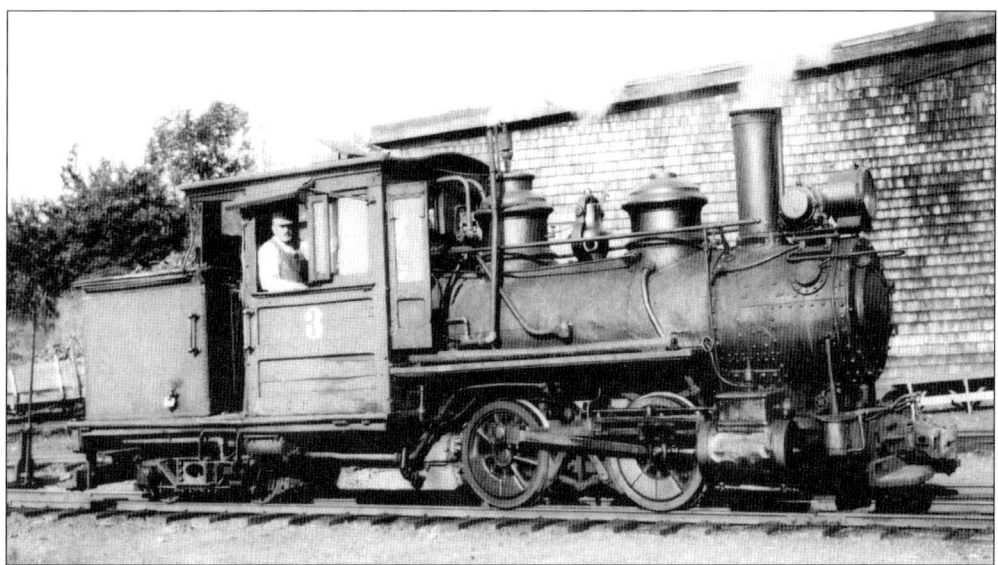

Here we see Wiscasset, Waterville & Farmington Railway locomotive No. 3 simmering beside the engine house. Originally built in Portland for the Wisscasset & Quebec Railroad as shop No. 627 in 1894, it was the next-to-last steam locomotive ever to be built by the Portland Company. Only two Portland locomotives are known to still exist. One is a sister to the above engine, and one is a standard-gauge Canadian National Railroad engine and is at a museum in Ottowa.

37

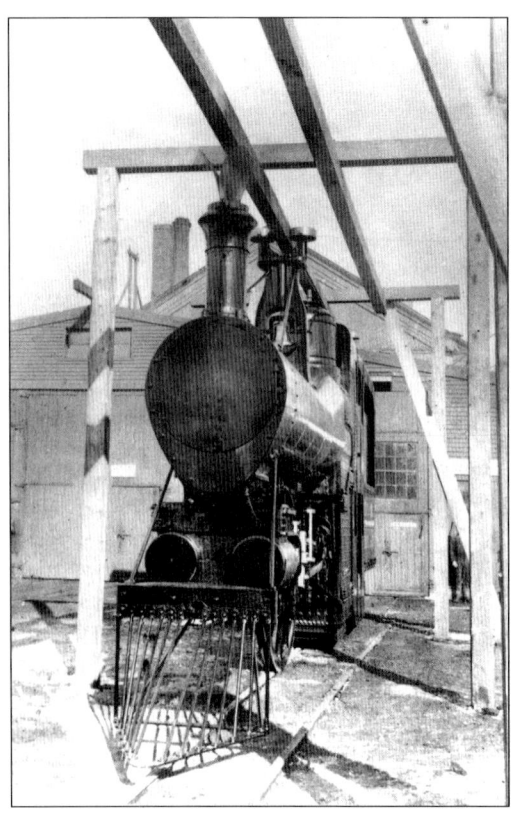

This 1889 monorail steam engine, *Cycle*, No. 1, was the brainchild of Eben Moody Boynton of West Newbury, Massachusetts. He had it built along with a second engine for his Boynton Bicycle Railway in Coney Island, New York. It had a two-story cab and a 93-inch double-flanged single driver. The two trailing wheels made it a 0-1-1-1 wheel arrangement. Here we see it on a test track with a wooden overhead rail to stabilize it at the Portland Company yard.

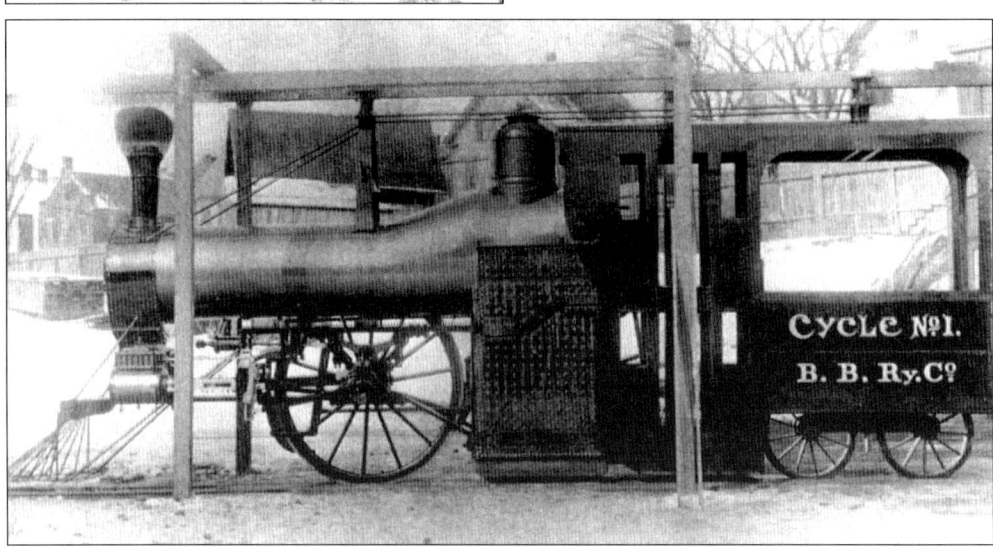

Shown here is a side view of Eban Moody Boynton's *Cycle*, No. 1, built for his Boynton Bicycle Railway. The monorail engine had a double-flanged 93-inch-diameter single driving wheel. The engine weighed 22 tons and was 15.5 feet high and 4 feet wide. It was built in 1889 and ran on a line to Coney Island, New York. The Portland Company also produced a second engine, dissimilar to this one, as well as a least one 4-foot-wide double-decker passenger car that carried 118 passengers and was boarded from both sides of the individual vis-à-vis seat compartments from the outside.

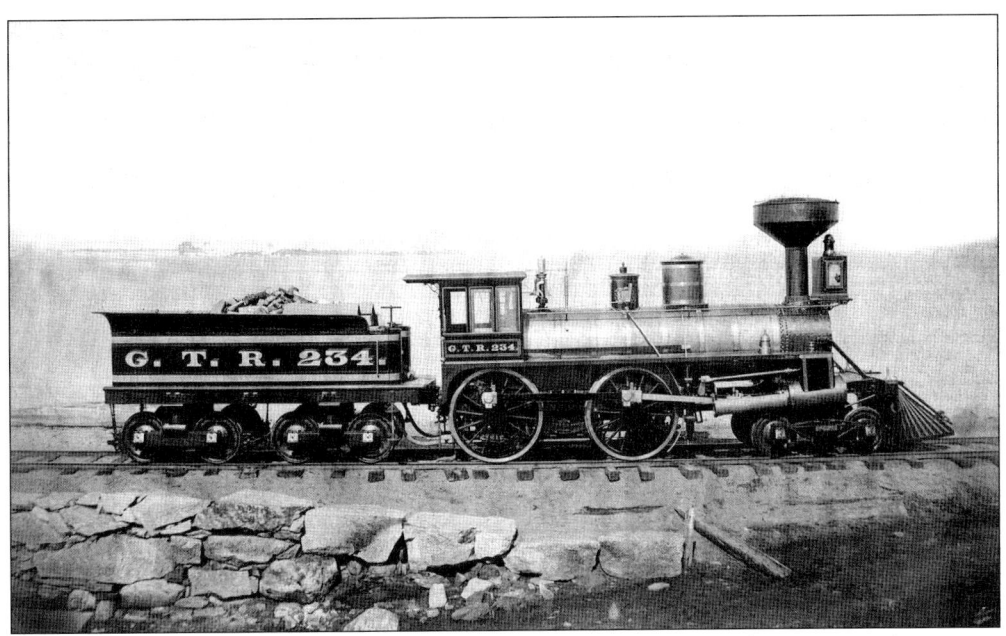

An early Grand Trunk Railroad engine is shown *c.* 1873. Its road number is 234, and it rests in front of the Portland Company for an official builder's photograph.

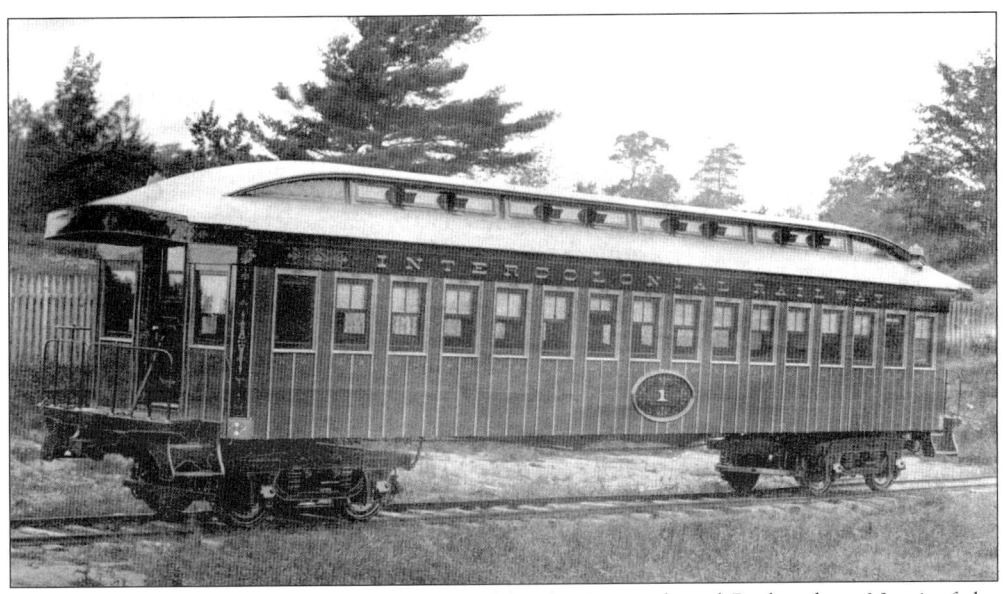

The car shops also turned out passenger cars like this Intercolonial Railroad car No. 1 of the 1870s. The decorating masters, or "trimmers," in the paint shops did superb work detailing both railroad cars and engines with many colors of paints as well as with gold and aluminum bronzing powders simulating gold and silver leaf. After the early 1880s, when many engines now burned the dirtier coal instead of wood, the colors on the exterior of railroad equipment shifted to darker shades, and less ornate and colorful details were used.

39

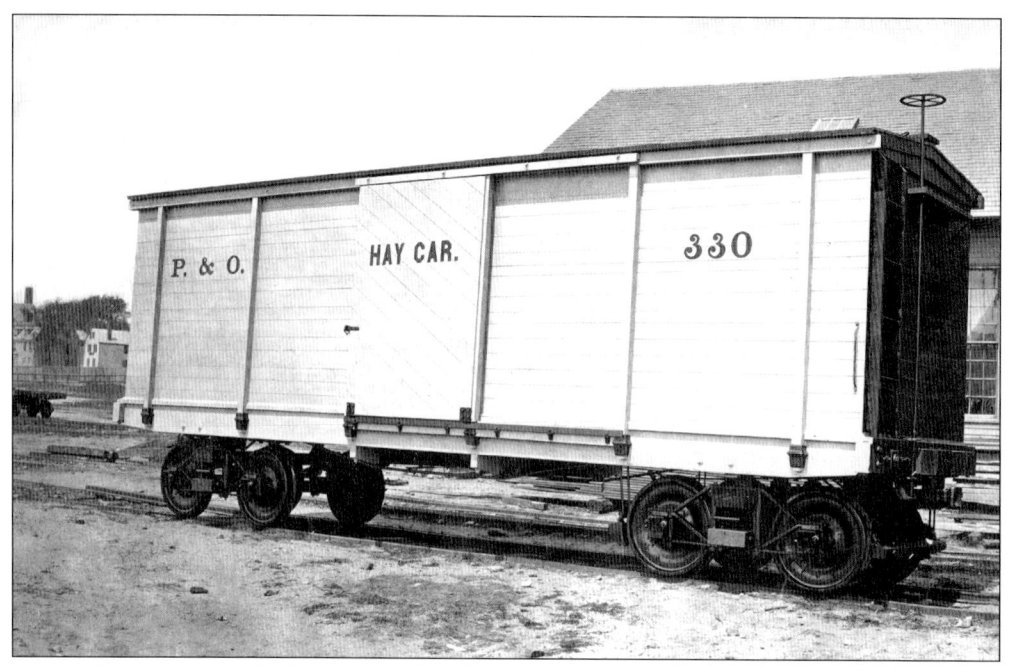

Pictured is Portland & Ogdensburg Railroad hay car No. 330. The hay cars were unique in that when the loose hay was to be unloaded at its destination, the whole car body could be lifted off the car's platform from the stake pockets and the hay was then hauled off.

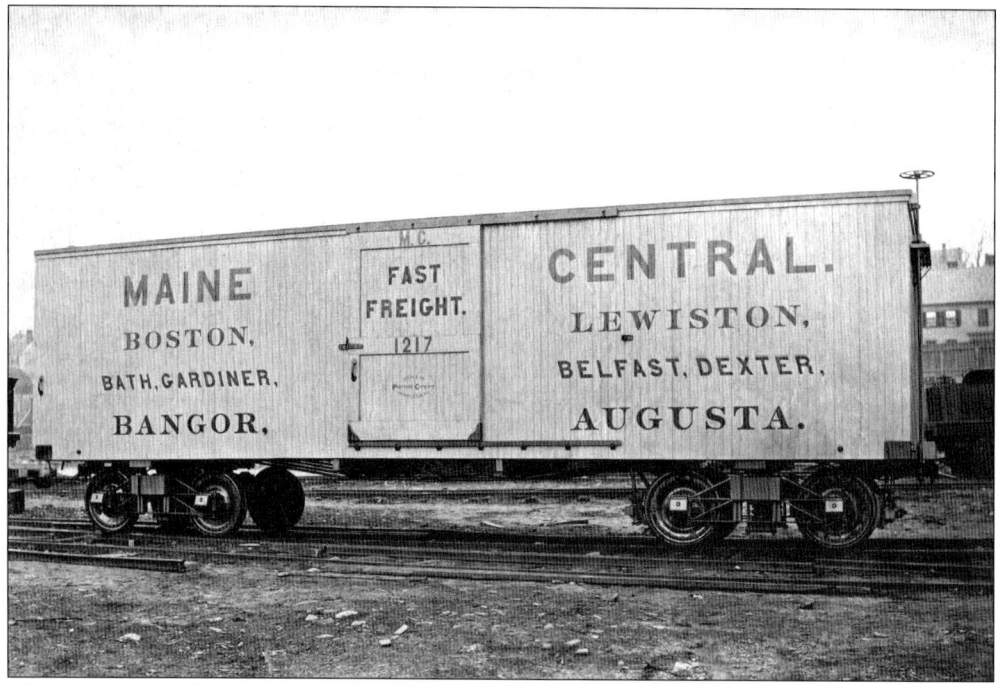

This photograph shows a very unusually decorated boxcar No. 1217. It was built for the Maine Central Railroad and decorated with the names of many of the cities that the railroad served. The Portland Company has its name very prominently displayed on the door of this "display or advertising car."

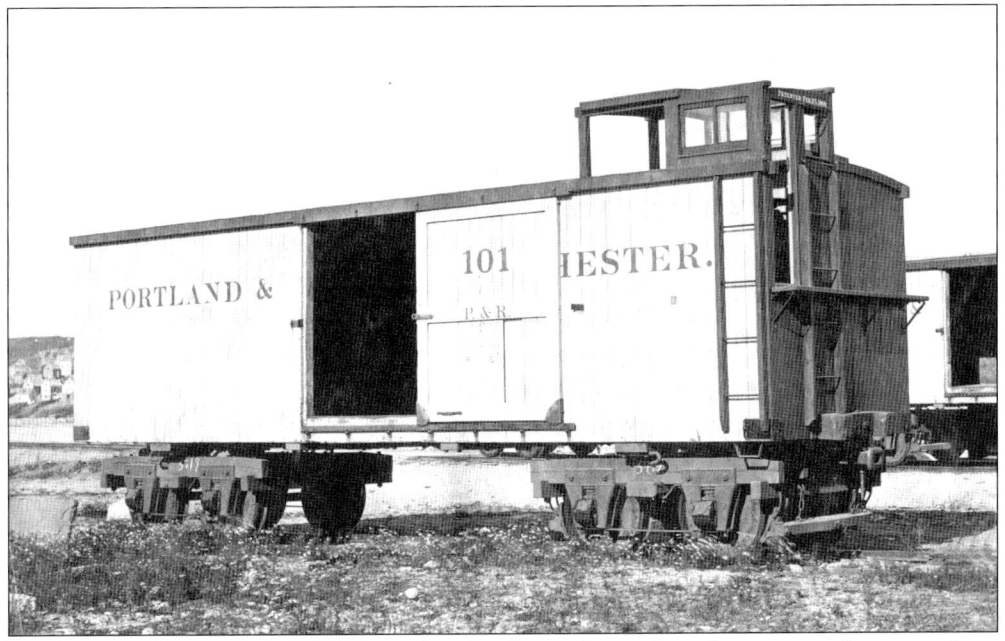

This unusual Portland & Rochester Railroad "caboose-boxcar" combination car has a cupola so that the brakeman can sit and watch over his train. The Portland Company designed, but never built, a similar narrow-gauge caboose with platforms at the turn of the century for the Wiscasset, Waterville & Farmington Railway. Now, the present Wiscasset, Waterville & Farmington Railway Museum in Alna, Maine, has built this planned two-foot caboose with its narrow end platforms and tiny windows and uses it today on the museums rail line.

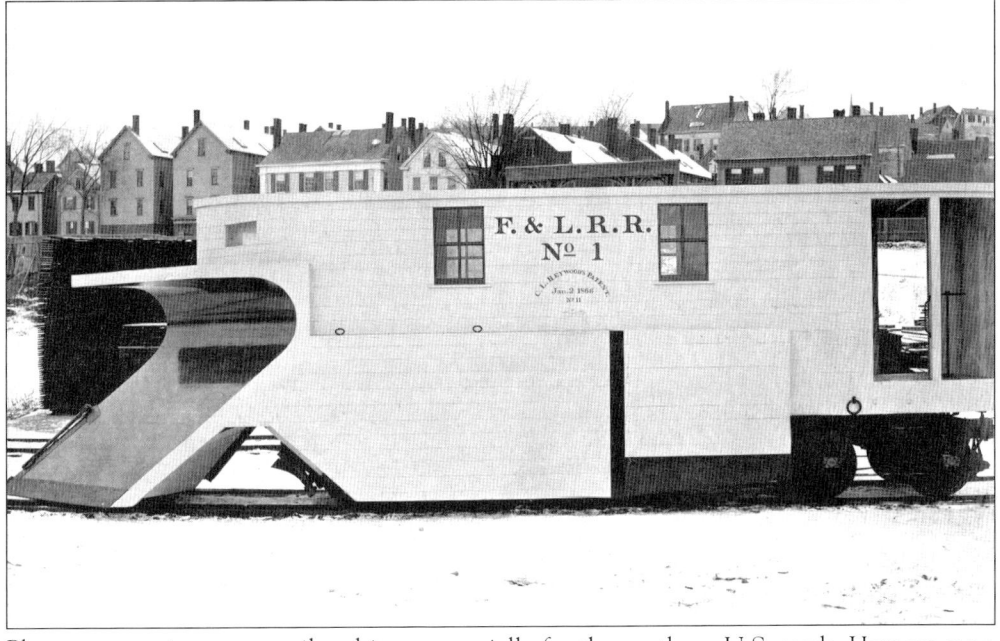

Plows were an important railroad item, especially for the northern U.S. roads. Here we see a wooden Fitchburg & Leominster Railroad wing plow needed to clear the line and push the snow well back to make room for the inevitable next snowfall.

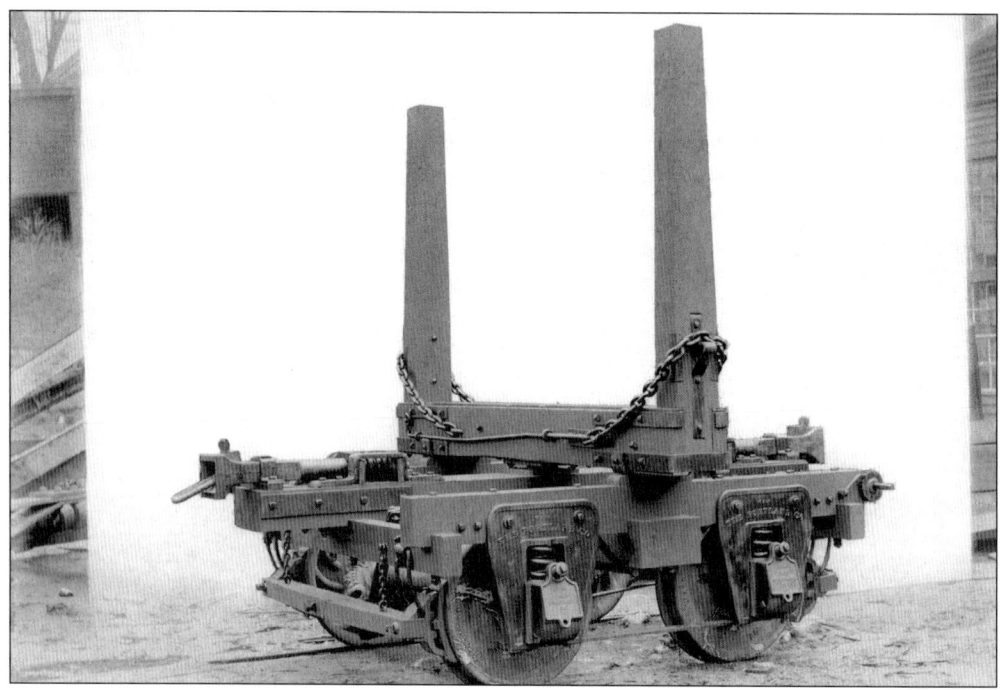

This completed log bunk built for the Somerset Railroad in 1906 is posed in front of a sheet for an official builder's photograph. The car shops turned these bunks out by the hundreds for hauling logs from Maine's timbering operations to the sawmills. One bunk was chained under each end of a load of long logs and coupled together with "reach poles" between the link couplers to make up a train of logs. The Sandy River Railroad in Phillips, Maine, used to haul logs at night and other freight and passengers during the daytime.

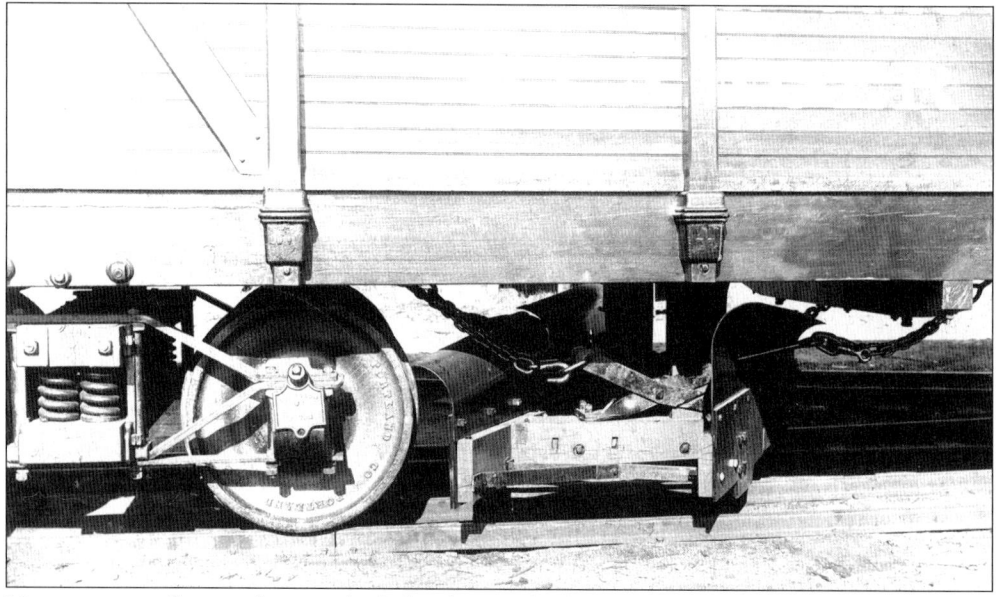

Here we see a flanger that was built by the Portland Company even down to its company-marked wheels. The scraping mechanism under the car was to clear ice and snow from between the rails to keep the trains from being derailed when snow packed down and froze.

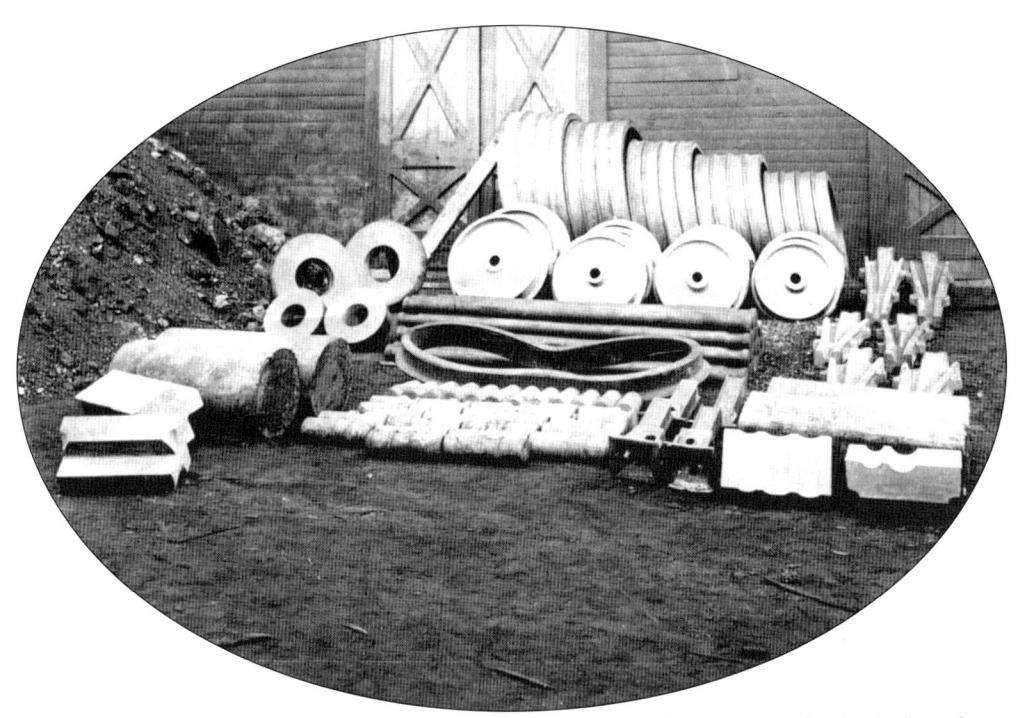

Outside the foundry we can see piles of locomotive flanged tires, car wheels, link and pin couplers, switch frogs, and other railroad-related castings.

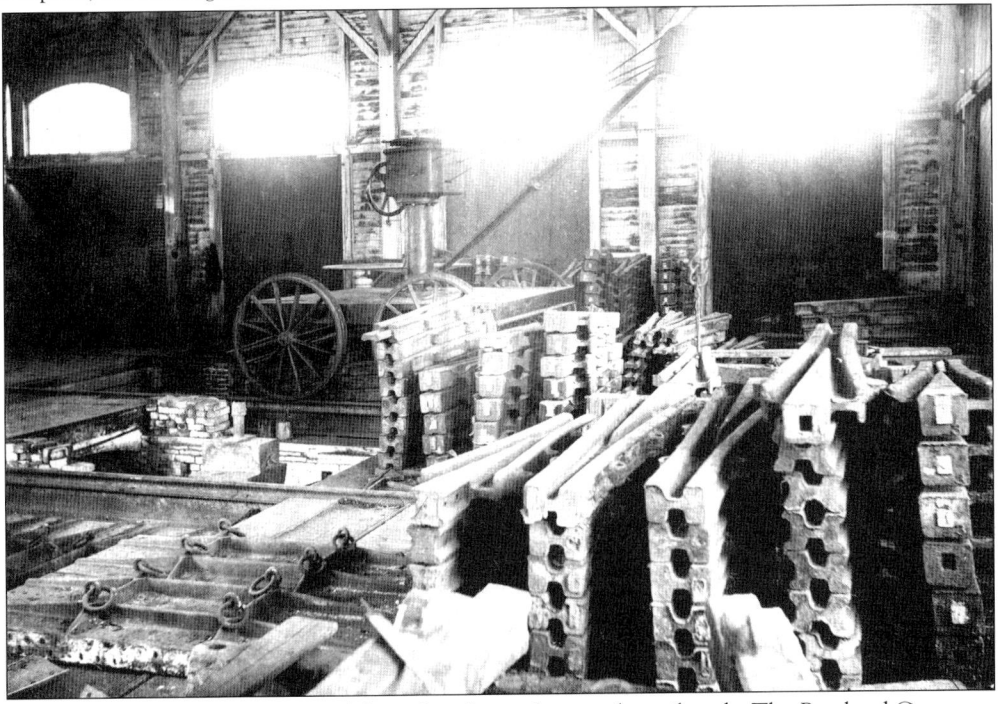

Many cast components were used for railroad switches on the railroads. The Portland Company had a special "frog shop" where these castings were machined after casting to fabricate the needed rail switches.

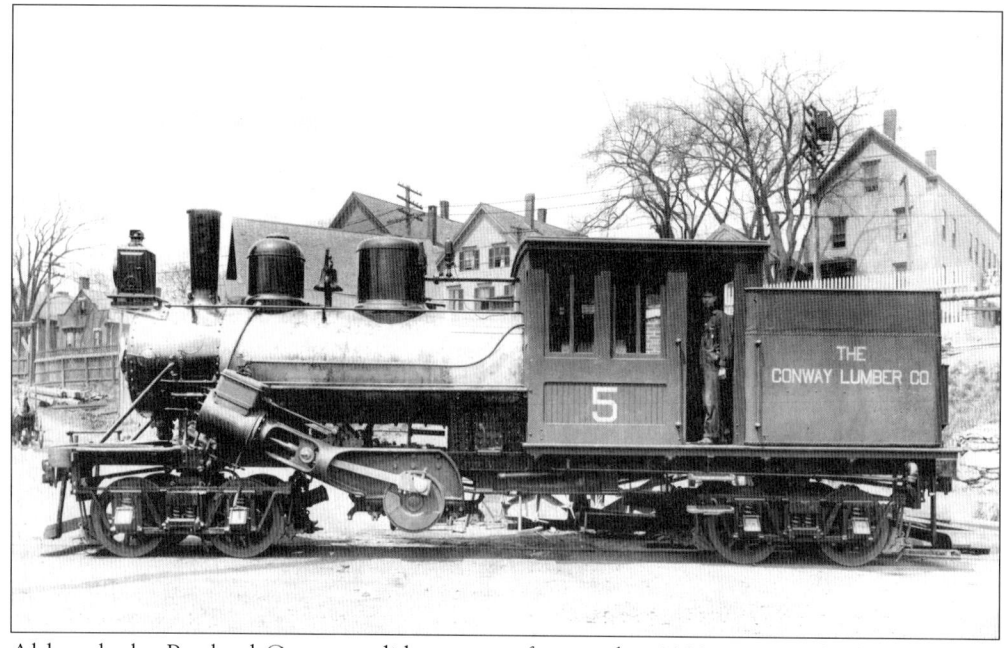

Although the Portland Company did not manufacture this 1900-era geared Climax logging locomotive, it did rebuild it in 1910 for the Conway Lumber Company. Geared locomotives, such as Shays, Climax, and Heislers, were able to move up greater grades than the more conventional rod locomotive and were therefore better suited for hauling heavy loads in hilly or mountainous country. The Portland Company also rebuilt an untold number of locomotives for many roads as they need to be reboiled or otherwise repaired.

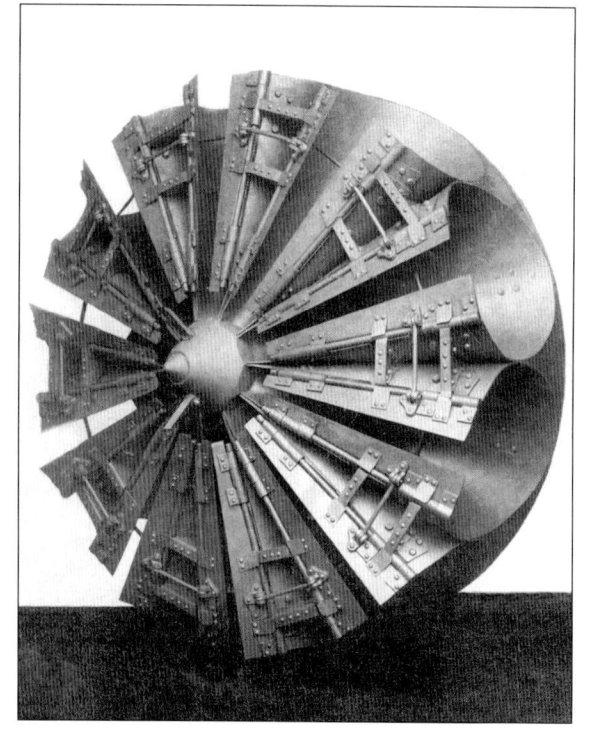

This view shows the auger fan for a Leslie rotary snowplow that the company made under a contract from the Leslie Company for the Northern Pacific Railroad. Several were built in two different gauges, and a couple of them are still in existence today in the West.

Three

VESSELS, MARINE ENGINES, AND BOILERS

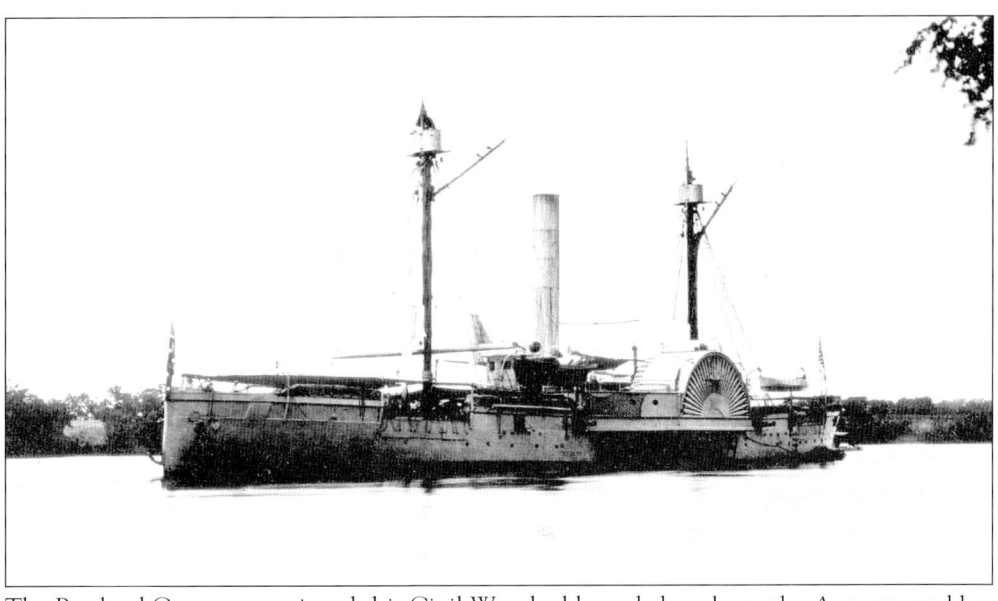

The Portland Company equipped this Civil War double-ended gunboat, the *Agawam*, and her sister ship, the *Pontoosic*, with boilers, engines, and other equipment in 1863. The *Agawam* was 205 feet in length and built for the U.S. Navy. She is shown "on station" at Trents Reach, blocking the entrance to the James River in Virginia in July 1864. The company also built several steam locomotives and cannon for the war.

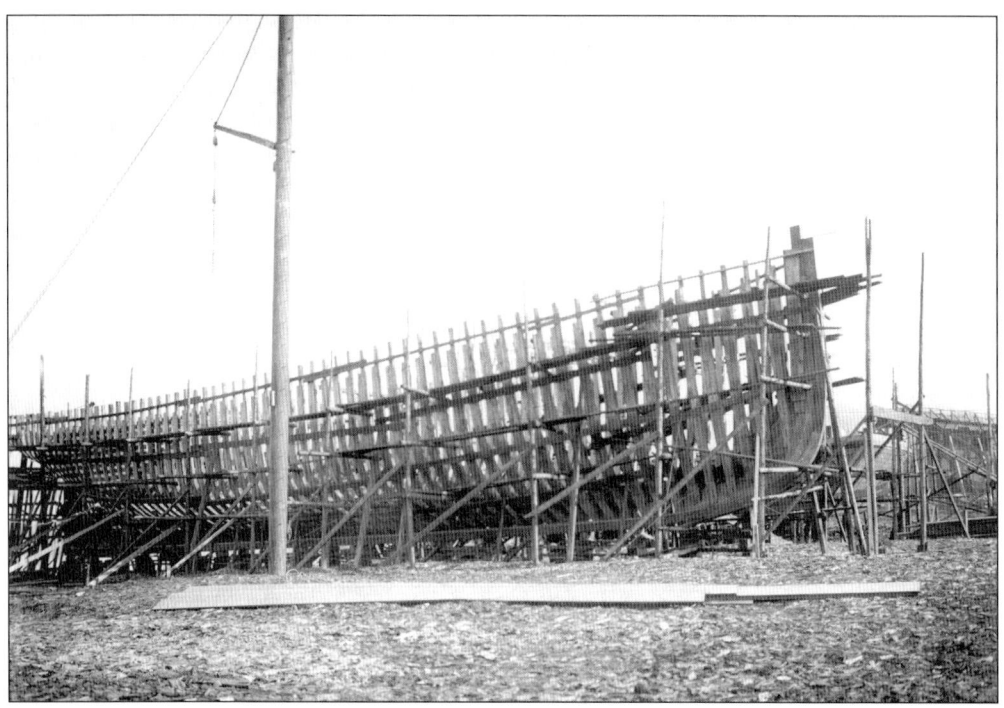

This view shows the very beginnings of the trawler *East Hampton* in a South Portland boatyard. She was built and equipped by the Portland Company in 1913 for Sickler & Meadows of the Atlantic Fertilizer Company.

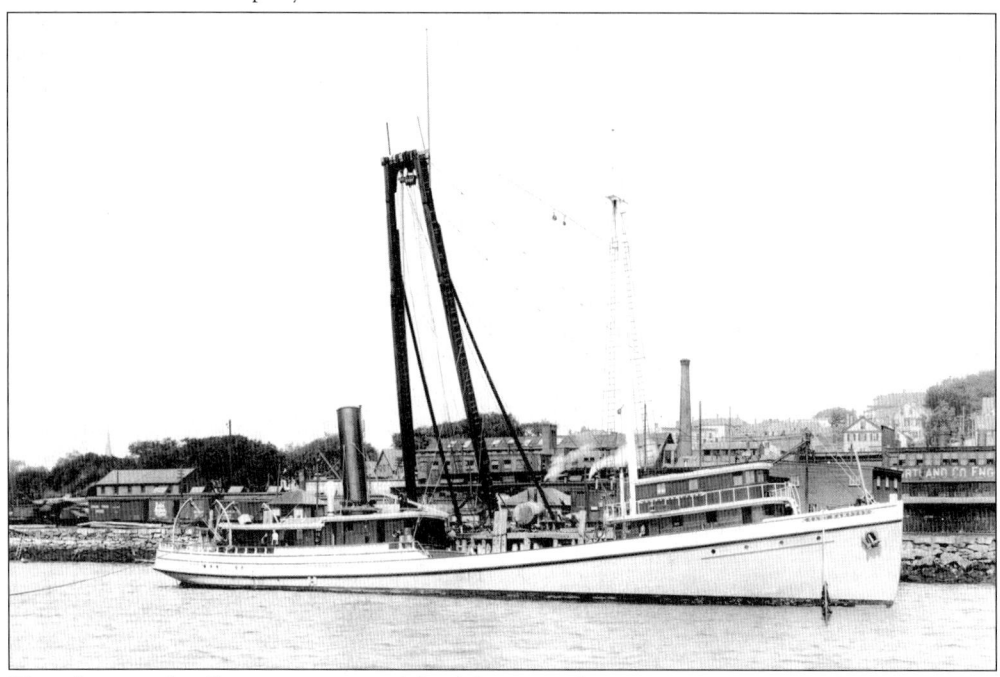

This photograph offers a great view of the fishing trawler *East Hampton* moored in front of the Portland Company pier after being built and equipped by the Portland Company in 1913 for Sickler & Meadows of the Atlantic Fertilizer Company. The trawler was 169 feet long overall.

Shown here is a view of the decks of the working trawler *East Hampton*. Along the forward rails we can see the doors, or "otter boards," under the gallows frames for use in trawling to keep the mouths of the nets open.

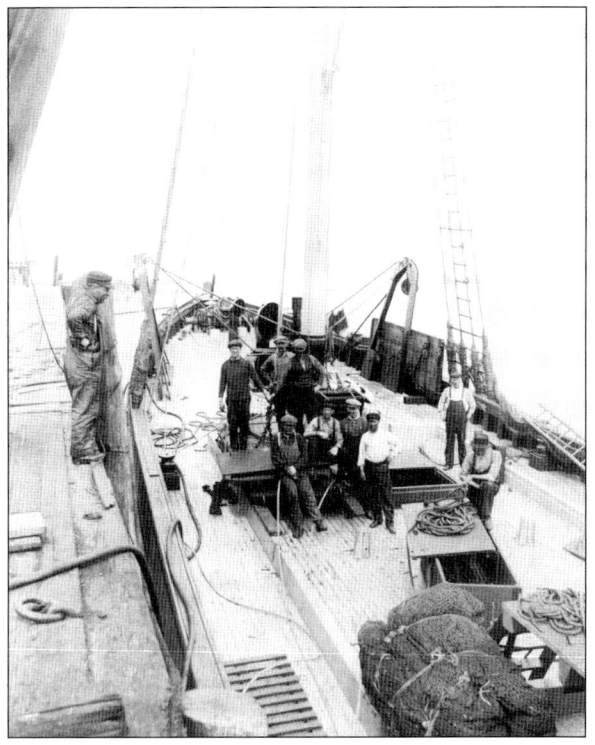

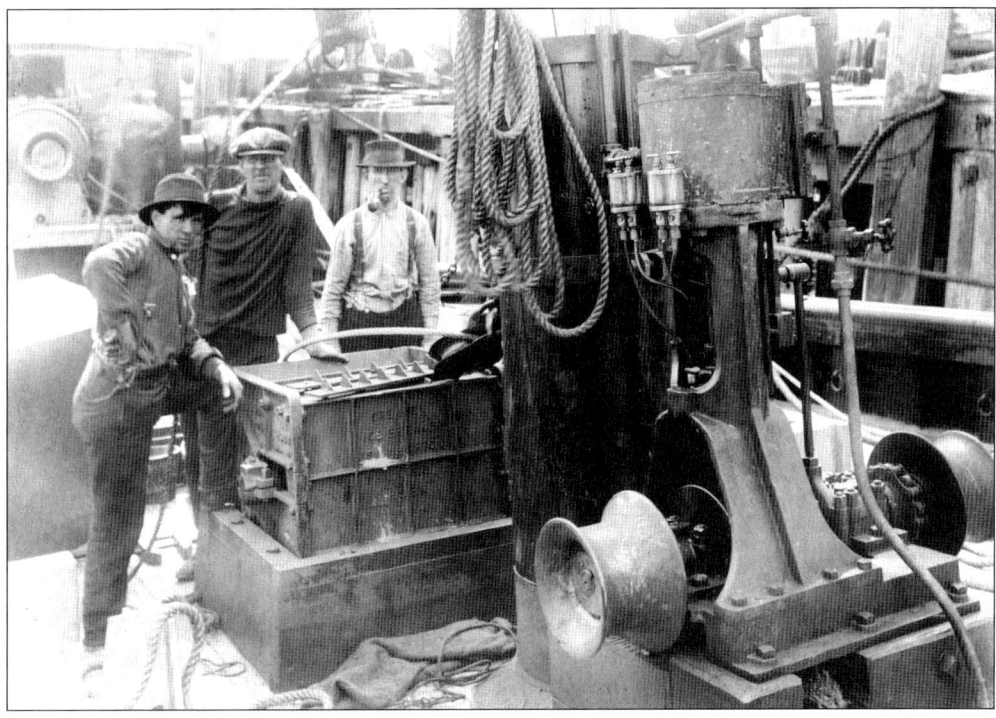

Some of the crew of the steamer *East Hampton* stop and pose for the photographer on the deck. Note the steam-powered windlass in the foreground and the ice-breaking machine that the men are leaning on for icing the holds of freshly caught fish.

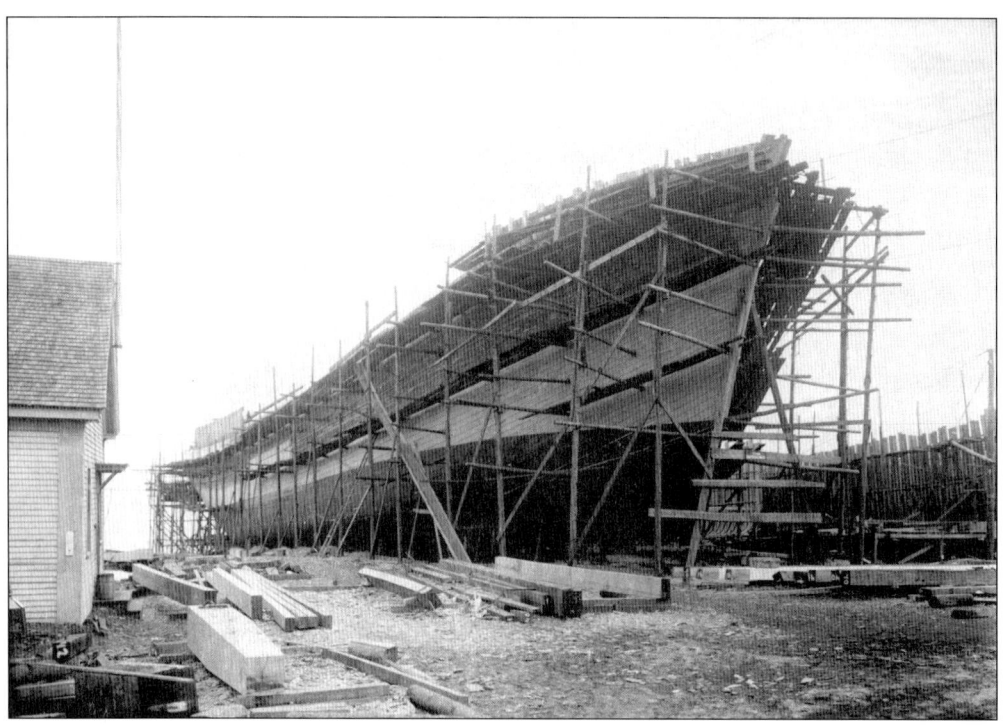

The hull of the steamer *Ripogenus* is nearly complete as we see it on the ways at the shipyard of the Francis Cobb Shipbuilding Company in Rockland, Maine. After launching, she will be towed to the Portland Company pier for outfitting with the necessary machinery.

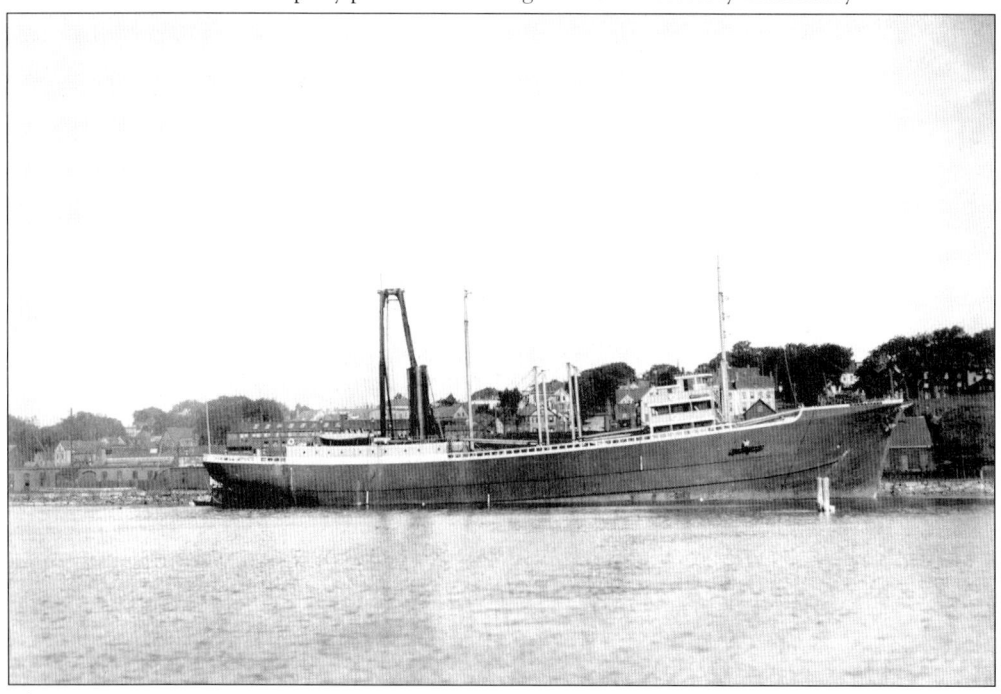

The twin-screw steamer *Ripogenus* is tied up to the company pier probably for outfitting. She was built in 1917 in Rockland for the Great Northern Paper & Pulp Company.

48

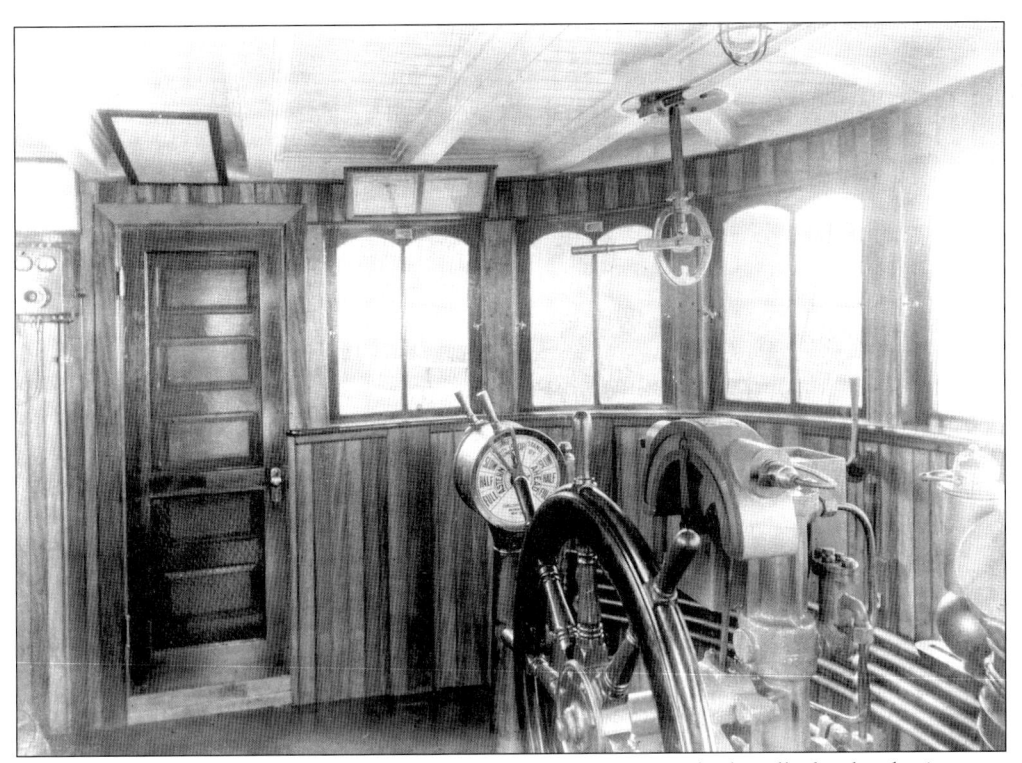

This view shows the pilothouse on the steamer *Ripogenus*. Note the handle for the ship's steam whistle mounted on the overhead above the wheel. The vessel even had a telephone on the wall near the door.

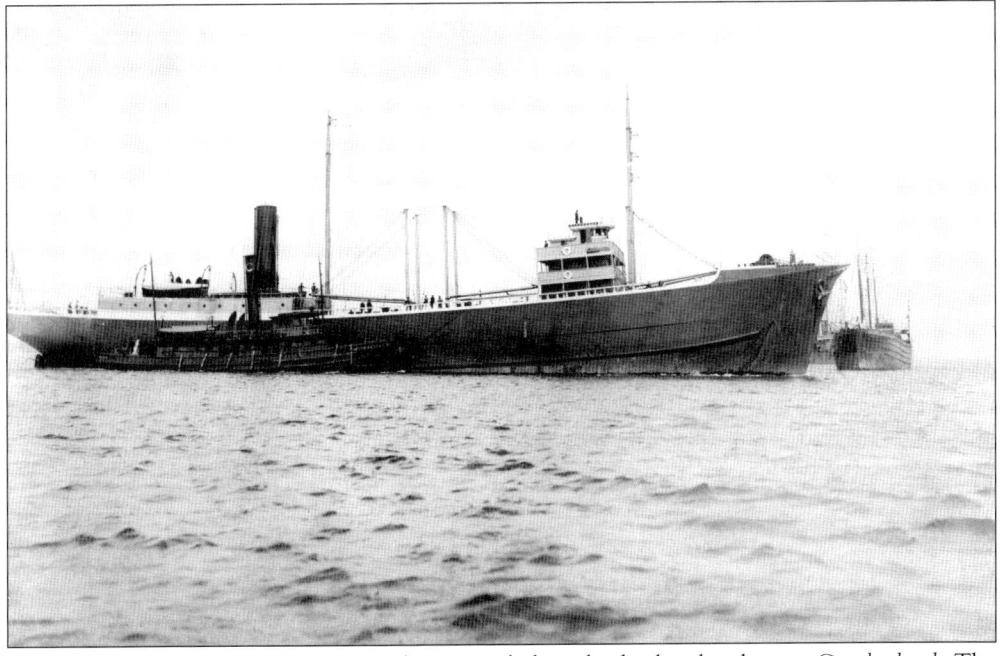

The twin-screw steamer *Ripogenus* is being guided in the harbor by the tug *Cumberland*. The *Ripogenus*'s home port was Belfast, Maine. At 267 feet in length, she was an impressive vessel.

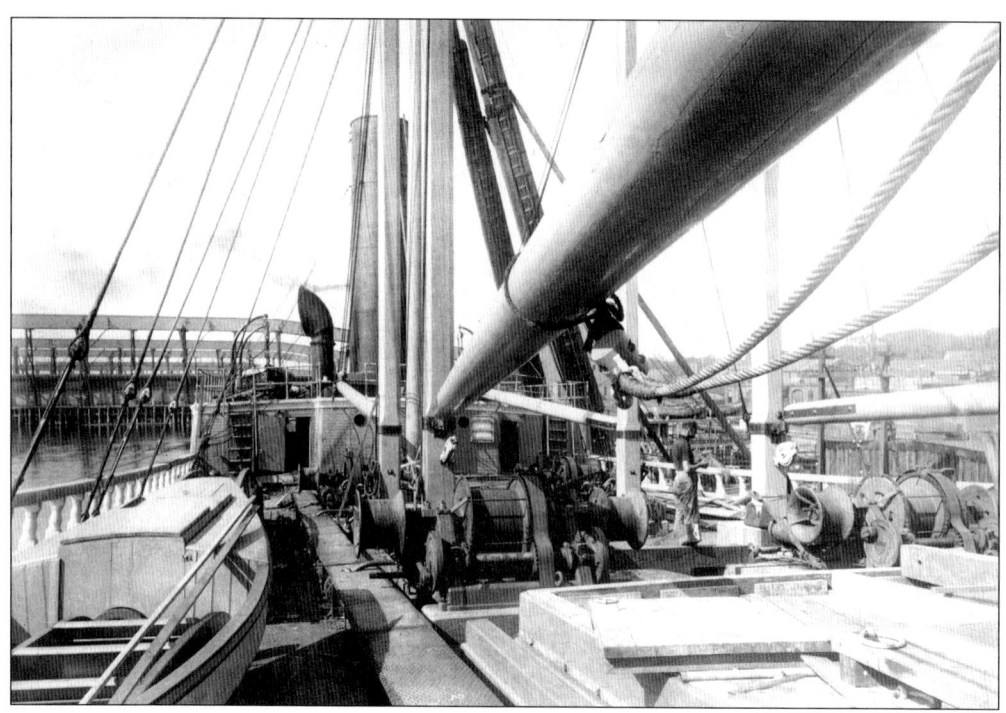

This view shows the deck of the steamer *Ripogenus* moored at the Portland Company pier. We can see the long grain conveyors from the Grand Trunk Railroad's grain elevators aft of the steamer.

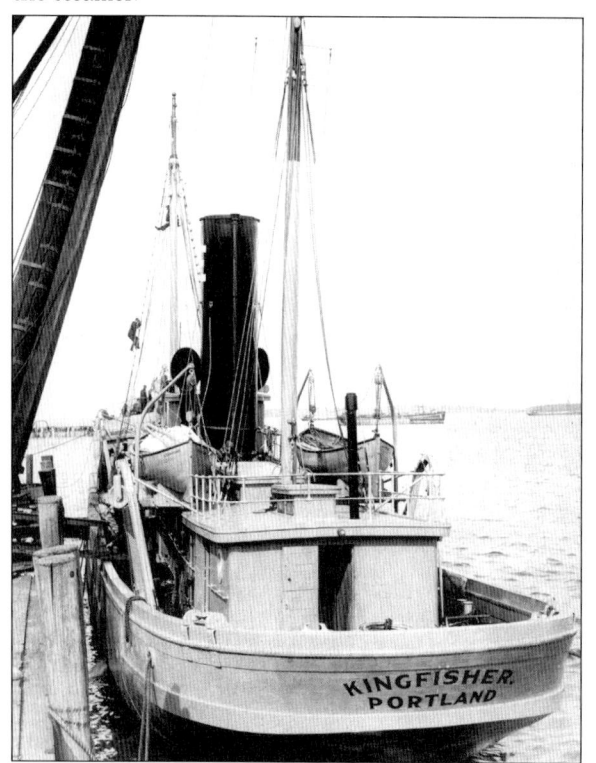

The fishing trawler *Kingfisher*, tied up at the company pier, was built in South Portland in 1917 for the East Coast Fisheries Company and was out of Rockland, Maine. All of her various equipment was built and installed by the Portland Company. She was 139 feet long stem to stern.

50

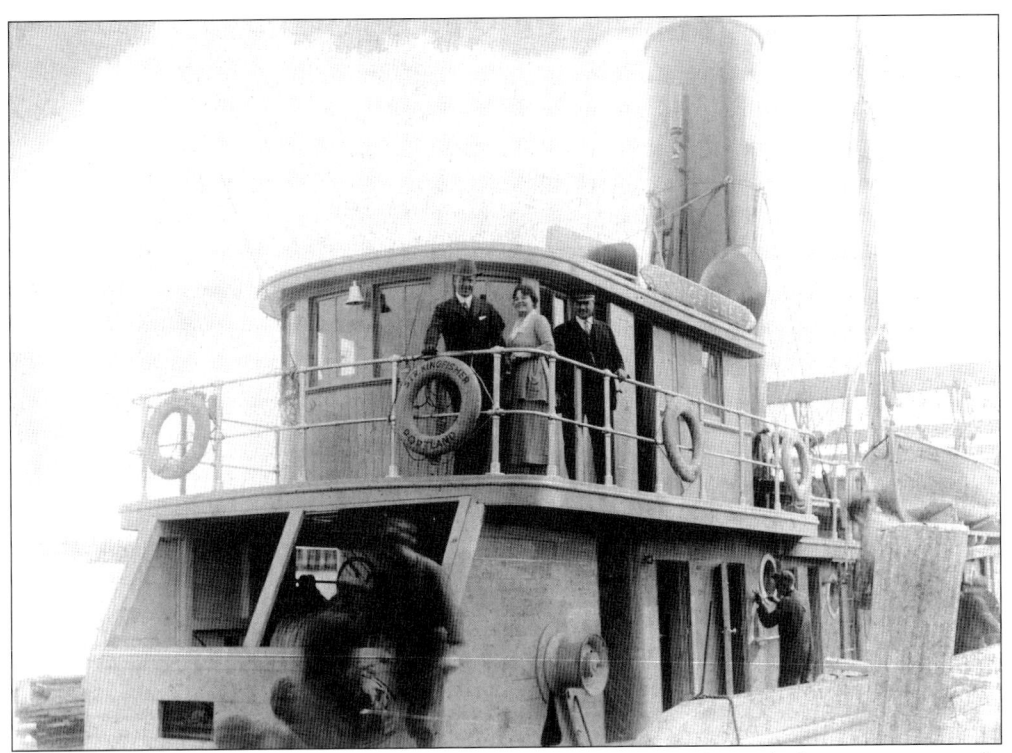

Shown is a closeup of perhaps the *Kingfisher*'s owner, his wife, and the captain outside the pilothouse.

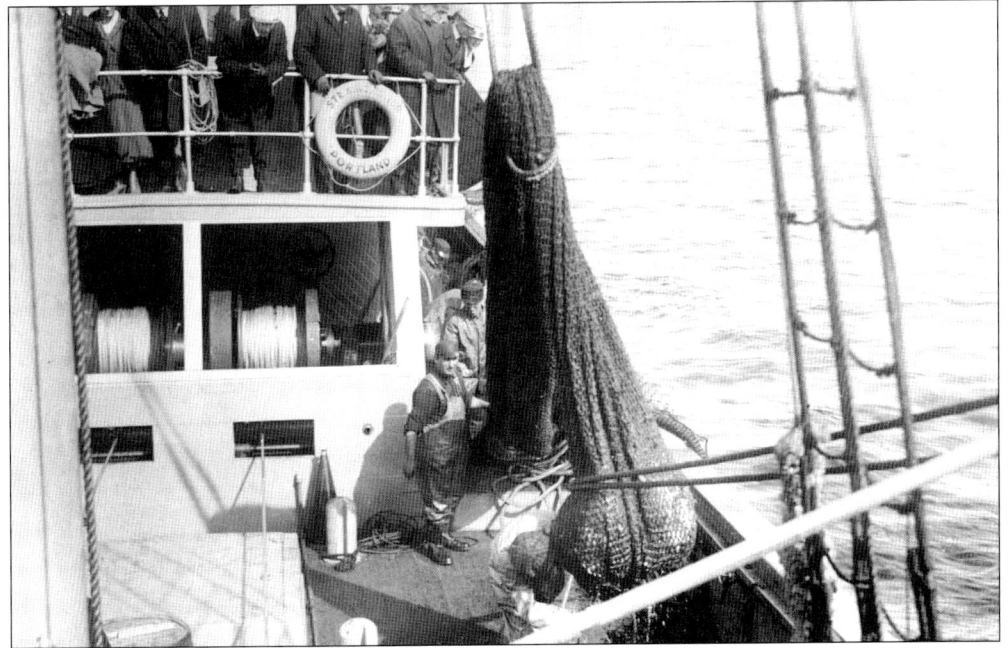

Perhaps on her first voyage, the trawler *Kingfisher* has just hauled a netful of small fish. The operation appears to be happening under the watchful eyes of interested guests aboard the vessel that day.

51

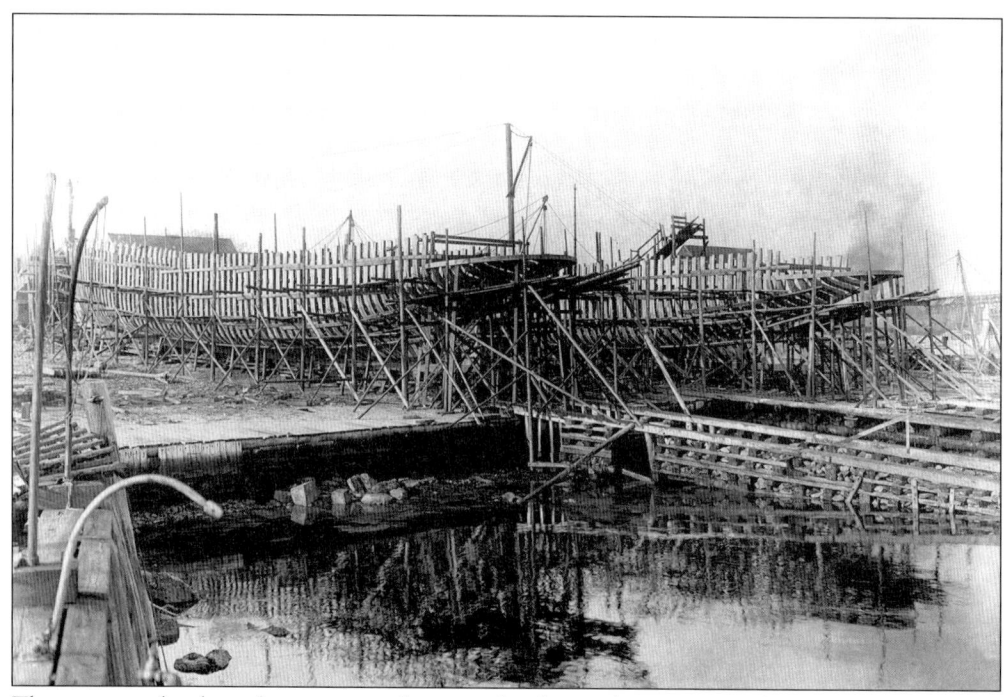

The two vessels whose frames we see here on the shipyard ways in South Portland are perhaps the twin fishing steamers *Herbert N. Edwards* and *Martin J. Marran*, built in 1911.

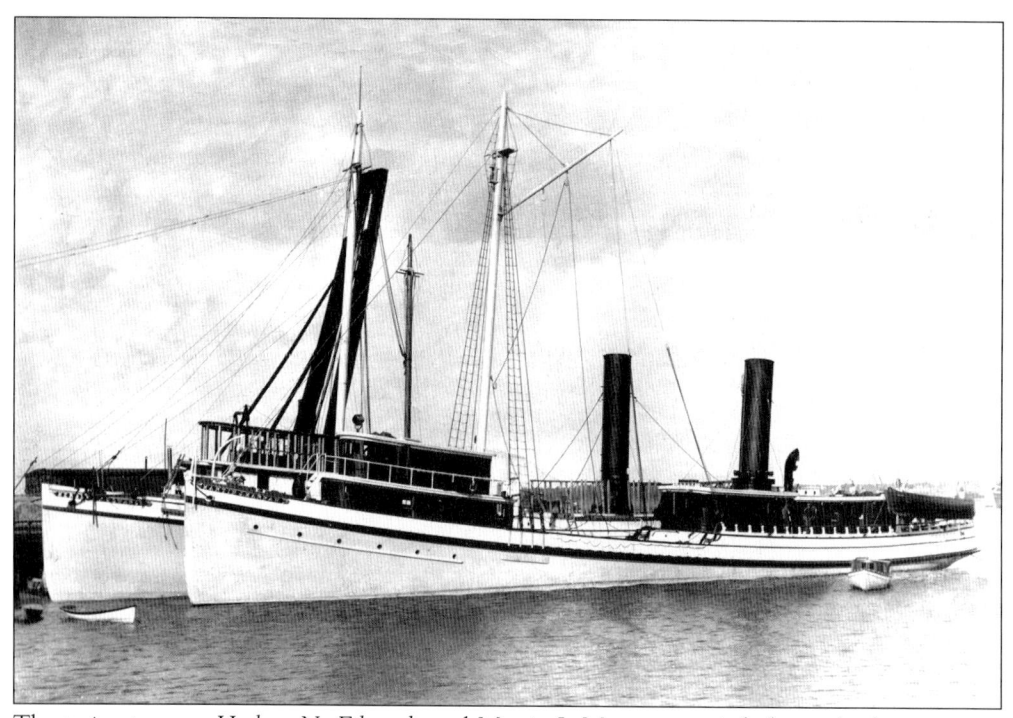

The twin steamers *Herbert N. Edwards* and *Martin J. Marran* are tied alongside the company pier. They were built by the Portland Company in South Portland, Maine, for the Atlantic Fertilizer Company in 1911.

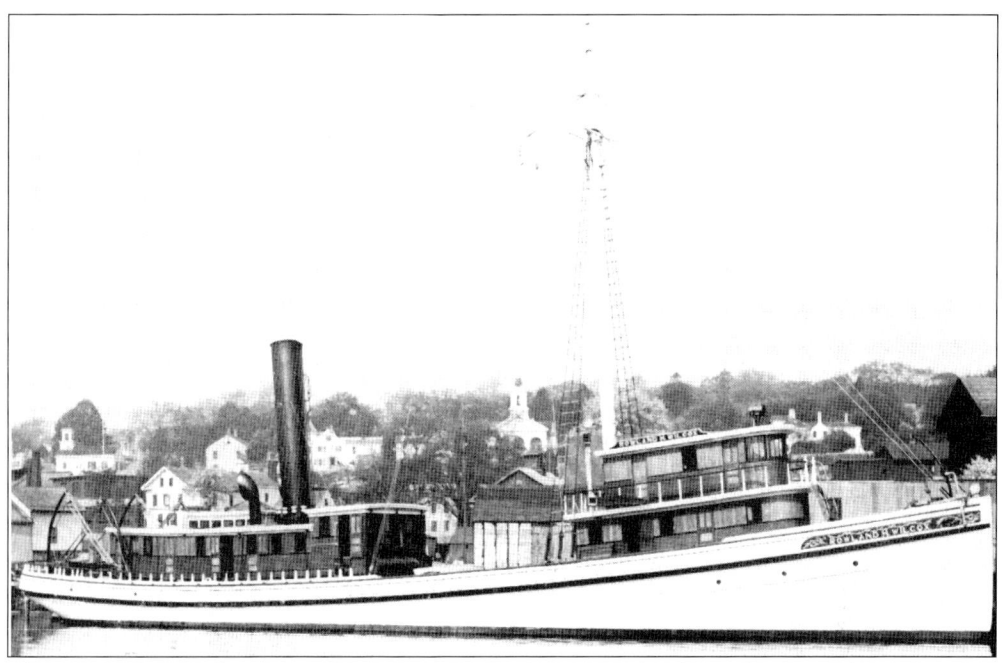

The *Rowland H. Wilcox* was a fishing steamer built in 1906 for the Wilcox Fertilizer Company of Mystic, Connecticut, and was equipped with all Portland Company products. The boiler was a Scotch type with a 450-horsepower engine.

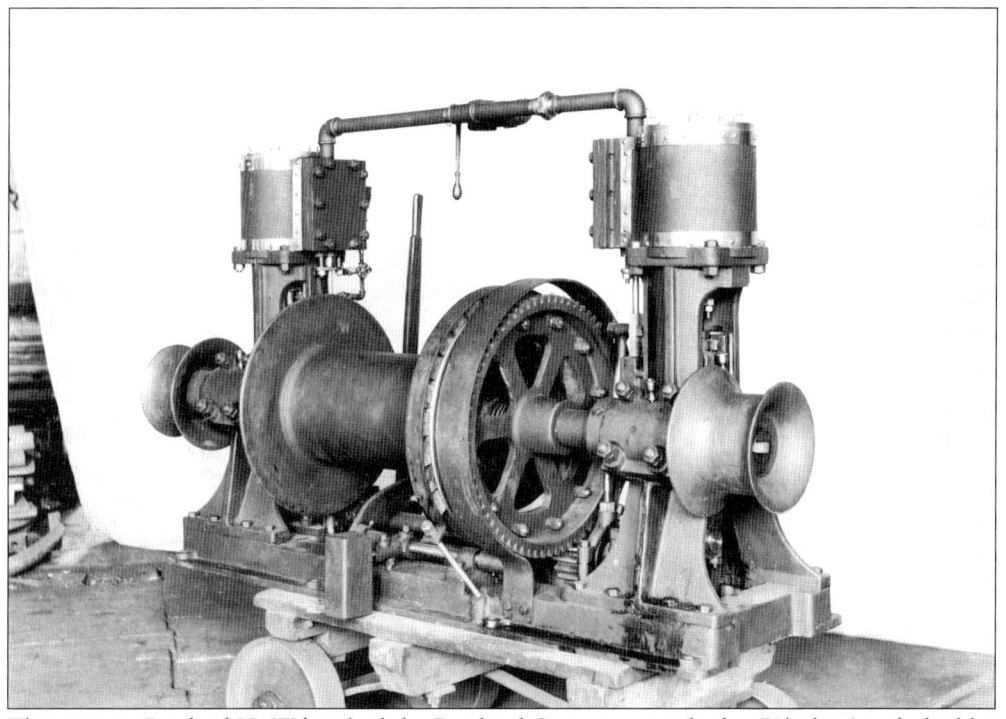

The steamer *Rowland H. Wilcox* had the Portland Company supply this 7½- by 6-inch double-cylinder steam-powered windlass with a friction-driven drum for use on the deck.

53

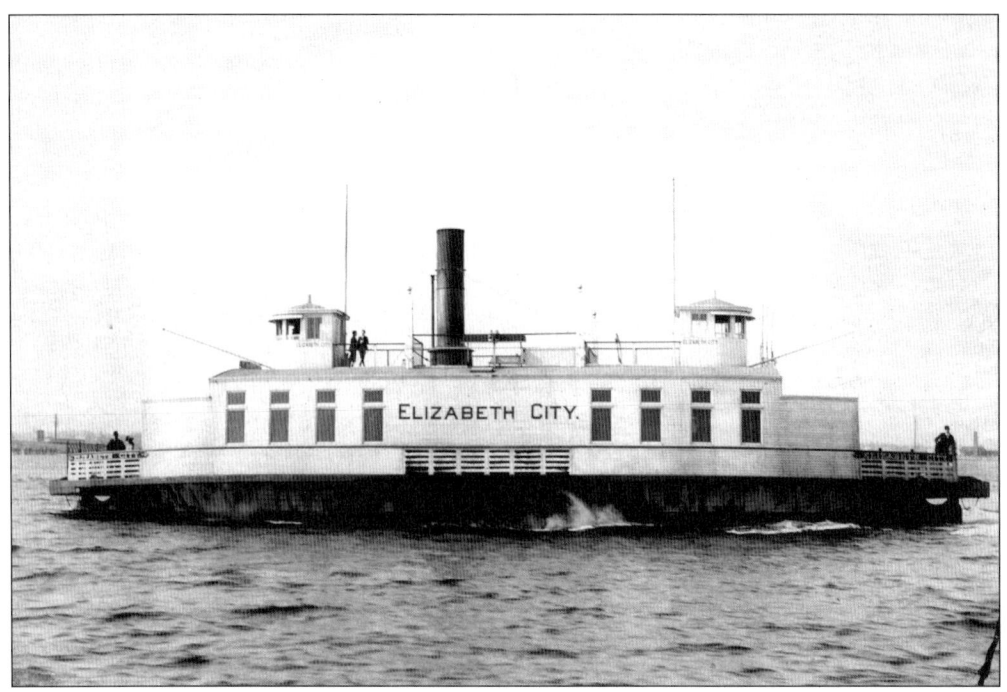

The *Elizabeth City* was a side-wheeled ferry berthed in Portland and built in 1893 in Bath, Maine, for G.S. Hunt and J.P. Baxter. She was 95 feet long from stem to stern and traveled among the islands of Casco Bay.

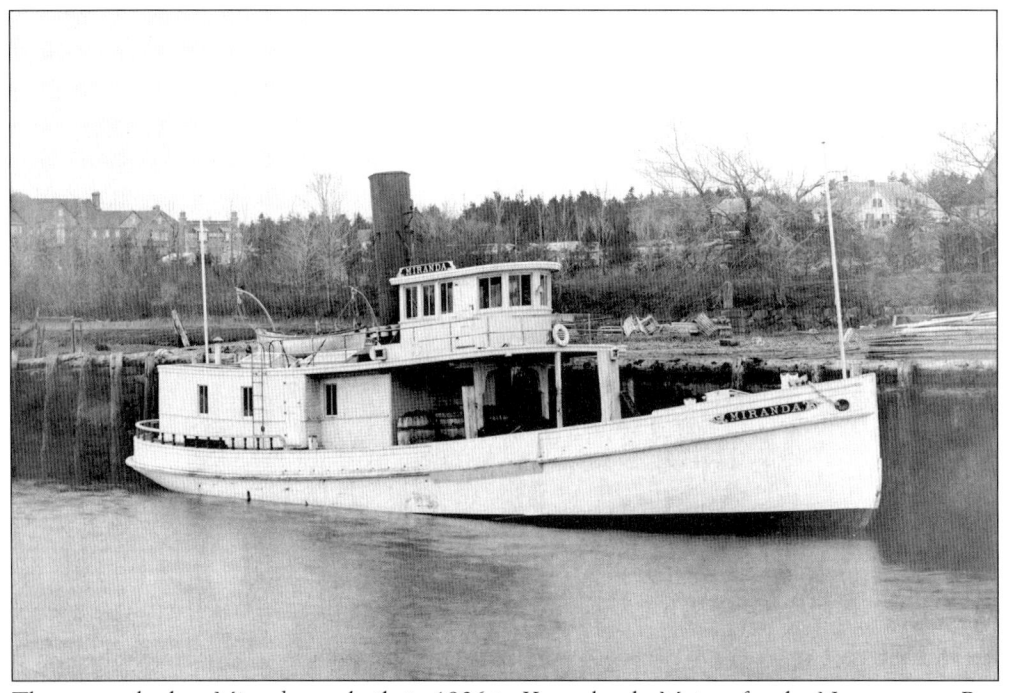

The oyster dredger *Miranda* was built in 1906 in Kennebunk, Maine, for the Narragansett Bay Oyster Company of Providence, Rhode Island. She was 80 feet long overall and was equipped by the Portland Company with a 200-horsepower compound engine and a vertical boiler.

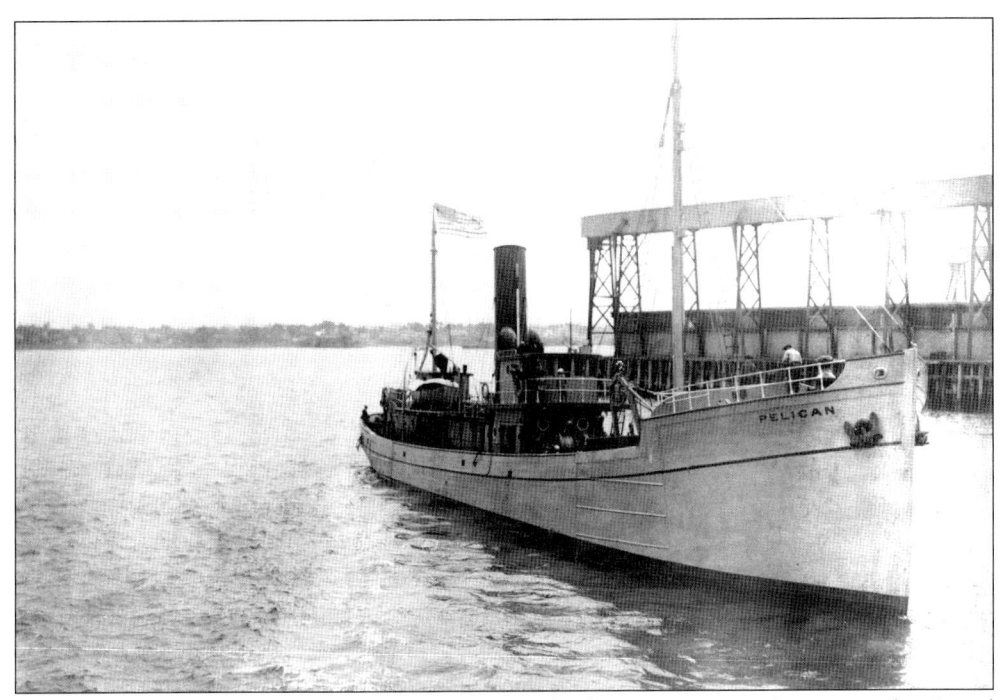

Pictured is another fishing trawler just off the Portland Company waterfront near the Grand Trunk grain conveyers, where Canadian grain was loaded aboard ships for Europe and the southern United States. The *Pelican* was built in South Portland, Maine, in 1919 for the East Coast Fisheries Company.

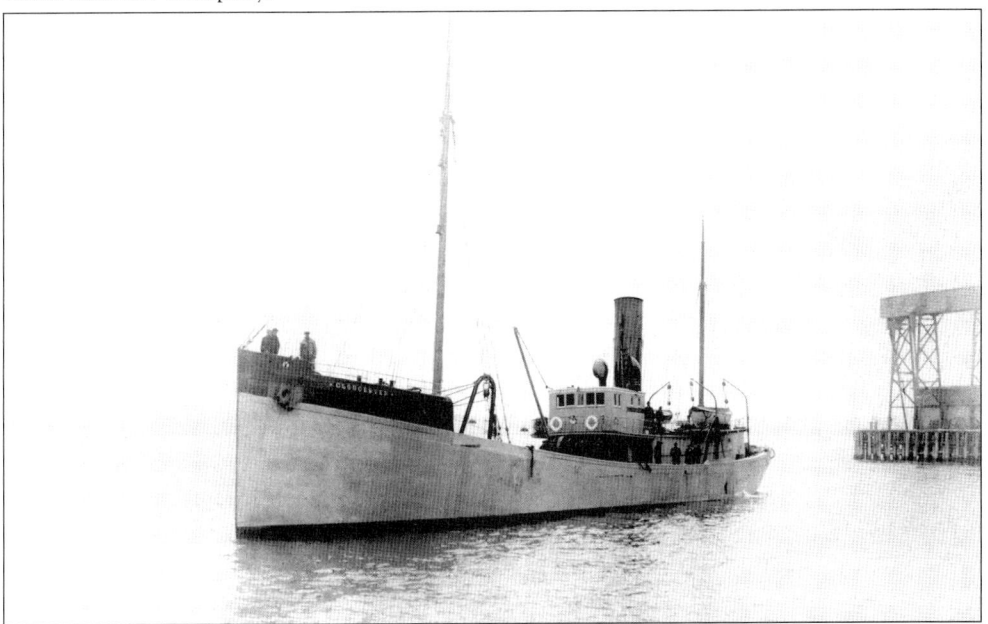

An "otter" trawler, the *Gloucester* out of Gloucester, Massachusetts, was built in Essex, Massachusetts, in 1919 for the Cape Ann Trawling Company. She was 164 feet long, 488 gross tons, and fully equipped by the Portland Company. "Otter" refers to the type of trawling gear using "doors" to keep the mouth of the net open.

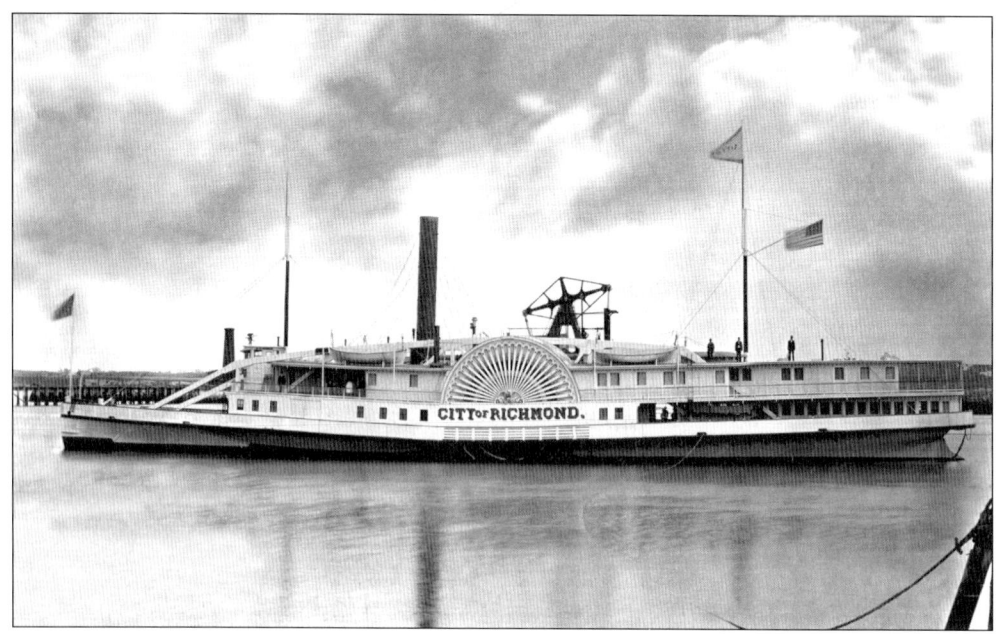

Another beautiful passenger side-wheeler that plied the waters of coastal New England and was equipped by the Portland Company was the *City of Richmond*.

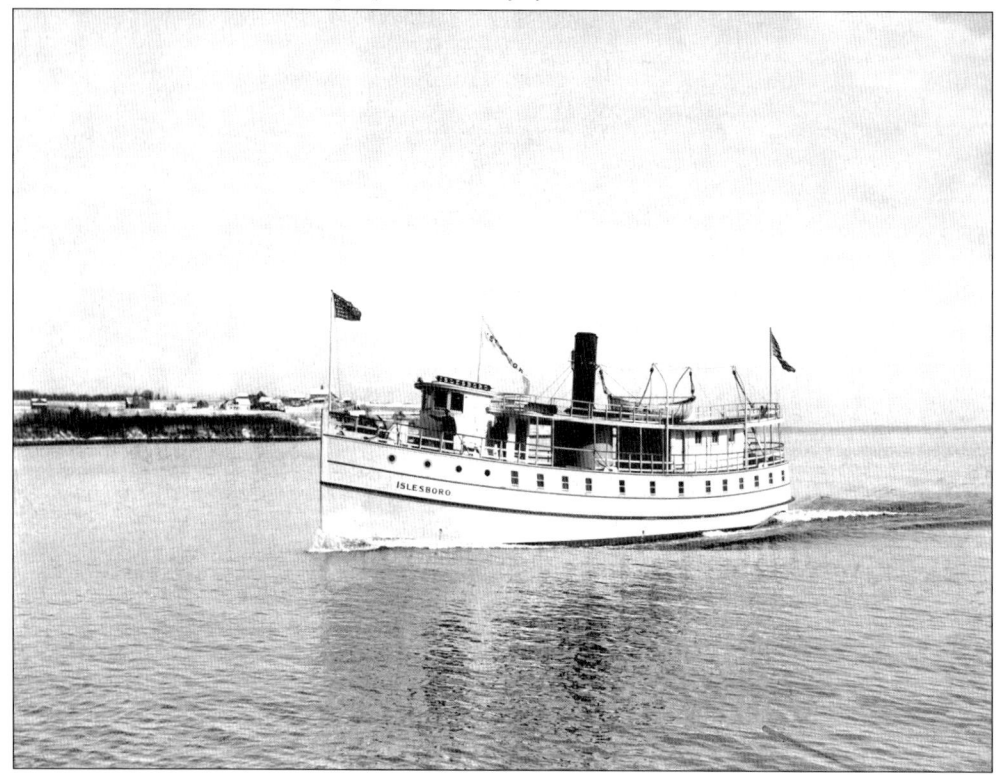

A small coastal passenger steamer is shown in service. The *Islesboro* was only 74 feet long from stem to stern. She was built in 1914 in Rockland, Maine, for the Penobscot Bay & River Navigation Company.

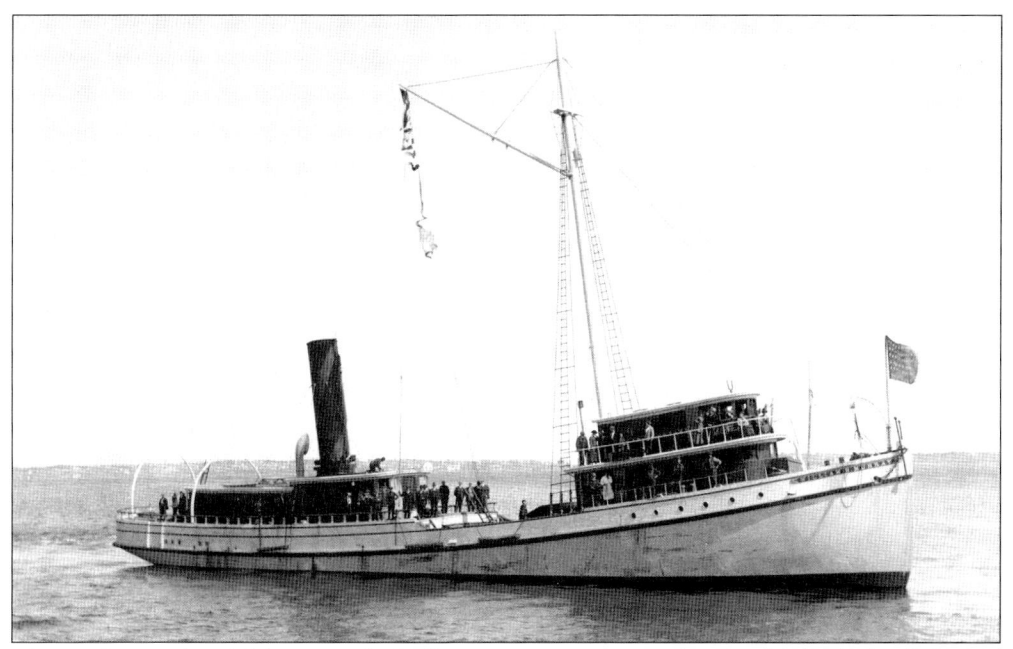

The newly completed fishing trawler *William B. Murray* steams along with a load of well-dressed passengers aboard in 1912. She was built in Rockland, Maine, for C.A. Stickler & Brothers and was outfitted by the Portland Company.

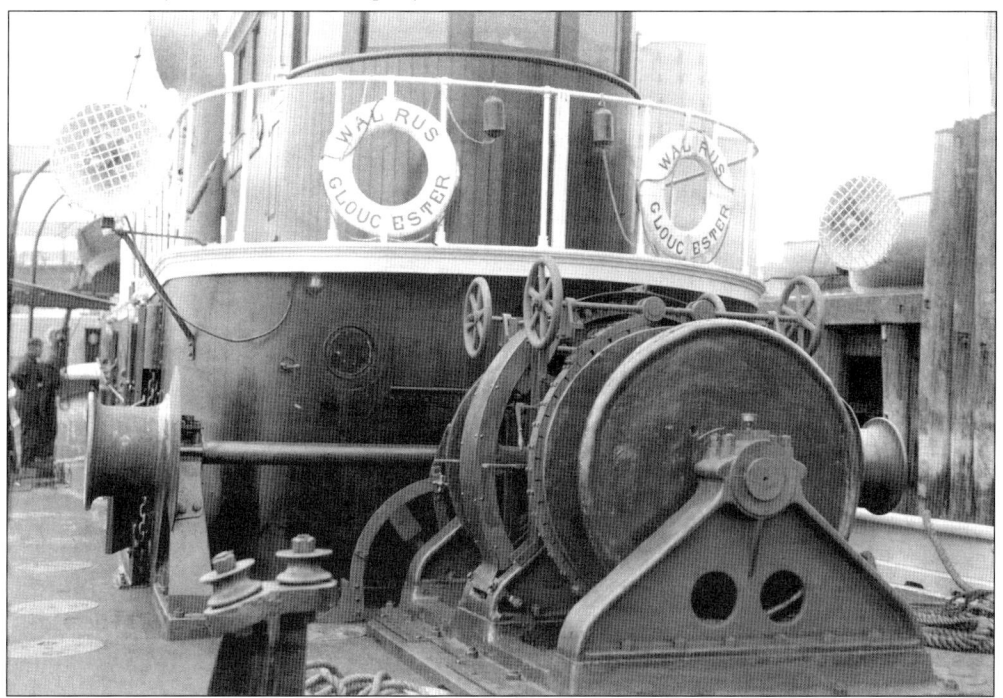

This photograph shows the pilothouse and deck winches of the steamer *Walrus* out of Gloucester, Massachusetts. She was built in the James boatyard in Essex, Massachusetts, in 1917 as a fishing trawler for the Cunningham & Thomson Company. She weighed 479 gross tons and was 163 feet long from stem to stern.

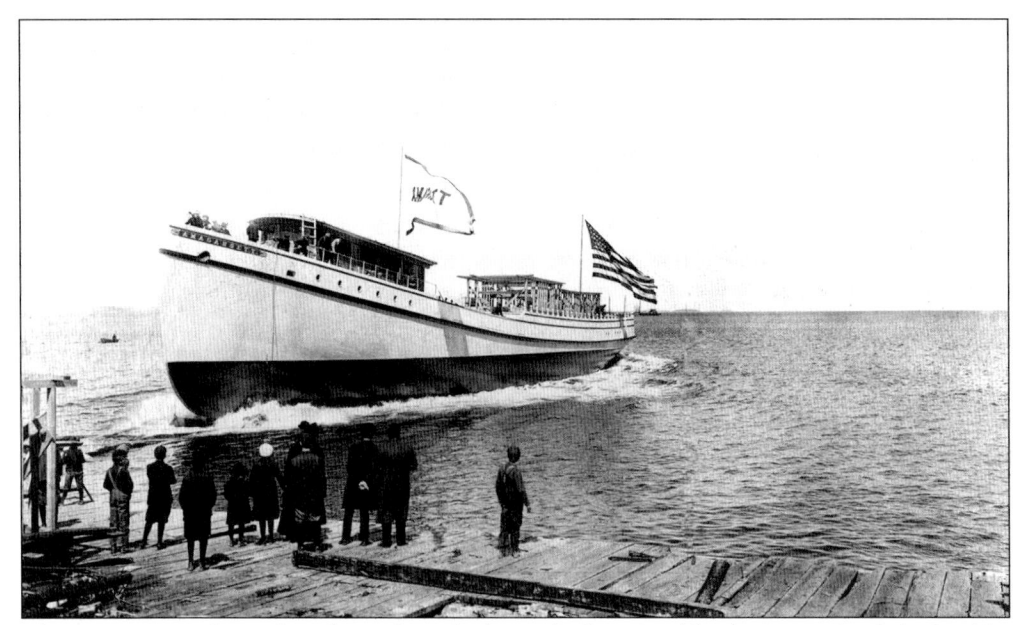

The *Amagansett*, shown here being launched, was built in Rockland, Maine, for C.A. Stickler & Brothers in 1912. She was a fishing trawler of 169 feet in length overall and was 390 gross tons in weight. Many of these fishing steamers were also called "porgy boats," as they were built to fish for menhaden, also called porgies.

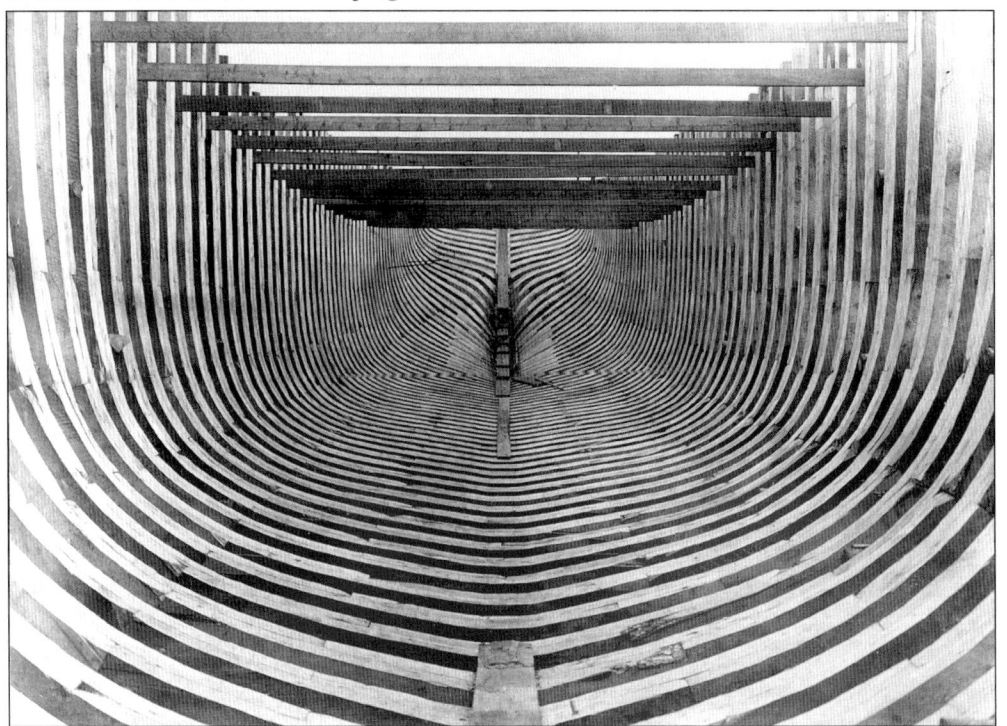

This photograph shows a keel-level view of the trawler *Amagansett* as her sturdy oak frame begins to take shape in 1912 in a Rockland, Maine boatyard. She is being built for C.A. Stickler & Brothers.

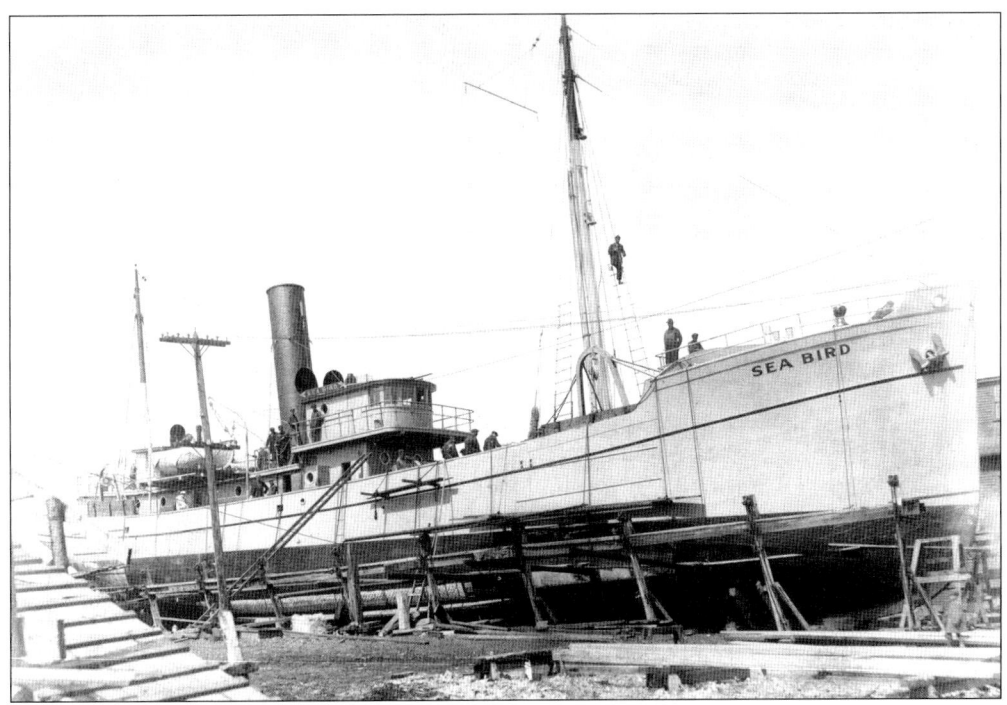

The nearly completed fishing trawler *Sea Bird* is still on the ways in the South Portland yard in 1919. She will be launched shortly after a few last-minute adjustments are finished. The 163-foot trawler weighed 383 gross tons and was built for the East Coast Fisheries Company of Portland, Maine.

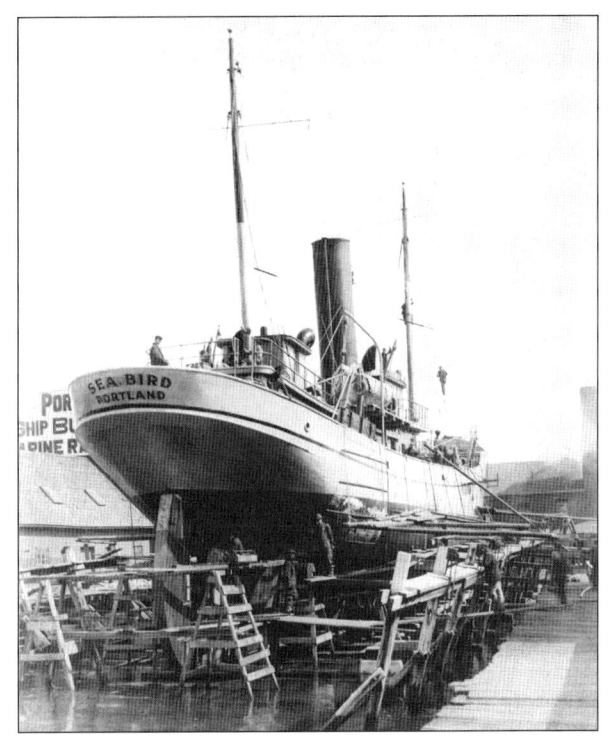

Shown here is a stern view of the trawler *Sea Bird* on the ways in South Portland, Maine.

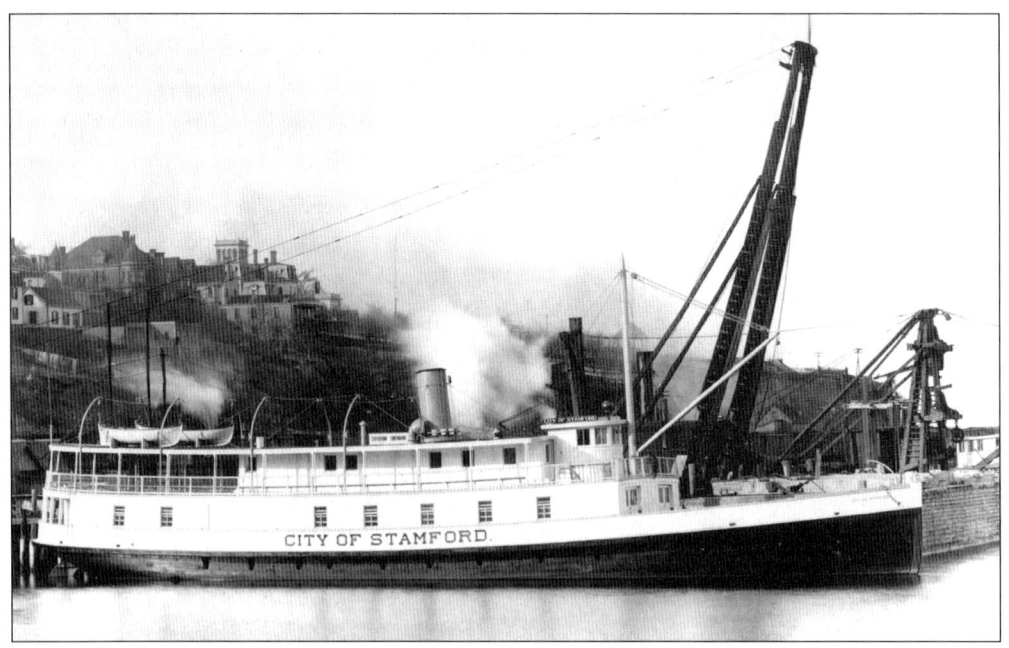

The passenger and freight steamer *City of Stamford* lies beside the Portland Company pier in 1906. She was built in Kennebunkport, Maine, for the North & East River Navigational Company of New York City. She was 145 feet long overall and was equipped with all Portland Company machinery and a three-furnace Scotch-type boiler. Also, this steamer had a complete electric plant (as did most vessels equipped in Portland), a 14-inch Rushmore searchlight, and a telescoping stack for going under the Harlem bridge in New York.

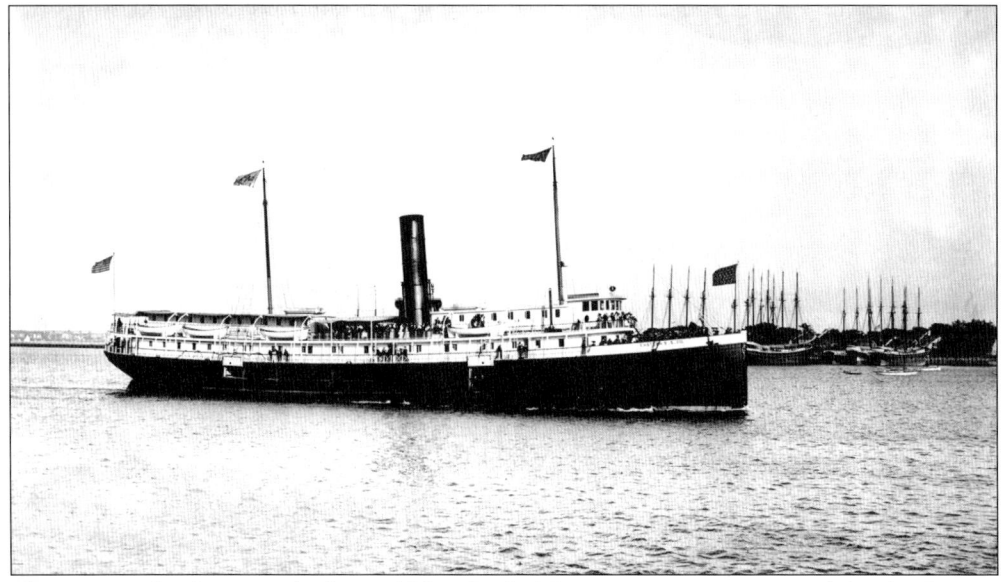

The steamer *St. Croix* was built in 1895 in Bath, Maine, as a passenger vessel for the Eastern Steamship Company of Eastport, Maine. She was 262 feet long overall and weighed 2,000 gross tons. The Portland Company built and installed all of her equipment as well as four three-furnace Scotch press–type 170-pound boilers. She is seen here entering Portland Harbor just below Eastern Prominade.

60

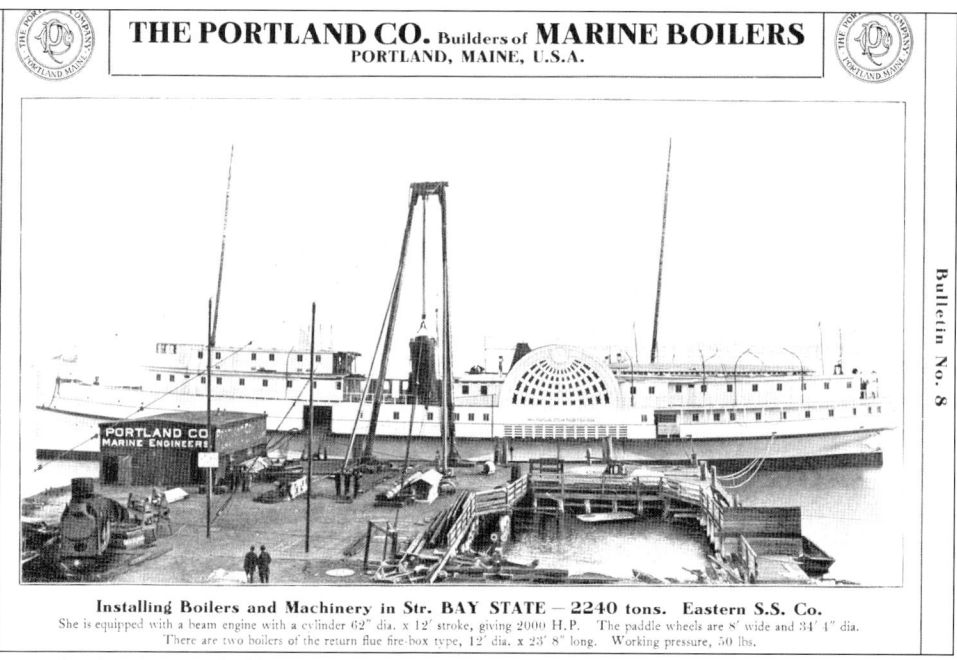

THE PORTLAND CO. Builders of **MARINE BOILERS**
PORTLAND, MAINE, U.S.A.

Bulletin No. 8

Installing Boilers and Machinery in Str. BAY STATE — 2240 tons. Eastern S.S. Co.
She is equipped with a beam engine with a cylinder 62" dia. x 12' stroke, giving 2000 H.P. The paddle wheels are 8' wide and 34' 4" dia. There are two boilers of the return flue fire-box type, 12' dia. x 23' 8" long. Working pressure, 50 lbs.

The Portland Company bulletin No. 8 shows the boilers and machinery being installed in the passenger side-wheeled steamer *Bay State*. The *Bay State* was built in 1890 for the Eastern Steamship Company. Note that at this time the great 33-foot-diameter paddle wheels have not yet been mounted. These paddle wheels were built by the company, and all of the engineering drawings are available at the Maine Historical Society in Portland.

One of the twin 40-ton Scotch-type marine boilers is being lowered into the boiler room of the great passenger side-wheeler *Bay State* by an A-frame derrick. She was built in 1895 in Bath, Maine, by the New England Ship Building Company and was then towed to Portland for installation of boilers, a walking beam engine, and other fittings and equipment—all of which was made by the Portland Company.

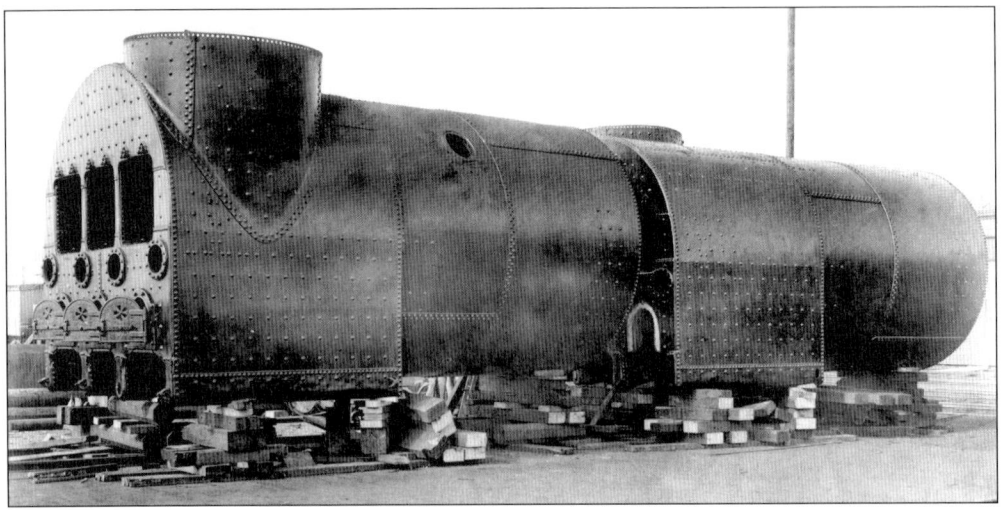

Two twin Portland Company marine boilers await installation into the passenger side-wheeler *Bay State*. She was built in 1895 by the New England Ship Building Company in Bath, Maine. The 12-foot-diameter, 23.8-foot-long boilers are a left and a right because of the placement of the exhaust or smokestack bases.

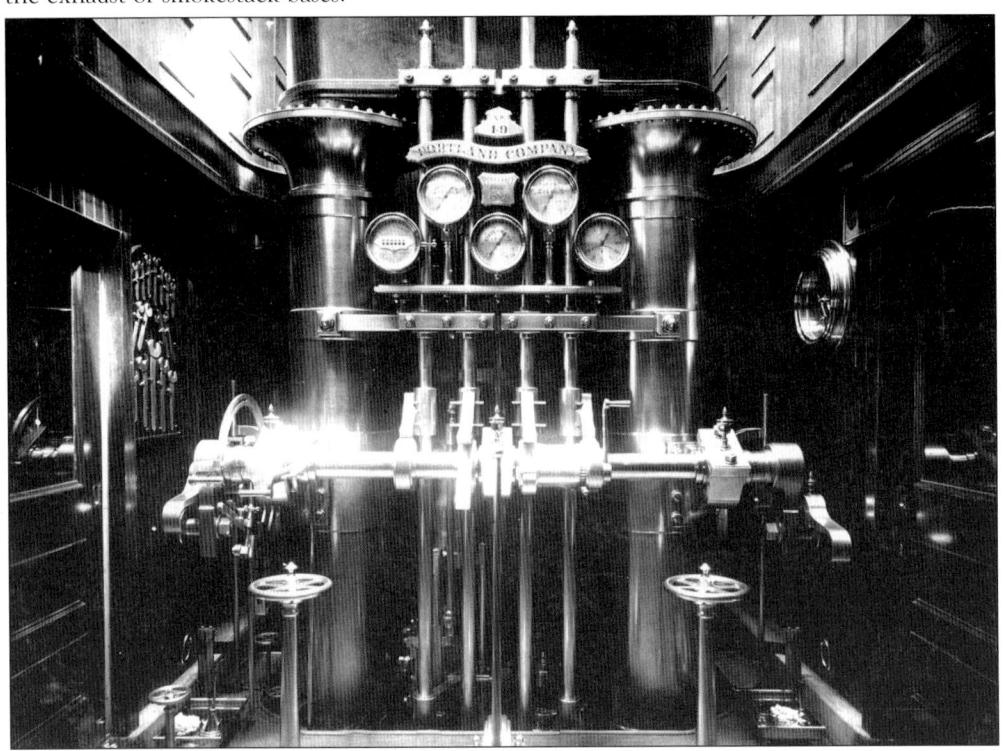

This photograph shows the splendid engine control room of engine No. 49, the passenger side-wheeler *State of Maine*. Note all of the beautiful mahogany woodwork and brass gauges and fittings. Even the wrenches were well displayed on the walls. The Portland Company was certainly proud of its contribution to this fine vessel. Built in 1882 in Bath, Maine, for the International Steamship Company, she was 241 feet in length stem to stern and weighed 1,410 gross tons.

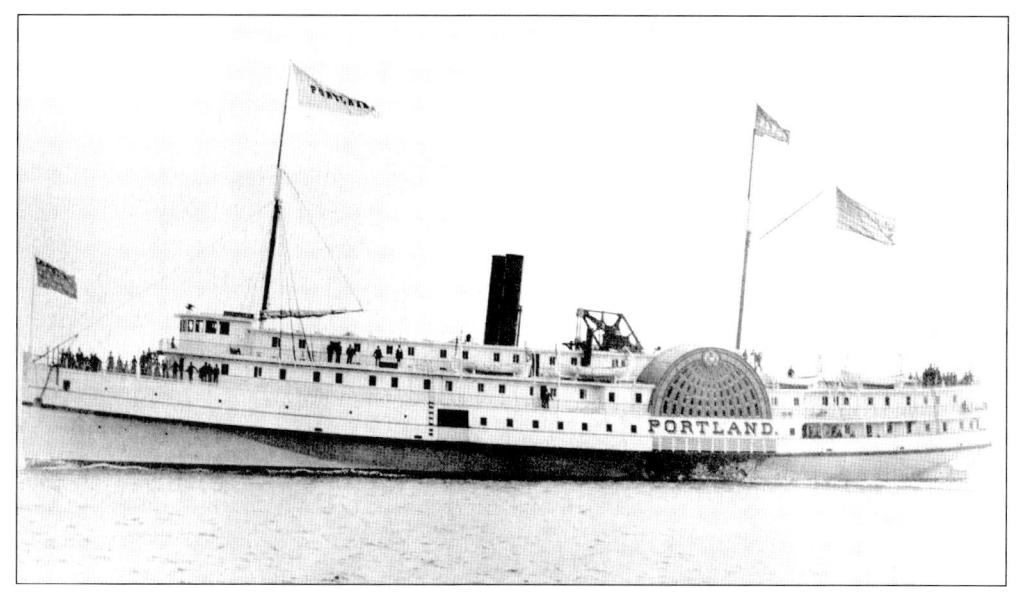

The passenger steamer *Portland* was one of the premier side-wheelers of the Eastern Steamship Company. She was fitted with twin 40-ton boilers and had a walking beam engine with a 62-inch-diameter cylinder and a 12-foot stroke, producing 2,000 horsepower. At 280 feet long, she made quite a picture as she plied the waters off the New England coast until one stormy night over a decade later when she simply disappeared with all aboard. In 2002, she was found upright and intact in the Stellwagen Bank National Marine Sanctuary off the coast of Massachusetts. She was a sister to the *Bay State*, which was also built in Bath, Maine, in 1890. After being towed to Portland from Bath, the Portland Company installed all her equipment and paddle wheels.

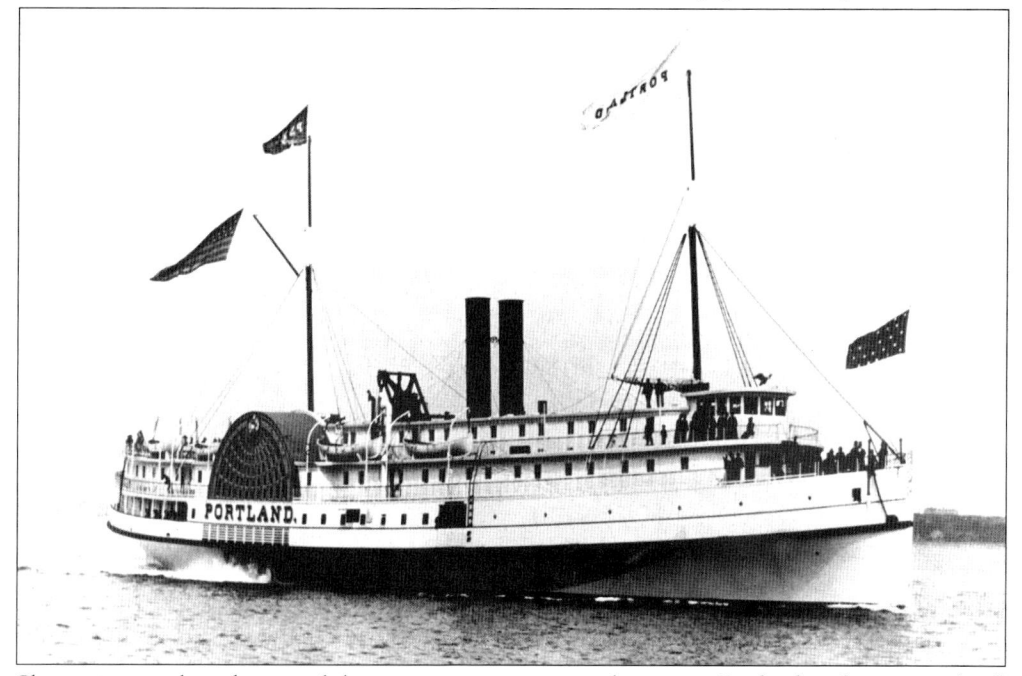

Shown is a starboard view of the great passenger coastal steamer *Portland* under way with all flags flying. She weighed in at a hefty 2,253 gross tons.

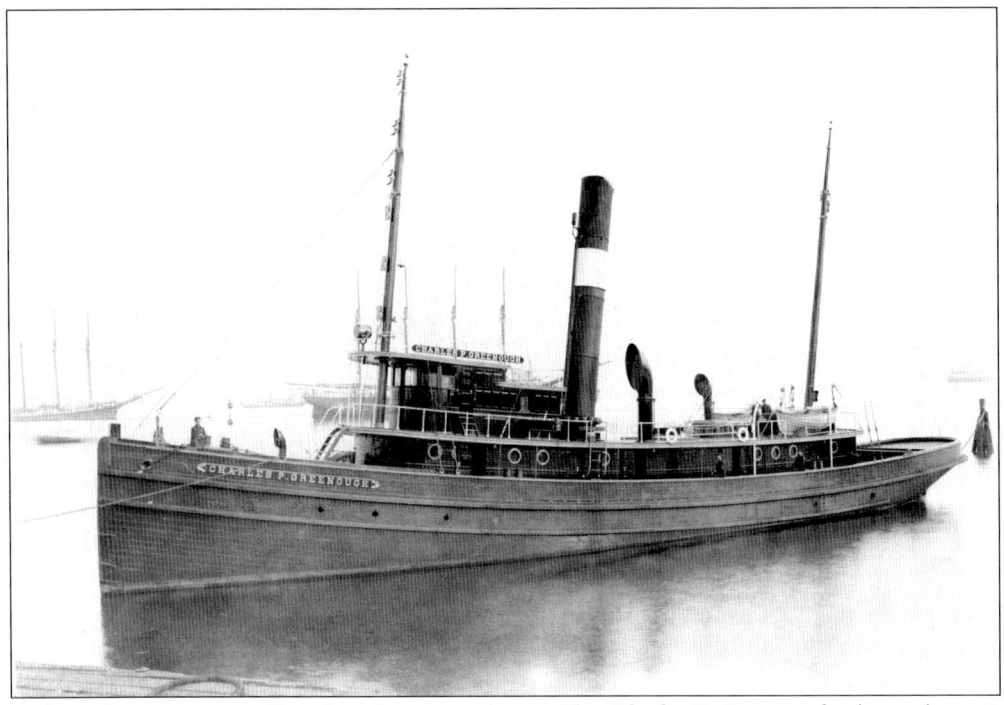

Early tugboats were usually referred to as towboats. The *Charles P. Greenough,* shown here, is obviously not equipped for "pushing," as her bow is lightly built and unprotected. The vessel was built in 1913 for the Commercial Towboat Company of Boston, Massachusetts.

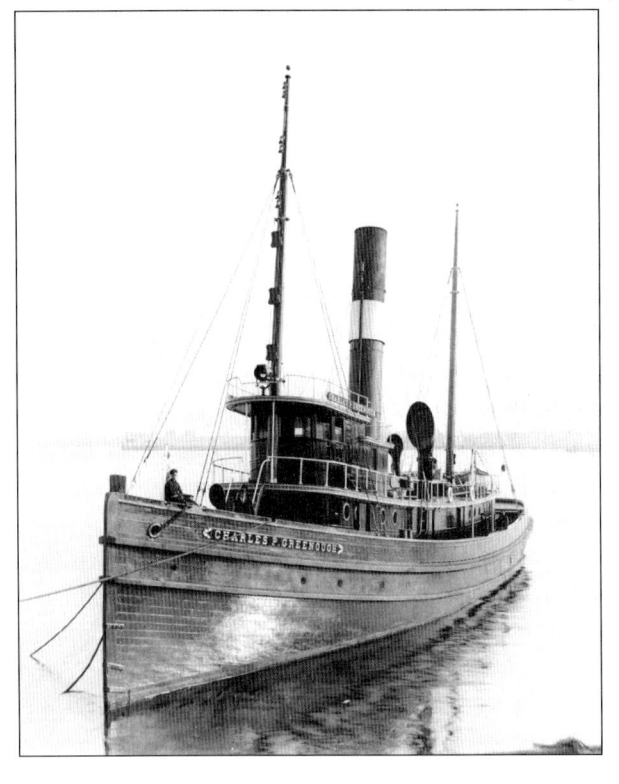

This view shows the bow of the towboat *Charles P. Greenough* resting near the shore in Portland.

A marine engine is rigged for lifting and is on the company pier, ready to be lifted by the derrick for installation in the tug *Charles P. Greenough*.

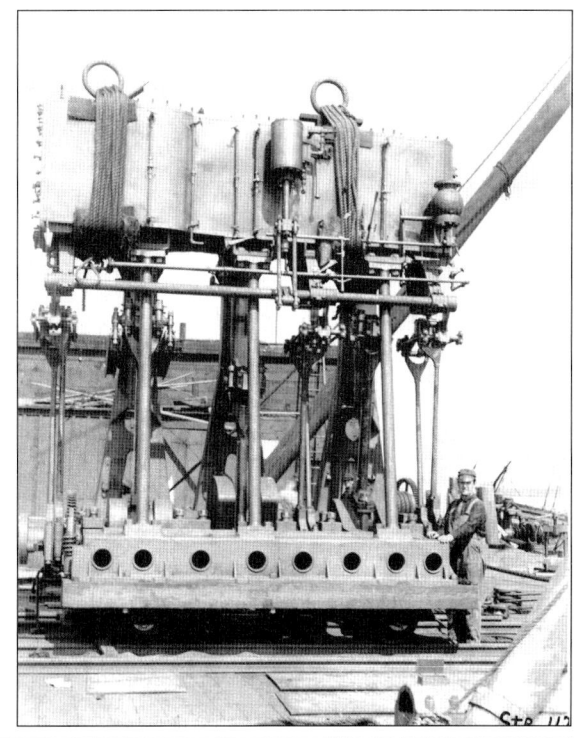

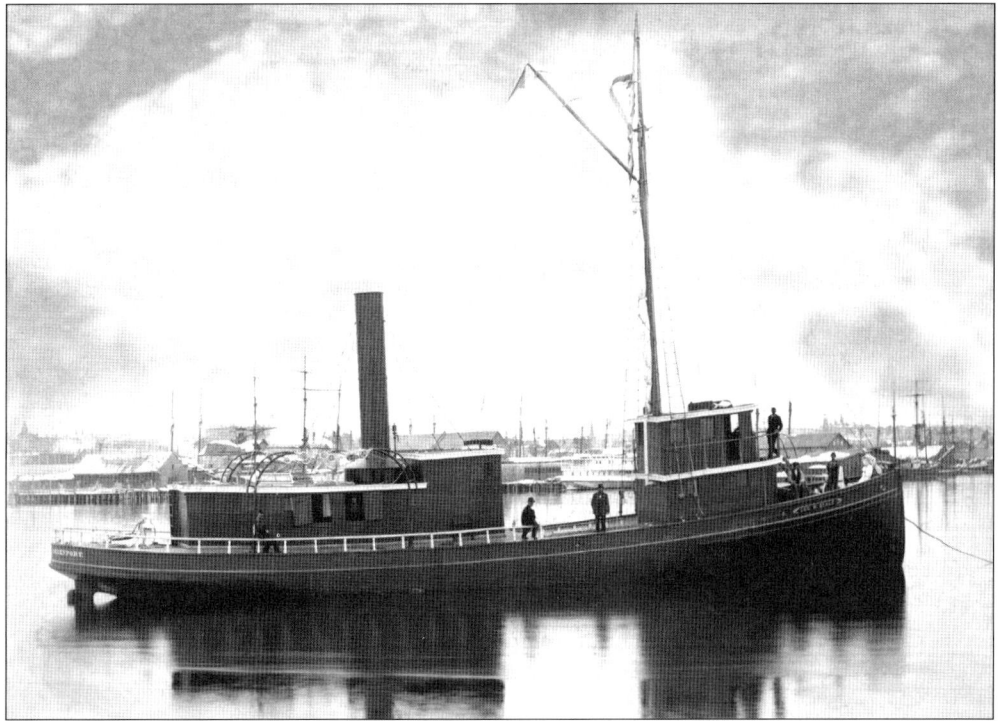

The fishing boat *George Beale* was built in 1879 for D.D. Wells & Sons of Greenport, New York, and outfitted with Portland Company equipment. This steamer was also called a "porgy boat" and was built to fish for menhaden, also called porgies.

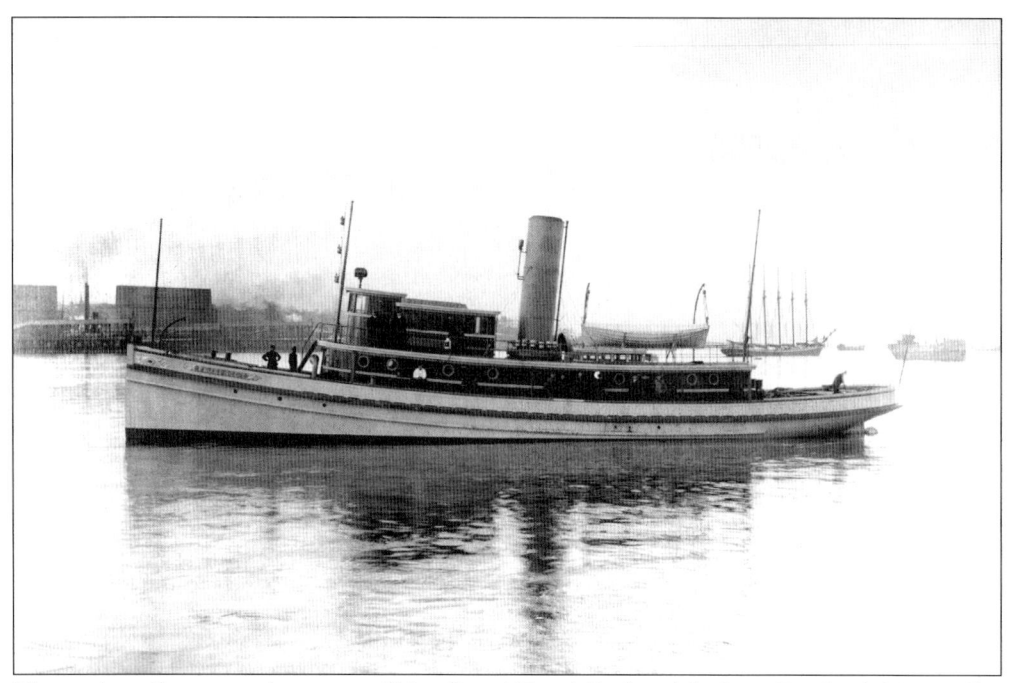

The towboat *Pejepscot* is lying just off the Grand Trunk Railroad docks in Portland, Maine. She was 109 feet long and built for the Sagadahoc Towing Company in Bath, Maine. She was equipped with a 450-horsepower Portland compound engine and had a steam-driven hawser.

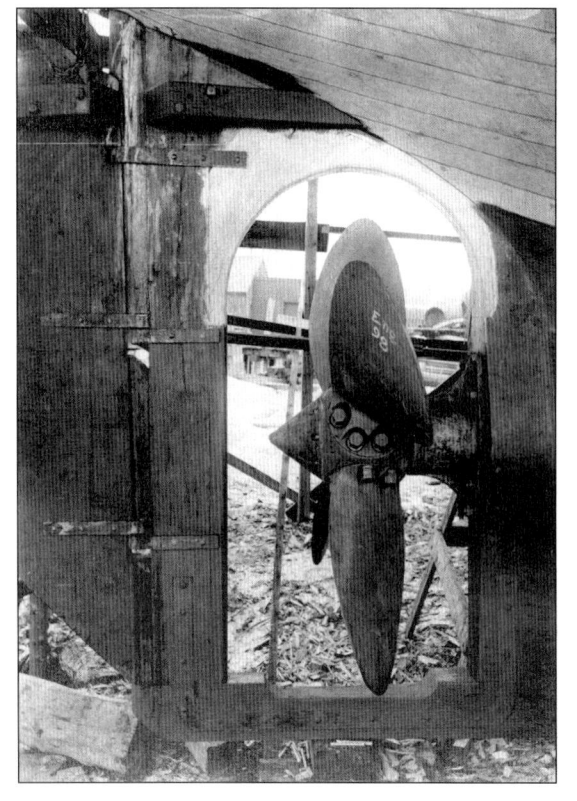

The Portland Company kept track of the vessels it built or equipped by the shop numbers of the company's engines installed in them. Here we see a new propeller with "Eng. 98" chalked on it. This denotes that the vessel attached was the towboat *Pjepscot*, built in 1907.

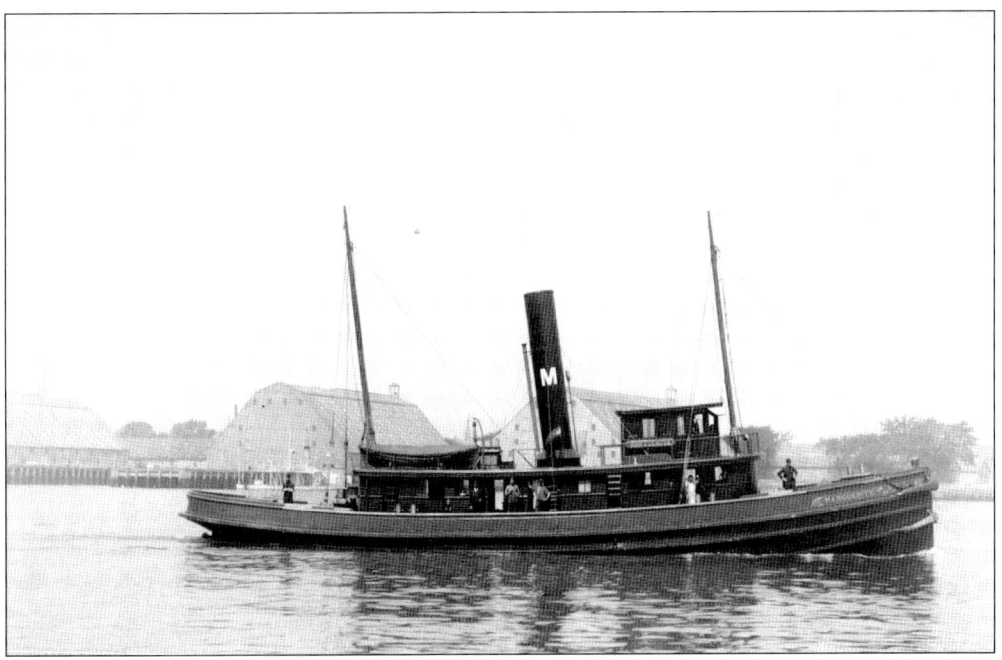

This early towboat was built in 1893 in Kennebunkport, Maine, for the New England Dredging Company in Boston, Massachusetts. The *Marguerite* was 96 feet in length overall and weighed 128 gross tons.

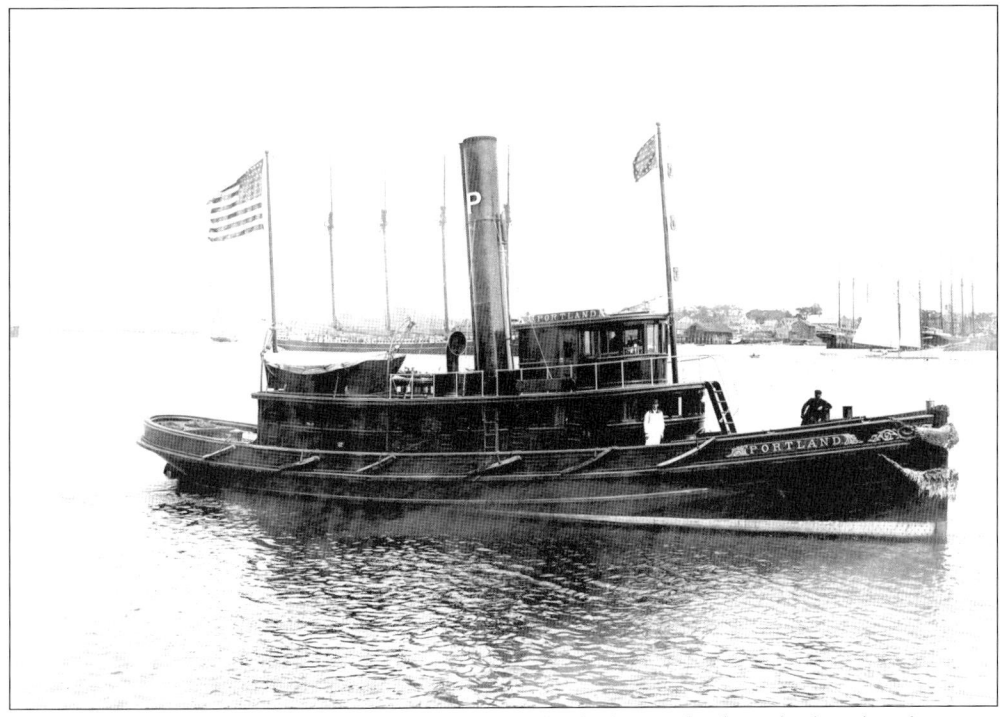

Almost an identical sister to the steam tug *Cumberland*, the *Portland* was built only a few years earlier in 1902 in South Portland, Maine, for the Central Wharf Towboat Company of Boston, Massachusetts. She was 87 feet long stem to stern and also Portland Company equipped.

67

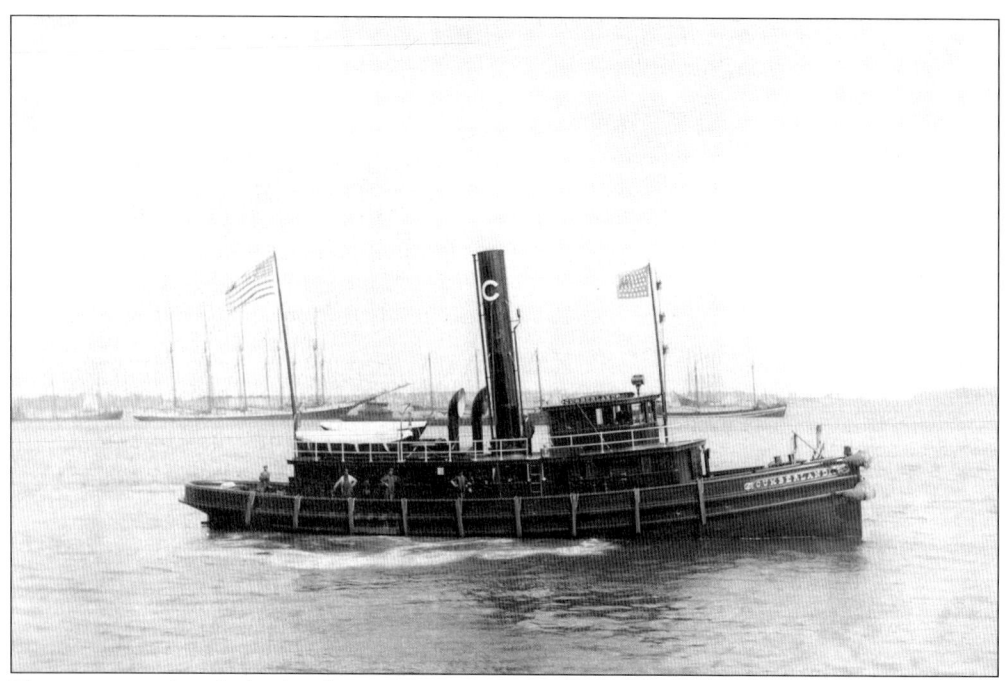

The steam tug *Cumberland* makes its way across Portland Harbor after she was built in 1910 in Rockland, Maine, for the Central Wharf Towboat Company of Boston, Massachusetts. She was 87 feet long stem to stern and Portland Company equipped.

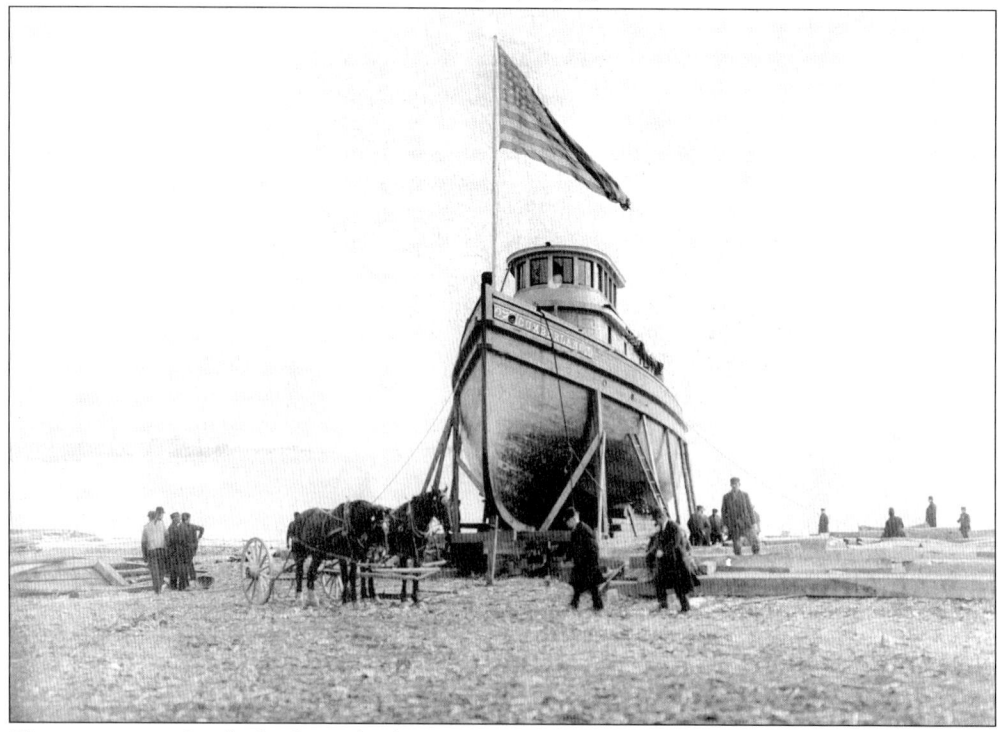

The steam tug *Cumberland* was built in 1910 in Rockland, Maine, for the Central Wharf Towboat Company. Here we see her in a lonely austere boatyard about ready for launching.

68

This view shows the 18-inch, 32- by 22-inch compound marine engine built as shop No. 105 by the Portland Company and soon to be installed in the towboat *Cumberland*. The engine had 440 horsepower and operated with 150 pounds of steam pressure.

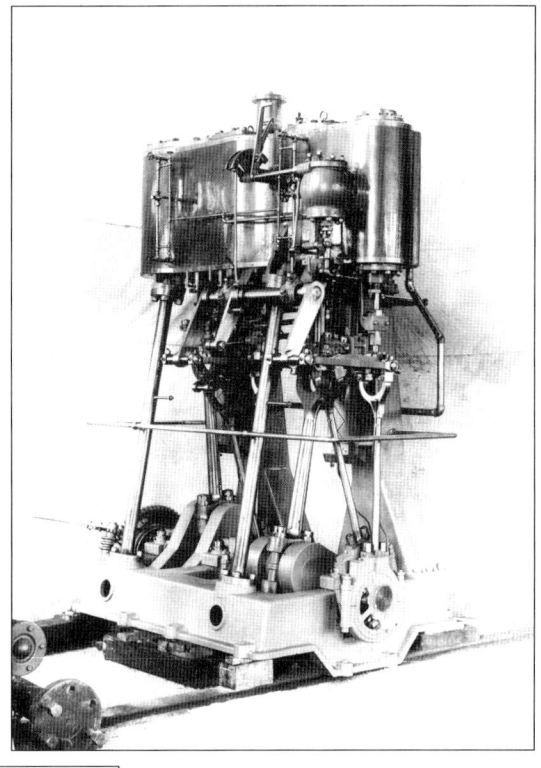

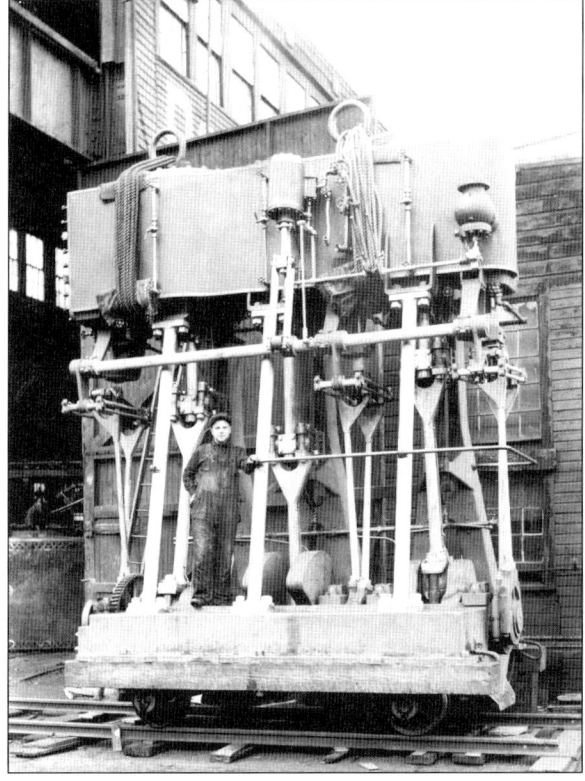

The 900-horsepower marine compound engine No. 114 was built by the Portland Company for the fishing trawler *East Hampton* in 1913. Here it is rigged for lifting and is loaded on the dolly, ready to move from the company shops to the pier for installation aboard the vessel.

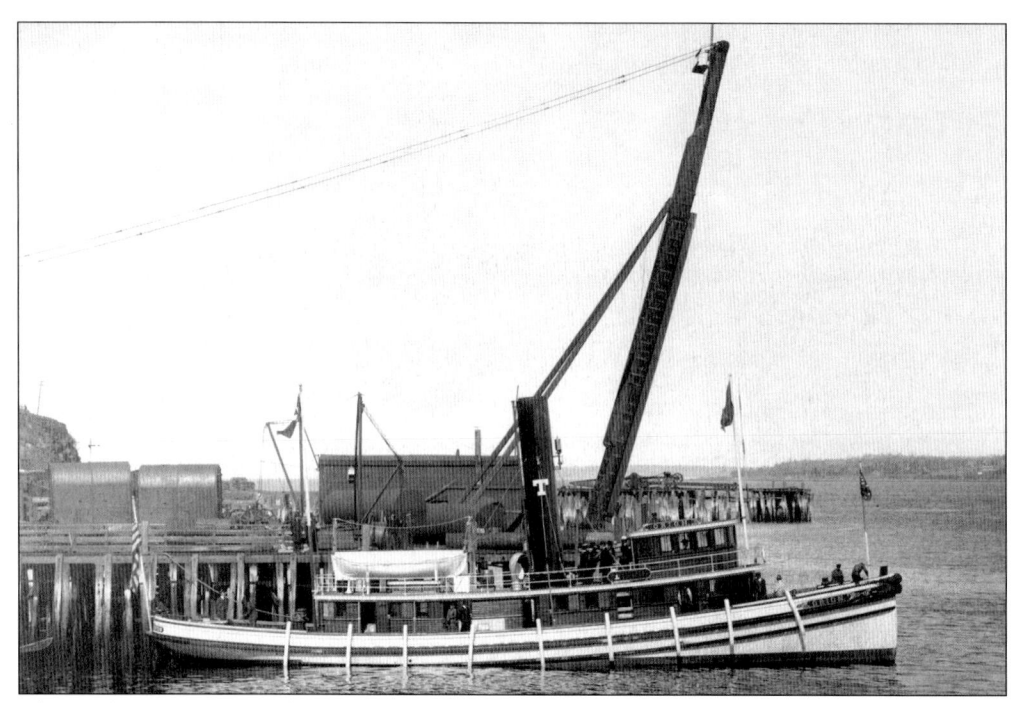

The towboat *Orion* rests beside the Portland Company pier. She was built and equipped in South Portland, Maine, by the company in 1905 for the Boston Towboat Company of Boston, Massachusetts.

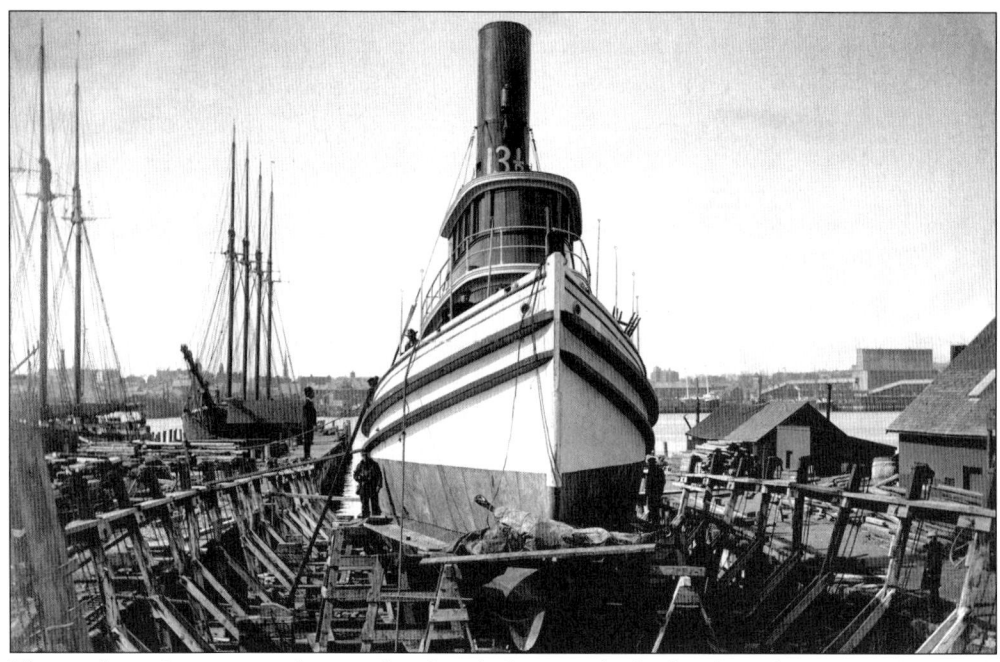

The towboat *Orion* is nearly completed and about ready for her launching from the South Portland boatyard where she was built and equipped by the Portland Company in 1905 for the Boston Towboat Company of Boston, Massachusetts. Beyond, we see the Portland skyline and the Grand Trunk Railroad grain elevators across the harbor from this busy boatyard.

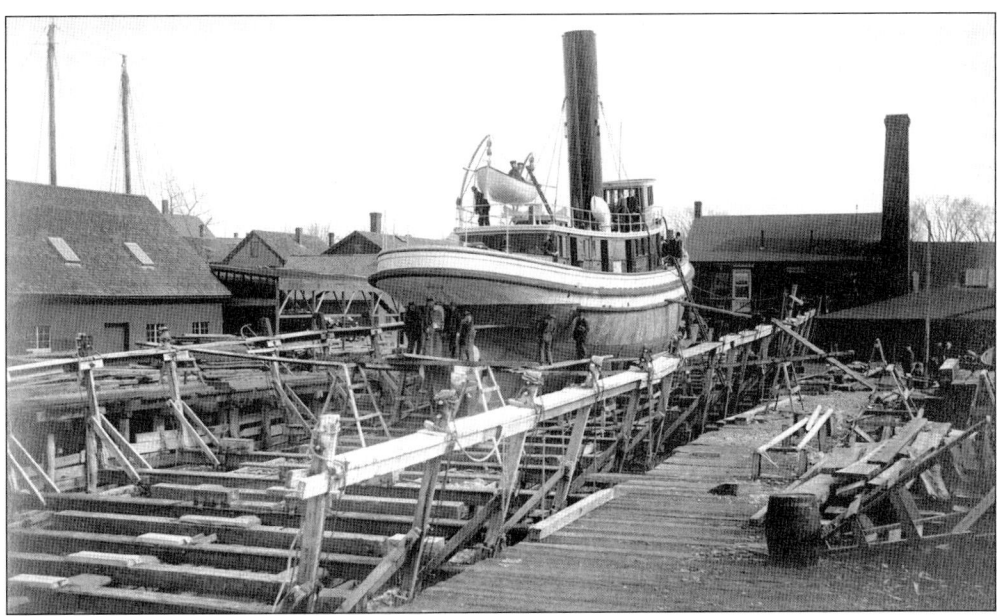

Pictured is a stern view of the towboat *Orion* nearly completed and about ready for her launching from the South Portland boatyard where she was built. After launching, she will be towed across the harbor to the Portland Company pier, where she will be equipped with boiler, engine, winches, pumps, and so on. She was built in 1905 for the Boston Towboat Company of Boston, Massachusetts.

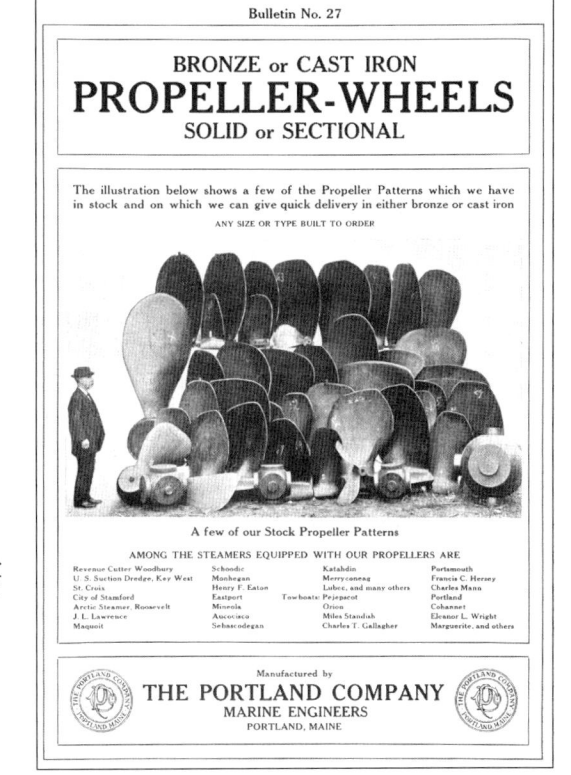

The Portland Company published bulletins about its wide range of products. Here is bulletin No. 27, showing many of the propeller patterns and some of the vessels equipped with Portland Company propellers. The company worked on hundreds of vessels, from yachts to freighters, trawlers, and the famous Liberty Ships of World War II.

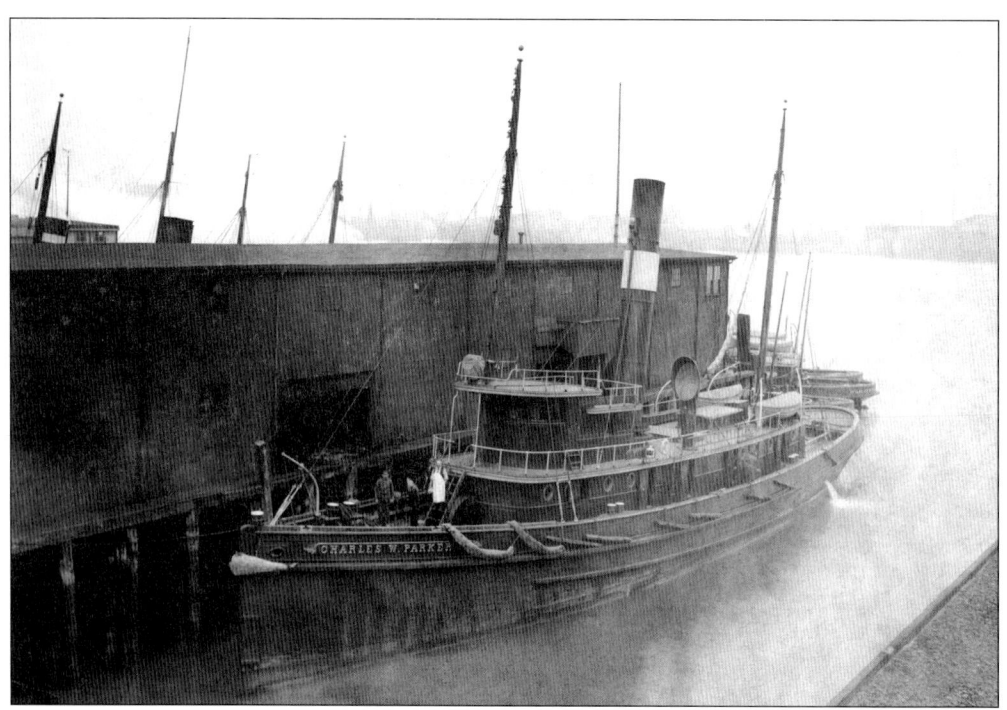

The tug *Charles W. Parker Jr.* was built in Bath, Maine, in 1909 for a Boston towboat company. She was 125 feet in length stem to stern and weighed 277 gross tons.

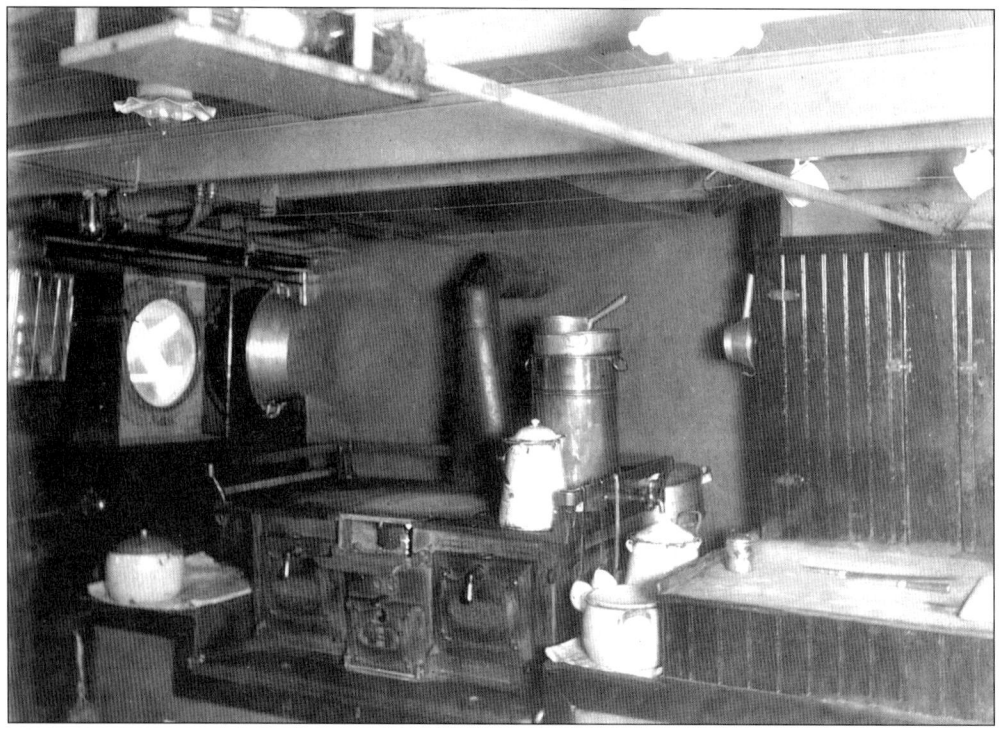

This view offers a look inside the 1909 tug *Charles W. Parker Jr.* at the galley with its coal-fired cook stove and the usual pots and pans for preparing meals for the crew.

72

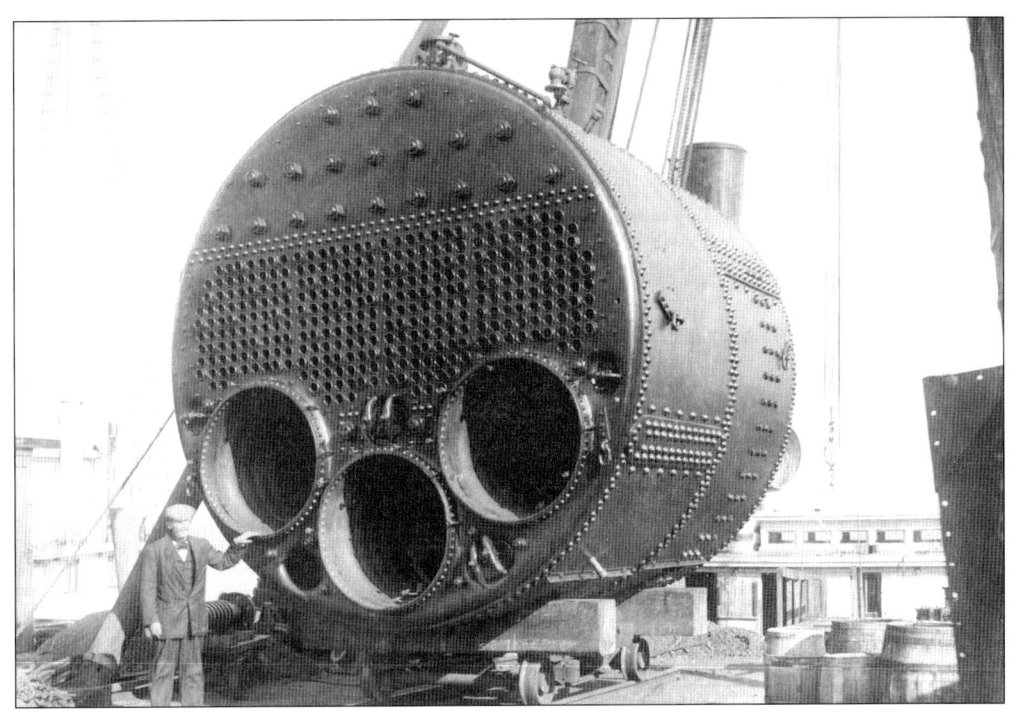

This Scotch-type marine boiler has just crossed the Grand Trunk Railroad main line as it travels on a dolly and rails from the Portland Company boiler shop to the company pier. The Portland Company maintained a right-of-way across the railroad's tracks to move equipment, materials, and employees to its pier, where the customers' vessels were equipped or repaired.

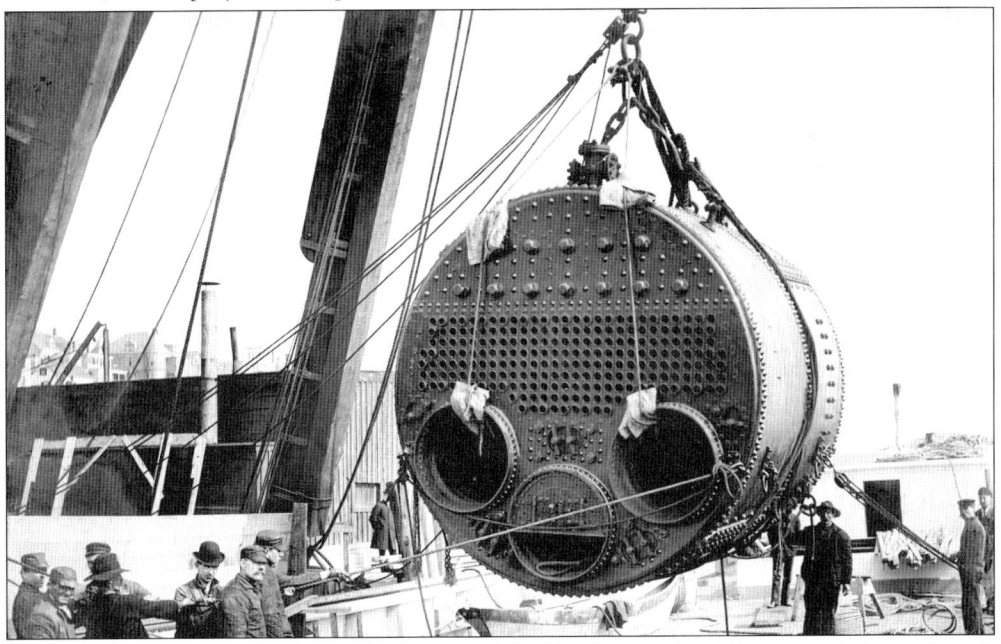

Here we see a Scotch-type marine boiler being lifted by the Portland Company A-frame derrick and about to be lowered below through an opening in the decks of a vessel tied up at the company pier.

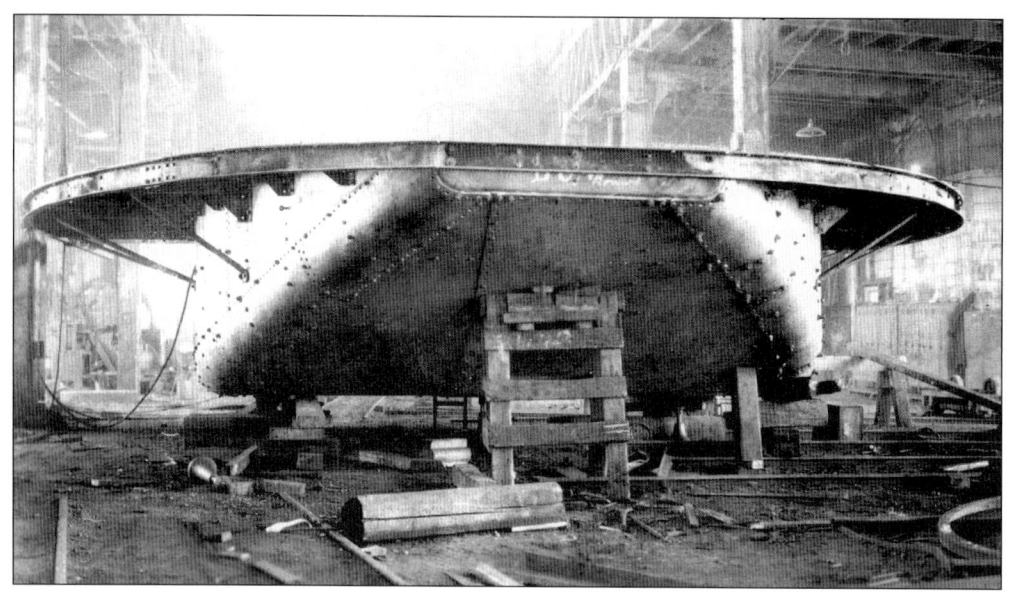

Here in the Portland Company erecting shop, we see the bow section of an 80-foot boat being fabricated of iron in January 1921 for the Great Northern Paper & Pulp Company. The boat, with a broad rounded bow, was presumably for moving logs around in the waterways.

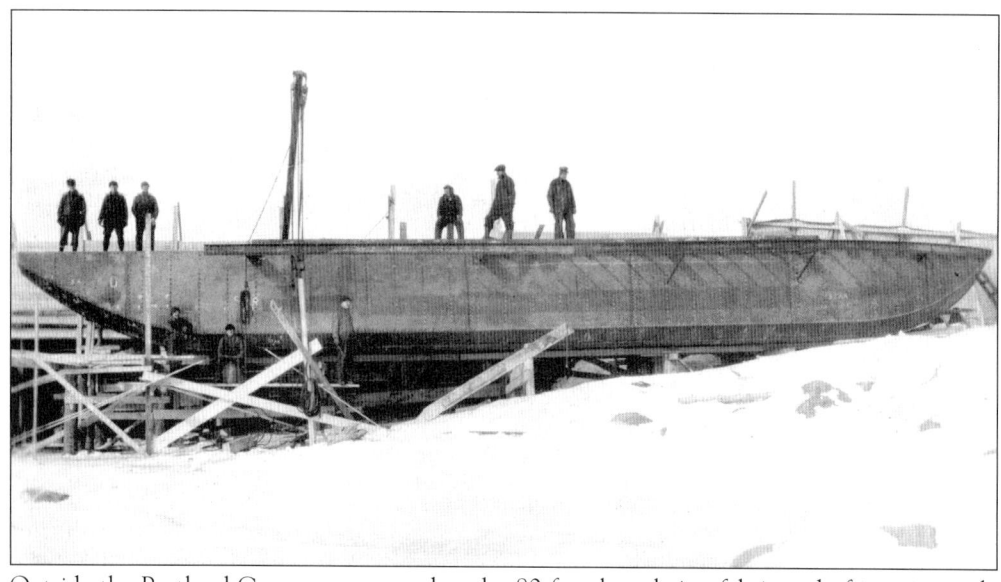

Outside the Portland Company we see that the 80-foot boat being fabricated of iron is nearly completed. It was built in 1921 for the Great Northern Paper & Pulp Company.

Four
AUTOMOBILES AND TRUCKS

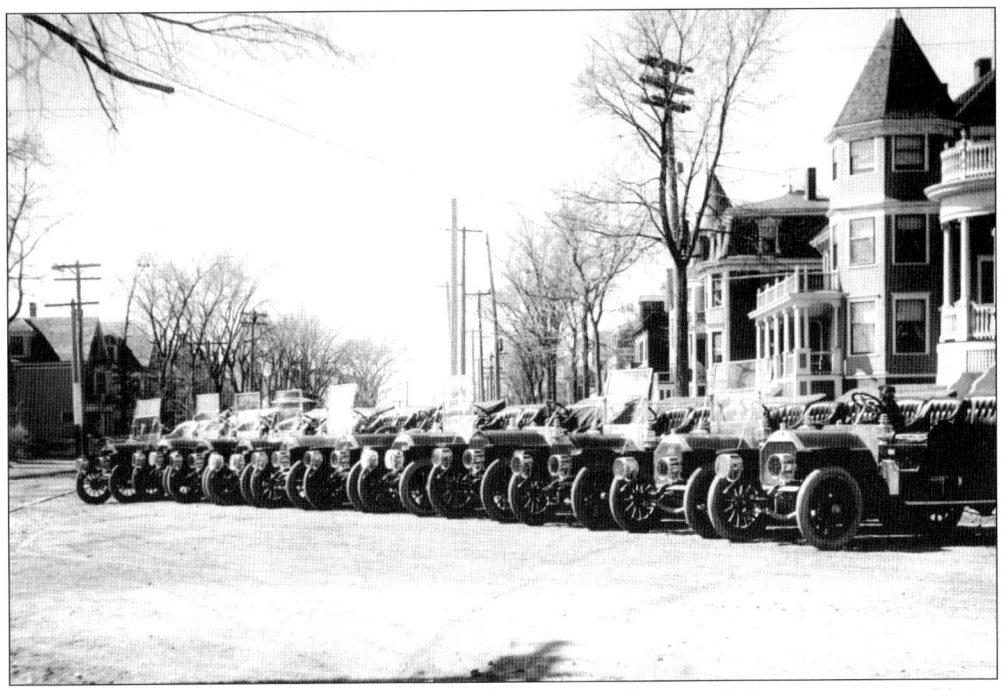

Eleven new Knox automobiles are lined up along Eastern Prominade for a company publicity photograph. All of these automobiles have just been sold, as all have 1909 Maine license plates with consecutive numbers hanging from their front axles. The Portland Company was the sole distributors of Knox automobiles and trucks in the state of Maine.

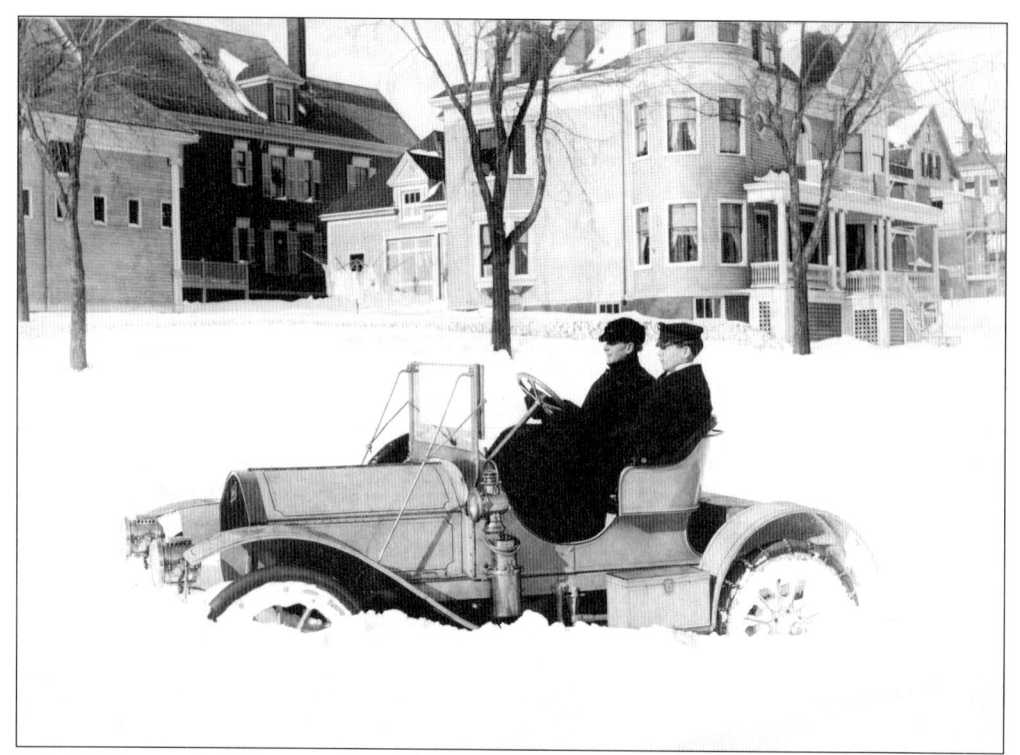

This 1907 air-cooled Knox runabout was sold by the Portland Company and is being driven by A.L. Dennison, a racecar driver for the Knox Automobile Company in Springfield, Massachusetts. His passenger is E.H. Cushman of the Portland Company. This wintery scene is located on Eastern Prominade, Portland, Maine, at the corner of Fore Street just above the Portland Company. The fine house in the background still graces the Munjoy Hill neighborhood today.

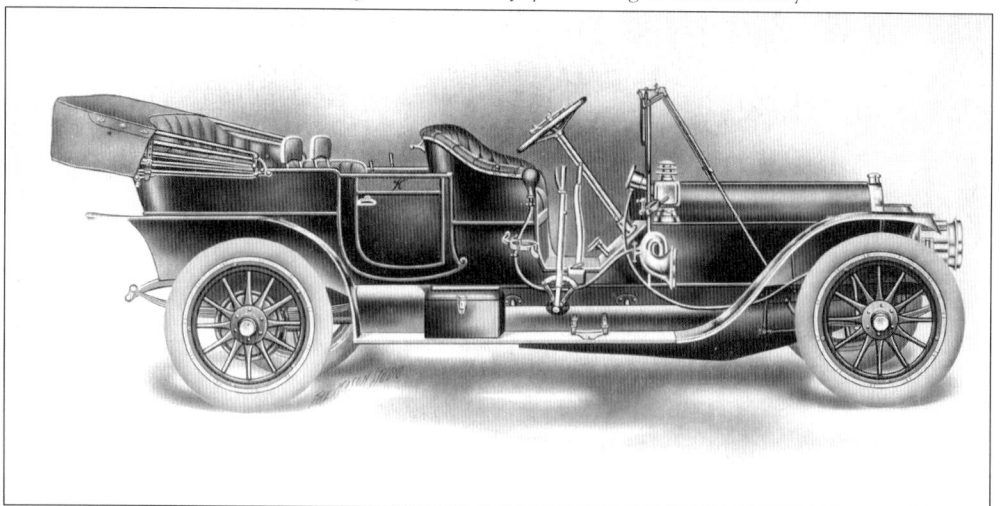

This closeup shows the Knox Automobile Company seven-passenger touring car sold by the Portland Company starting in 1908. These large and grand automobiles sold for several thousand dollars at the time, which was a substantial expenditure of money for even a wealthy businessman to spend. Notice the right-hand drive feature, a standard practice in the automobile industry at the time.

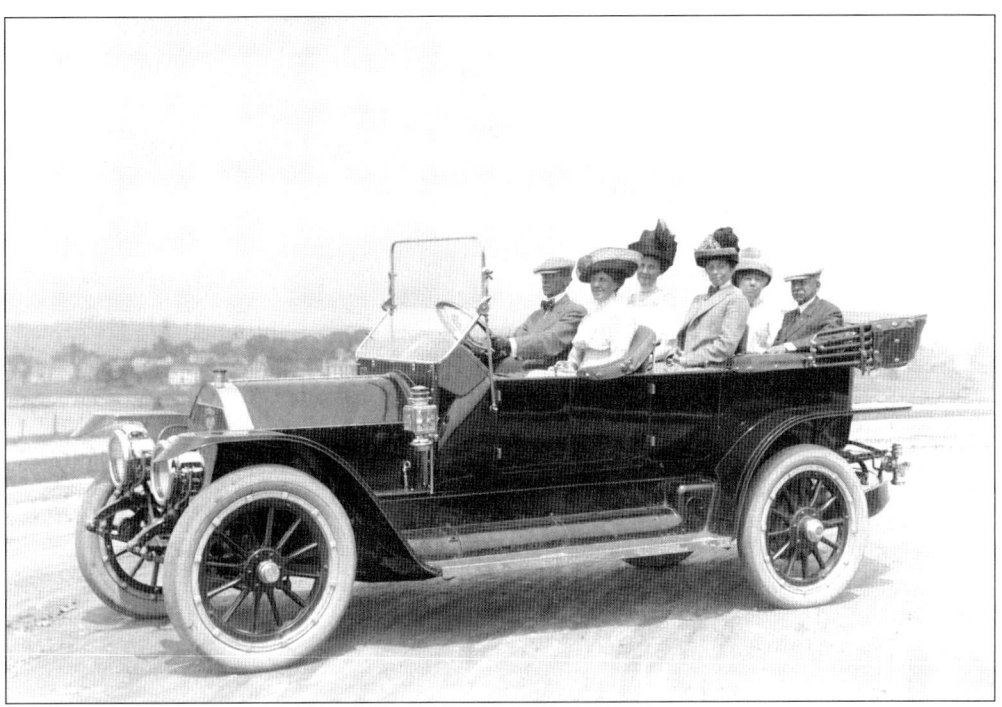

A Knox Automobile Company seven-passenger touring car is being enjoyed by several ladies and men as they motor along the highways in Maine.

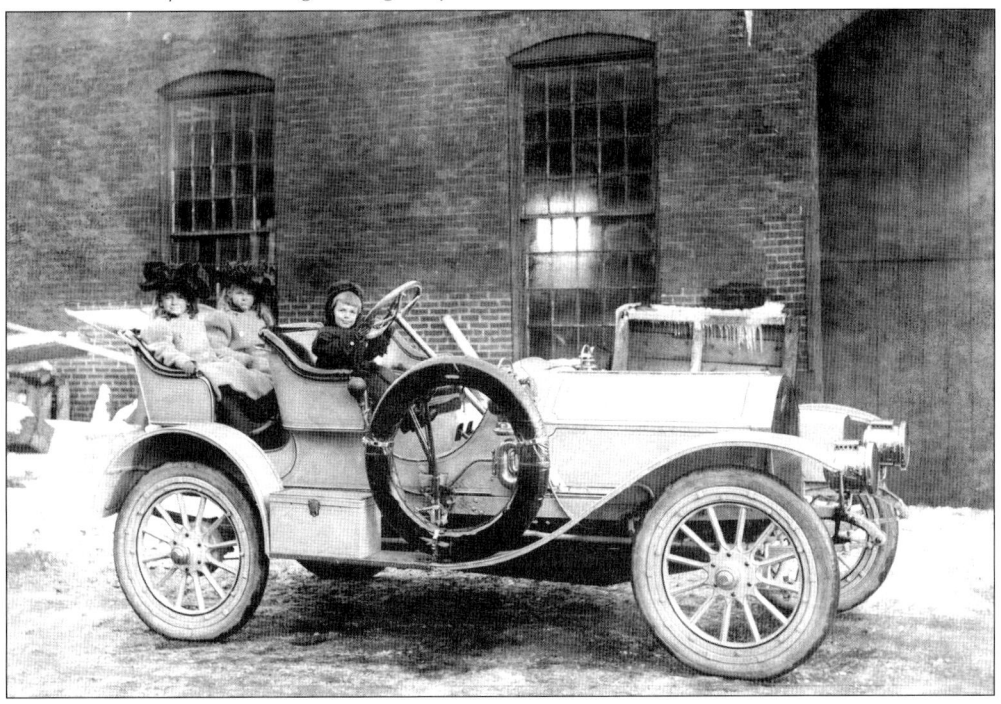

Parked beside the Portland Company shops is Richard Conant Payson's personal 1909 Knox five-passenger touring car. Payson was the general manager of the Portland Company at that time. Seated in his car are two of his children, Richard and sister Emma, with her friend.

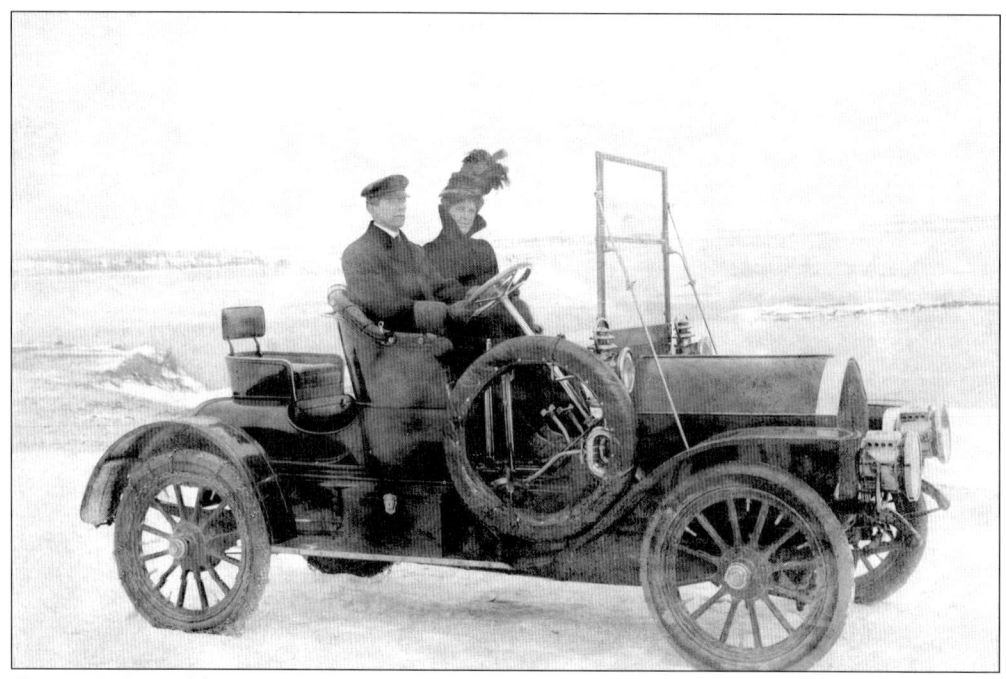

George F. Reynolds, assistant manager of the Portland Company, and his wife are driving in a 1907 air-cooled Knox runabout with a rear mother-in-law seat in Cape Elizabeth, Maine. Many automobiles of this era carried two, three, or more spare tires, as the rubber and roads were both so bad that one might have several flats to contend with on a single motor trip.

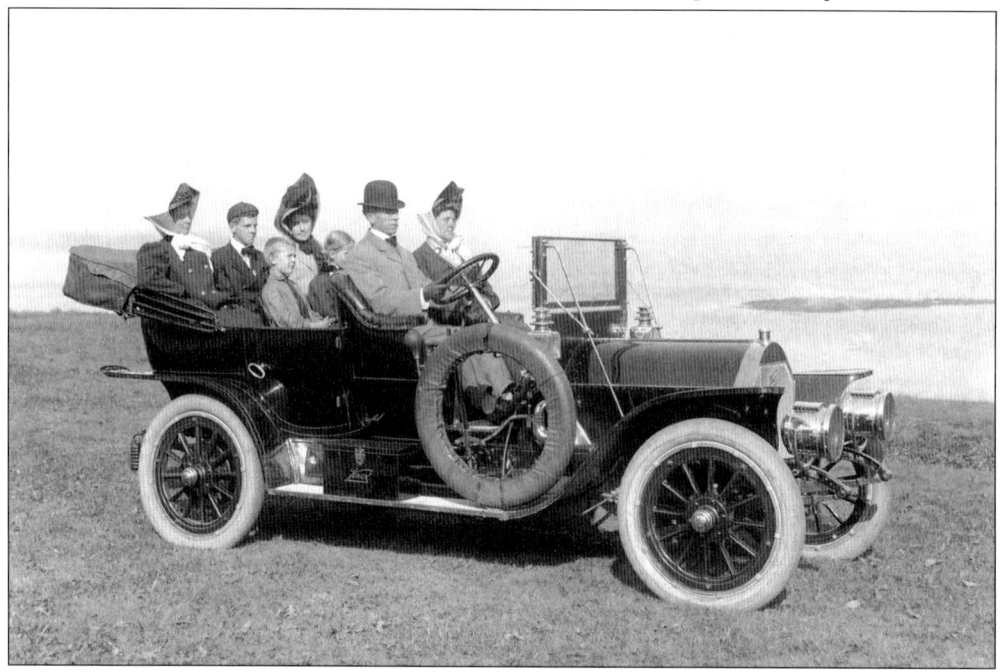

Another Knox seven-passenger touring car is being driven along the waterfront of Casco Bay. The two children in the rear are sitting on the "jump seats" that could be folded away for extra legroom when they were not needed. The front seats on this sporty model have no doors.

Here we see the front view of a Knox touring car with a porcelain 1909 Maine dealer plate on it. The prefix letter "B" denotes it as a Maine dealer plate. Note that many of the occupants are wearing dusters to keep their fine clothes from being soiled by the dust and dirt from the gravel roads. The driver even has a pair of goggles on his cap.

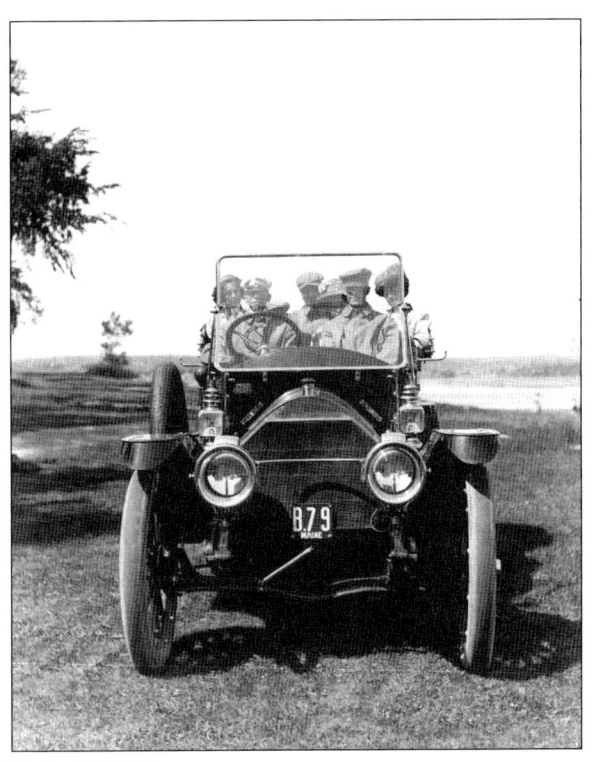

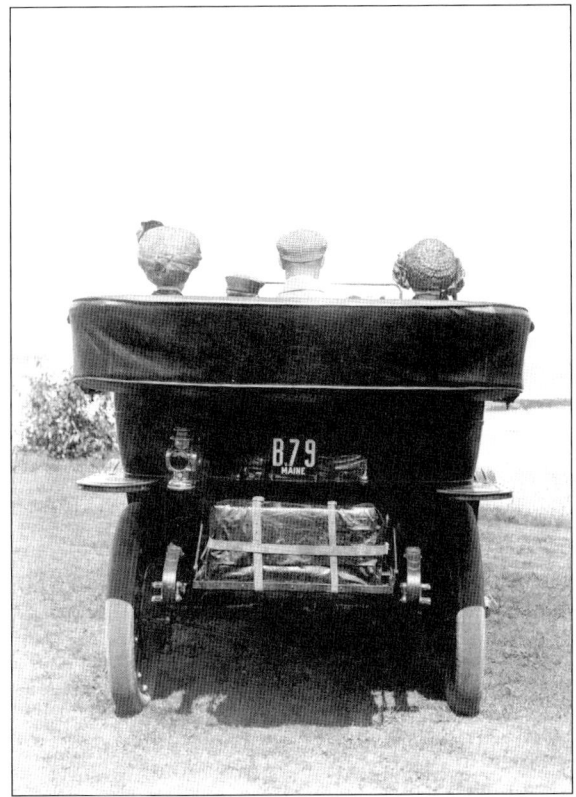

This view shows the rear of the same Knox touring car as in the above photograph. The luggage trunk on the rear platform is from the era when the trunk was literally a trunk. Also, these early automobiles usually had no front or rear bumpers as yet, as perhaps tailgating had not yet been invented or at least not practiced on the road.

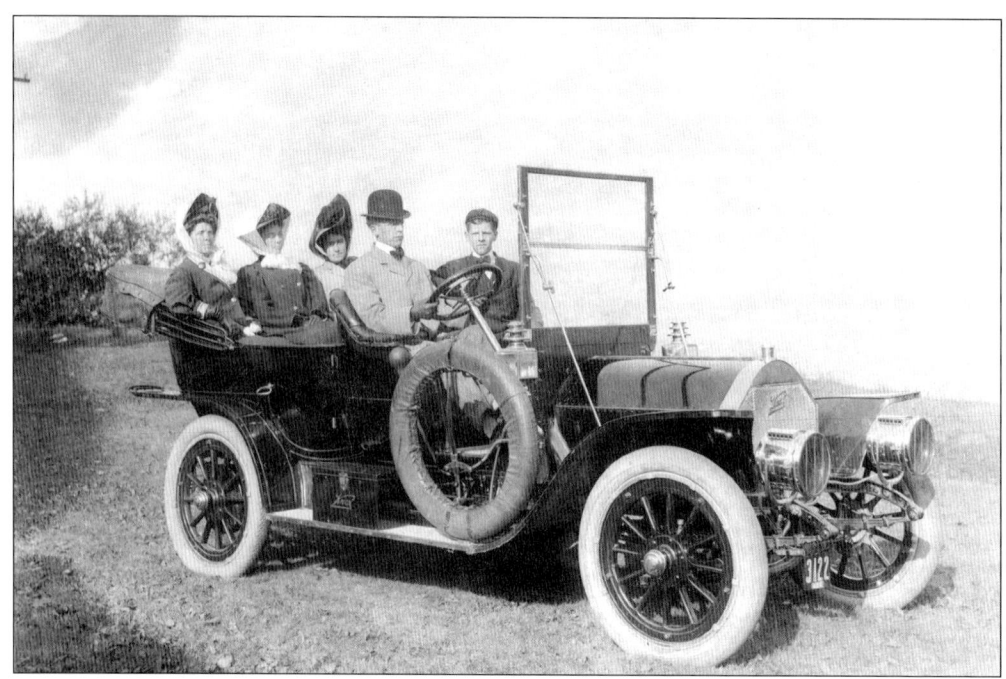

A new Knox automobile is being shown off c. 1909. The Portland Company sold these automobiles from early 1908 until 1914, when the Knox Automobile Company stopped producing automobiles. It did, however, continue to produce trucks until 1924, when the company ceased all vehicle production.

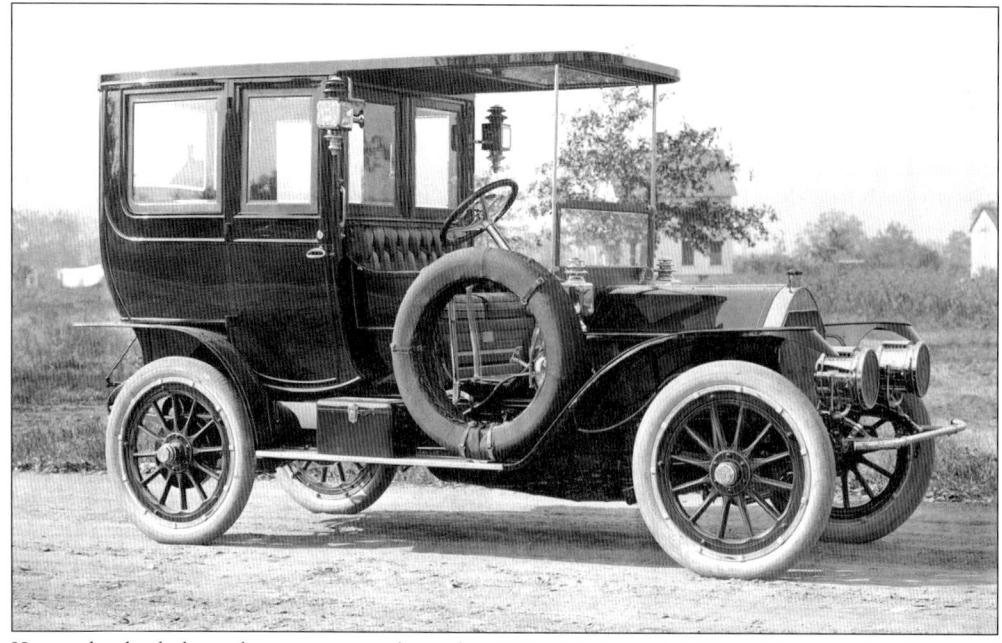

Knox also built large limousines, such as this 1911–1912 model. The driver or chauffeur had little protection from the elements as he drove his wealthy owners about in this "R" model. A Knox cost in the range from $3,000 to $5,000, while many other automobiles were being sold for only a few hundred dollars at the time.

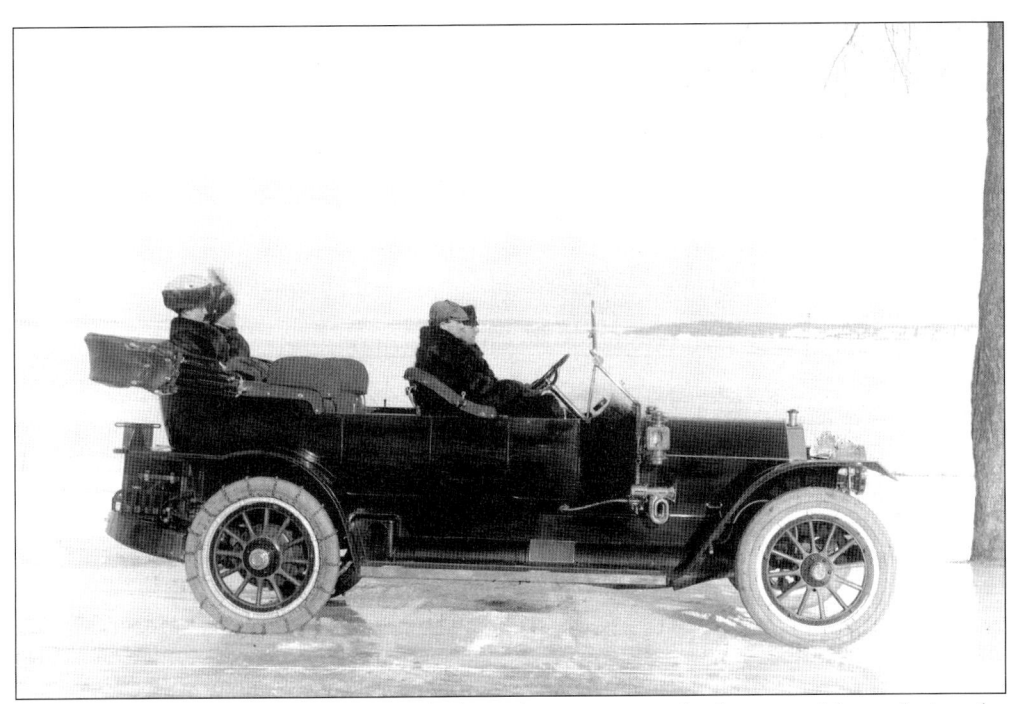

The Knox automobile was a heavy vehicle and was extensively driven in Maine during the winter. Driving along Casco Bay, this automobile has chains on the rear wheels as did most vehicles of the 1909 period, as the tires had no tread molded into them for that extra traction in the ice and snow. Most tires at that time were completely smooth.

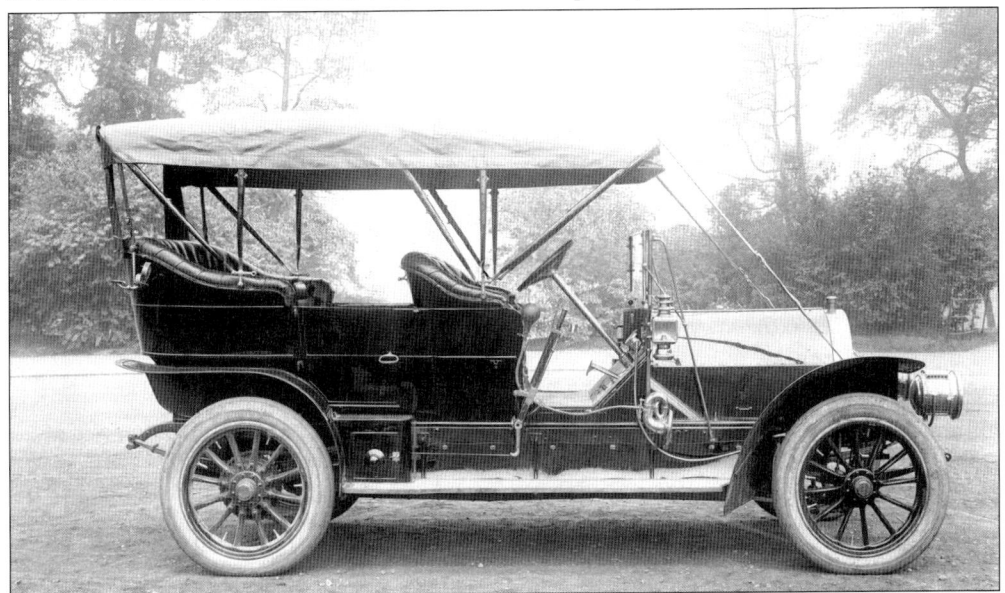

A 1909 Knox seven-passenger touring car sits here, awaiting someone to drive it away with its folding top up to protect the passengers from inclement weather. The large headlights were powered by acetylene produced by carbide generators and did give off quite a bit of light to drive by. The side or marker lamps were powered by lamp oil or kerosene and did not give off much light.

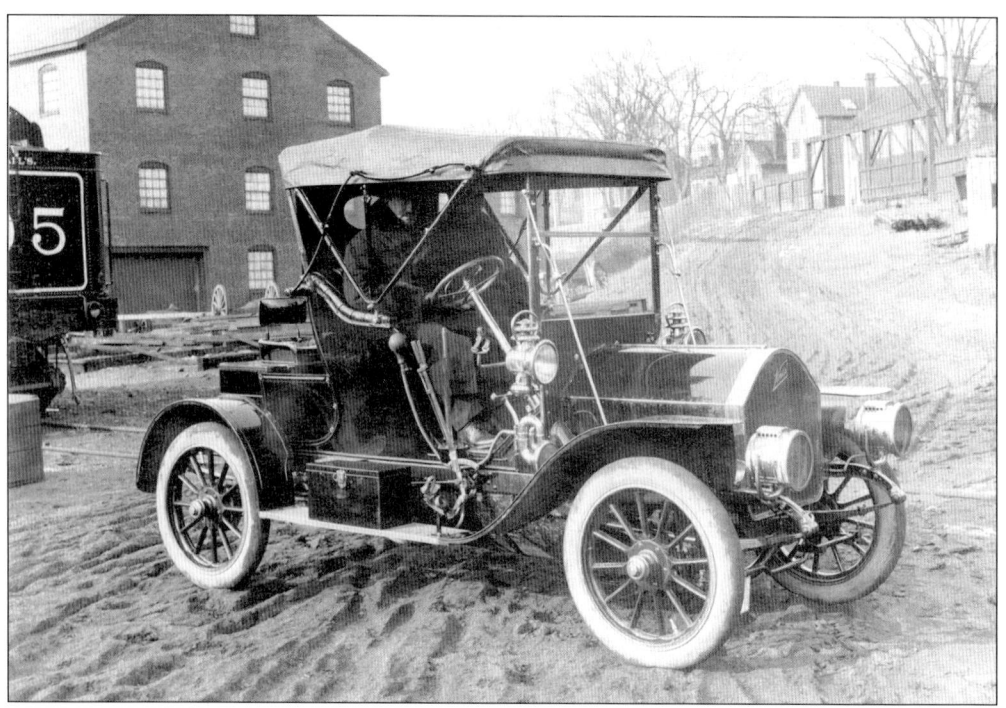

A 1907 air-cooled Knox runabout sits in the Portland Company upper yard. The gated entrance seen above is on Fore Street and is still the main entrance to the Portland Company complex and Maine Narrow Gauge Railroad & Museum at present. After 1907, Knox started building its vehicles with water-cooled engines as the horsepower was increased and more heat was generated. The pattern storage building is behind the automobile along with a locomotive tender.

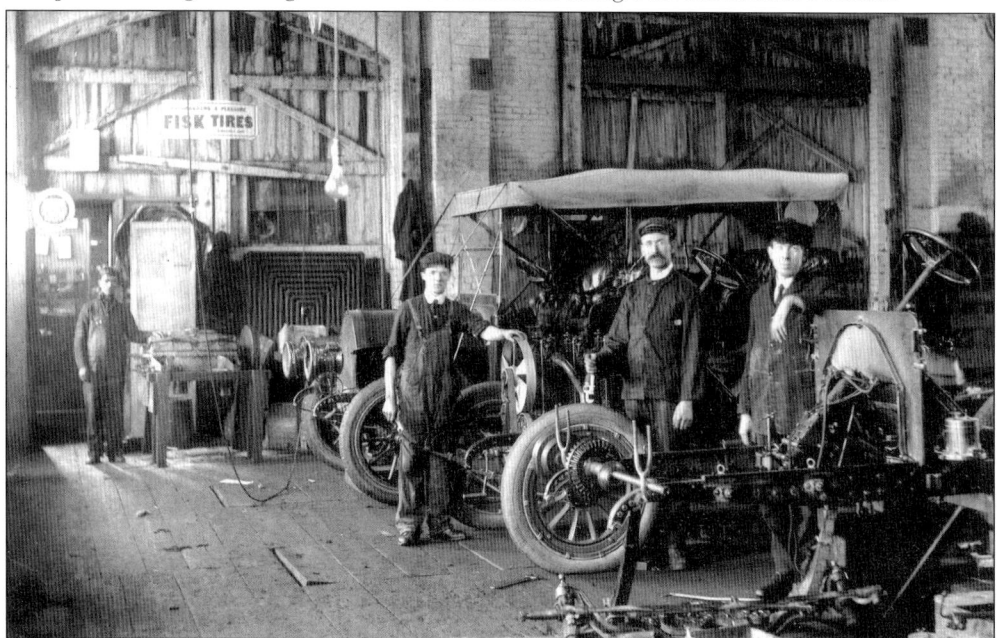

Here we find Portland Company mechanics working on Knox automobiles in the shop. They apparently also sold Fisk tires, according to the sign on the door at the rear.

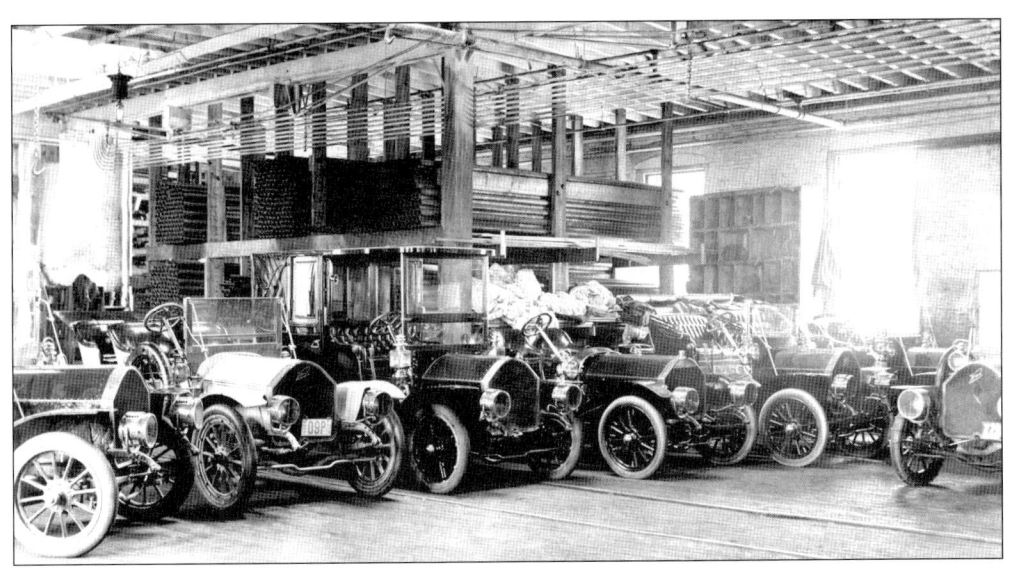

Pictured is a group of various models of new Knox automobiles in a Portland Company building, which still stands there today. The light-colored touring car with the "O9P" 1909 license plate on it probably is the one driven by general manager of the Portland Company, Richard C. Payson. This Massachusetts dealer license plate is from the Knox Automobile Company and was probably driven to Portland from the factory, as were most of the Knox units sold in Maine. It was common practice to drive these open cars in the dead of winter in February, through the cold and snow to Boston for the annual automobile show there and then to the Portland show one week later.

This closeup photograph of an early Knox "running chassis" reveals a fan and no radiator, as the engine is air cooled. The block has hundreds of pins sticking out of it for heat dissipation and resembles a porcupine. Also note that these early automobiles, as were most makes manufactured in America before 1920, were right-hand drive. It was not until later years that the American driver was moved to the left side, but the English never did get around to driving from the left side, even to this day.

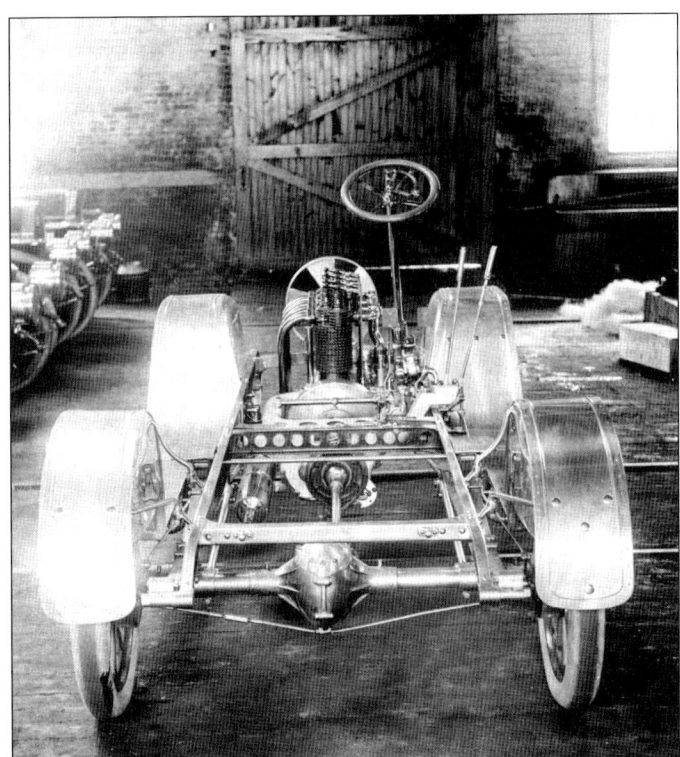

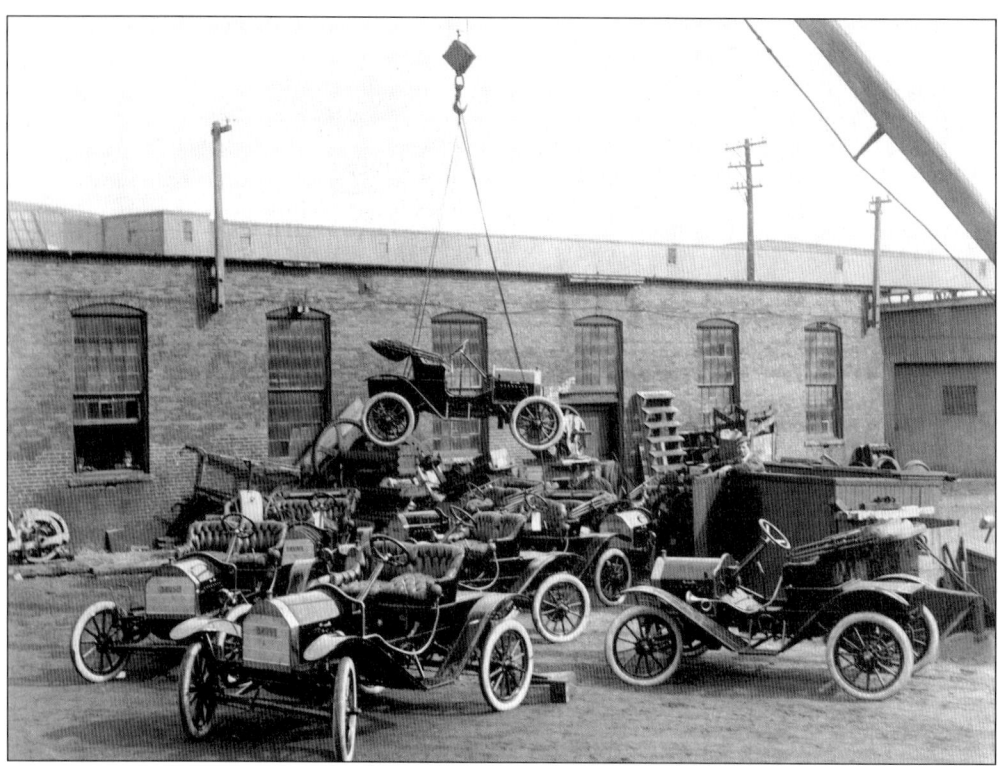

Brush and Cole automobiles are being unloaded from freight cars by the Portland Company's electrically operated track crane. In 1910, the Portland Company began selling these two makes of new automobiles as well as the Thomas. The Brush runabouts shown here were "the cars for the common man." They cost only $385 each and had wooden axles.

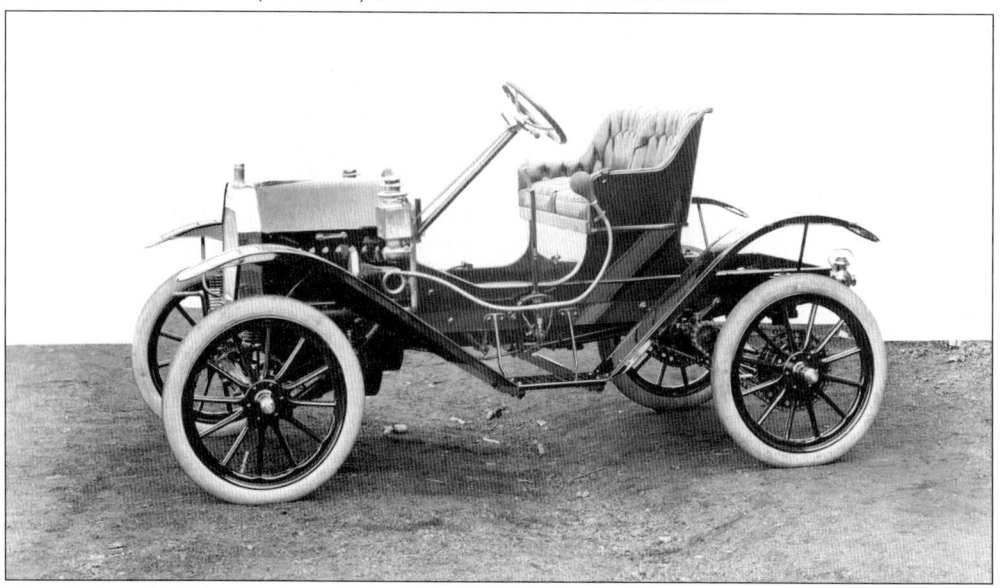

This closeup shows the Brush runabout sold by the Portland Company starting in 1910. Perhaps in an effort to keep the cost below $400, this automobile has no carbide headlamps, only kerosene lamps to mark its presence at night on the road.

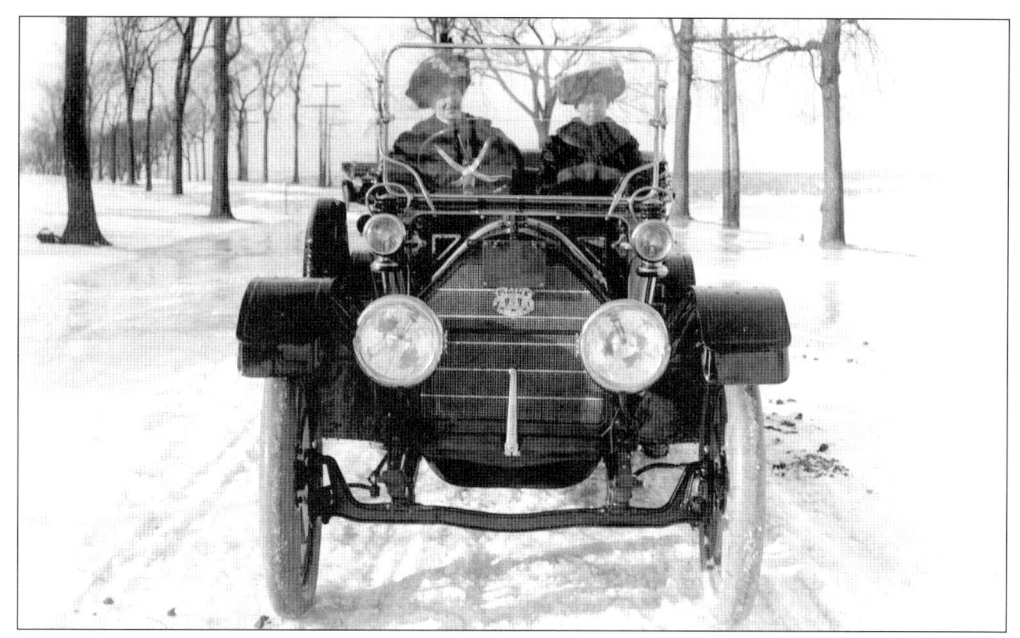

Another new automobile that the Portland Company started selling in 1910 was the Cole. Here we see two fur-clad society ladies enjoying a wintery ride in a "Cole 30-40" with the usual rear-wheel chains for added traction in the snow. We can also see the large brass monogram that owners could purchase to adorn the radiators of their fine automobiles.

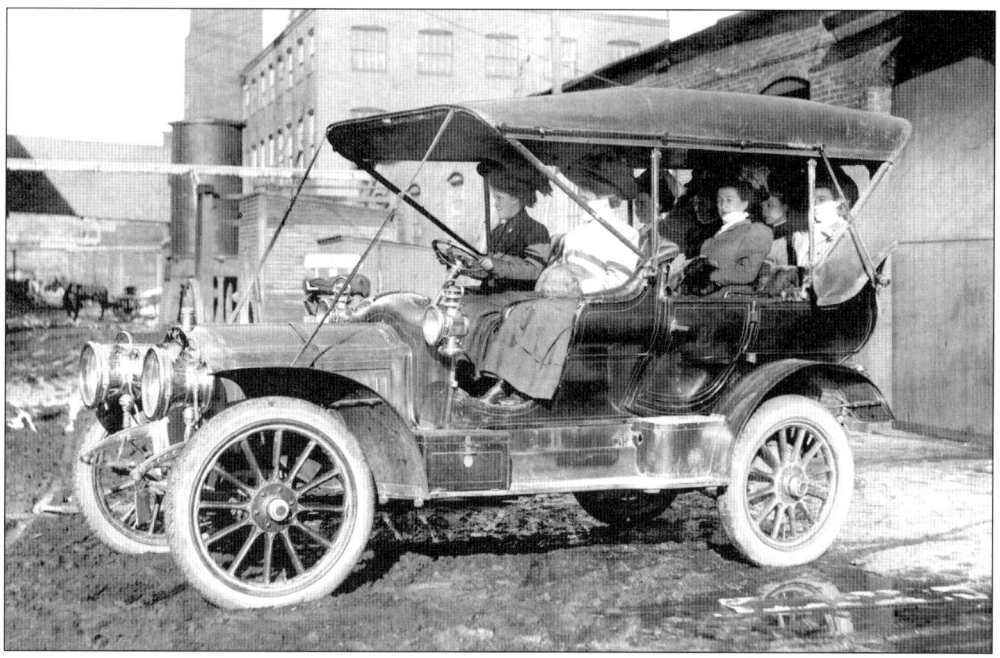

The four-story brick building behind this Thomas automobile is an original building of the Portland Company and now houses the Maine Narrow Gauge Railroad & Museum on the first floor. The ladies in this Thomas seven-passenger model are off for a ride during Maine's "mud time," when the roads are apt to be wet and deeply rutted with sticky mud and really a challenge to drive on. They have the top up just in case those spring showers appear.

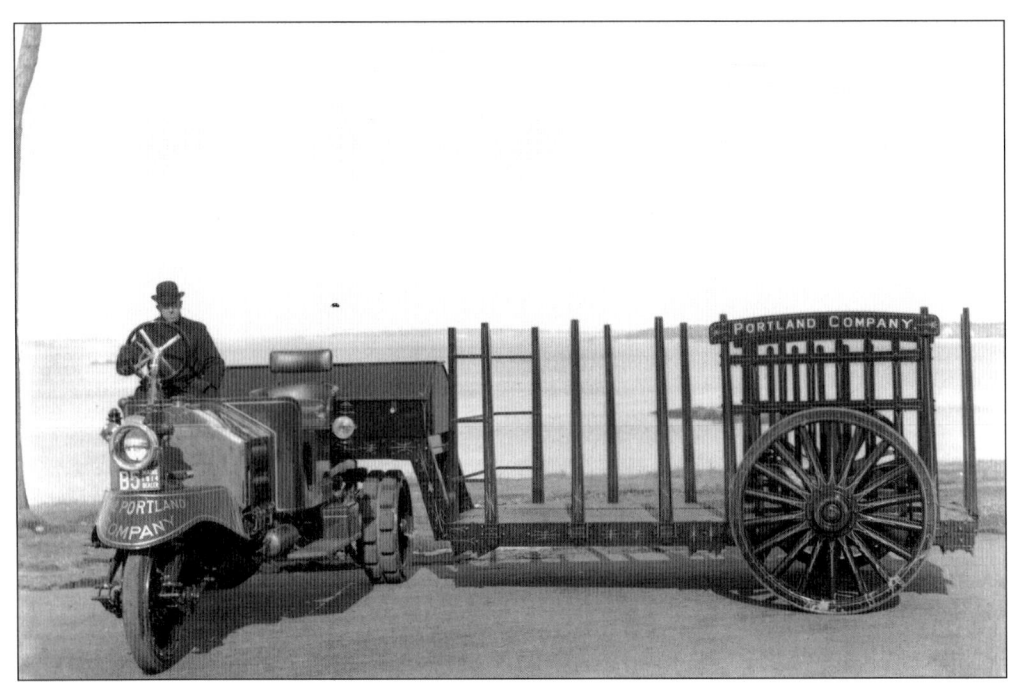

This view of the Portland Company's Knox-Martin tractor shows the Maine 1914 license plate "B5," which was the dealer's plate number of the Portland Company. The round-nosed tractor was the first model the Knox Automobile Company manufactured.

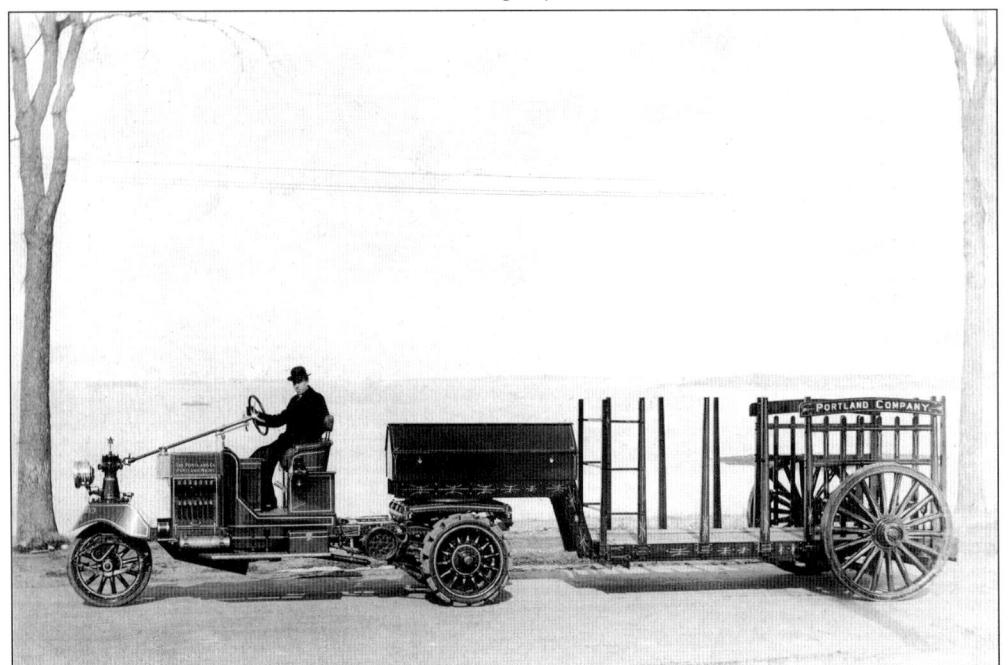

This Knox-Martin three-wheeled tractor and trailer was owned by the Portland Company to move heavy machinery and parts to local area businesses. The three-wheeled tractor was very popular with fire departments as a way to motorize their expensive horse-drawn steam engines without having to replace the whole fire engine to free themselves from the use of horses.

Five
ELEVATORS

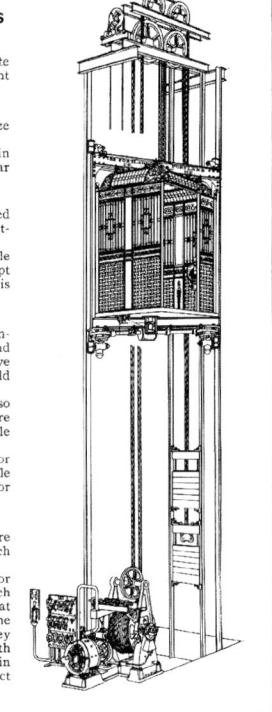

The Portland Company bulletin No. 36 gave a good overview of a complete electric elevator system installed as it would be installed in a multistory building. The passenger elevator cars of this period were particularly ornate and nothing like the uninteresting utilitarian elevators of today.

BULLETIN NO. 36

THE PORTLAND CO.
BOILER MAKERS, MACHINISTS, ELECTRICIANS
BUILDERS OF ELEVATORS
PORTLAND, MAINE, U. S. A.

STANDARD CONSTRUCTION FOR OUR ELECTRIC ELEVATORS

Foundations

All direct connected machines are complete on one bed plate, insuring permanent alignment of parts.

Worm and Gears

Drums are bolted directly to phosphor bronze gears.
Worm is cut on forged steel shaft and runs in oil bath with suitable thrust plates on single gear machines.

Brakes

Brakes on direct current machines are released by our double plunger type solenoid with adjustments all on top in readily accessible positions.
Alternating current machines have toggle mechanism with single plunger solenoid except for hand rope control where a mechanical brake is ordinarily furnished.

Motors

Motors for all direct current work are compound wound to obtain high starting torque, and for all passenger and some freight service have commutating poles and adjustable speed by field weakening.
Alternating current motors used are also particularly designed for elevator service and care is taken that they are the proper size to handle full rated elevator load.
We have devoted special attention to motor selection, and in addition are nearly always able to supply immediately from our stock parts for emergency service.

Controllers

Controller panels for the various services are made up as nearly as possible of standard switch units, facilitating both construction and repair.
We can furnish dash pot acceleration, but for most cases recommend series relay control which limits the starting current to a constant value at all loads. We wish to especially recommend the clapper type switches on these controllers. They embody simplicity and rugged construction with accessibility of contacts, powerful blowout field in arc chute, and vertical laminated brush contact

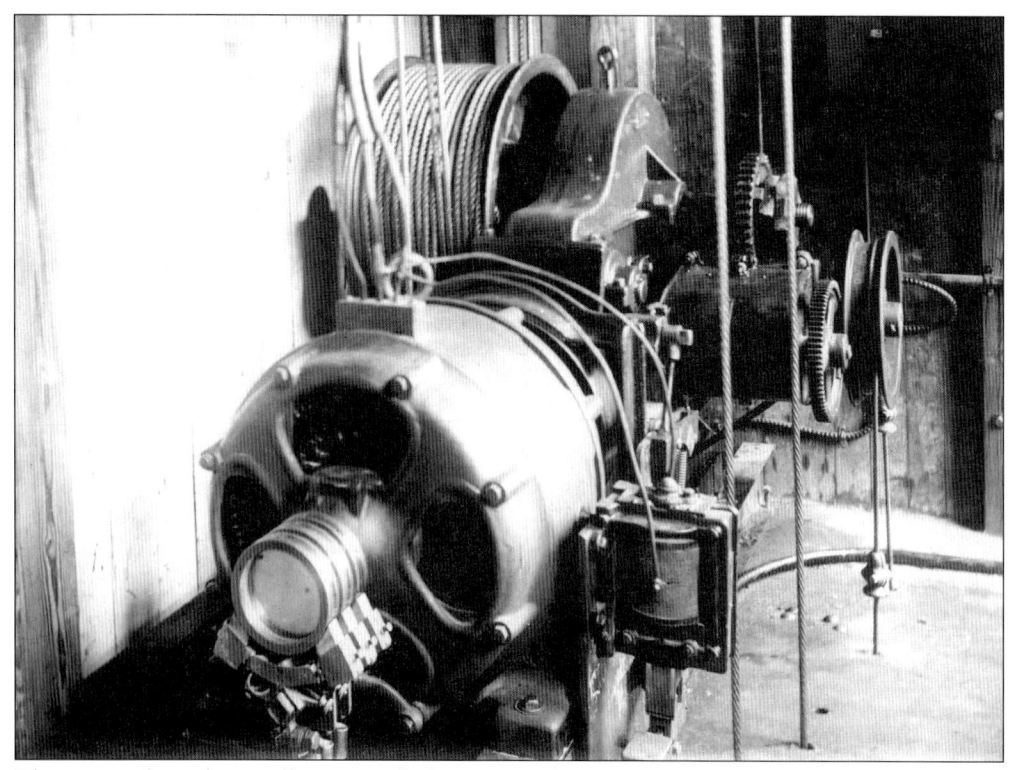

This view of an electrically operated elevator machine in operation shows the large electric motor, brake, cable drum, and cables.

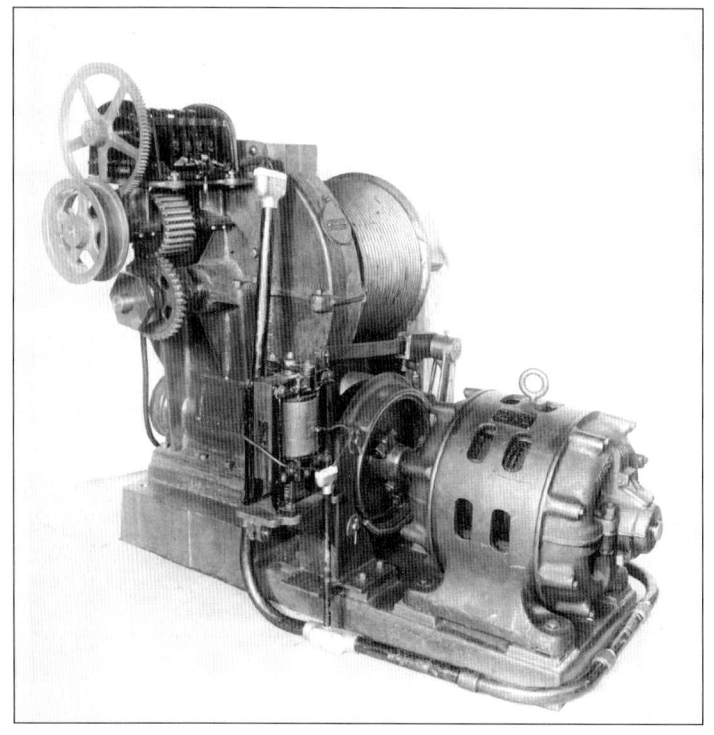

Pictured in a closeup of a Portland Company electric elevator machine is the braking mechanism between the large electric motor and the cable drum. Electric operating machines were used for both passenger and freight elevators.

88

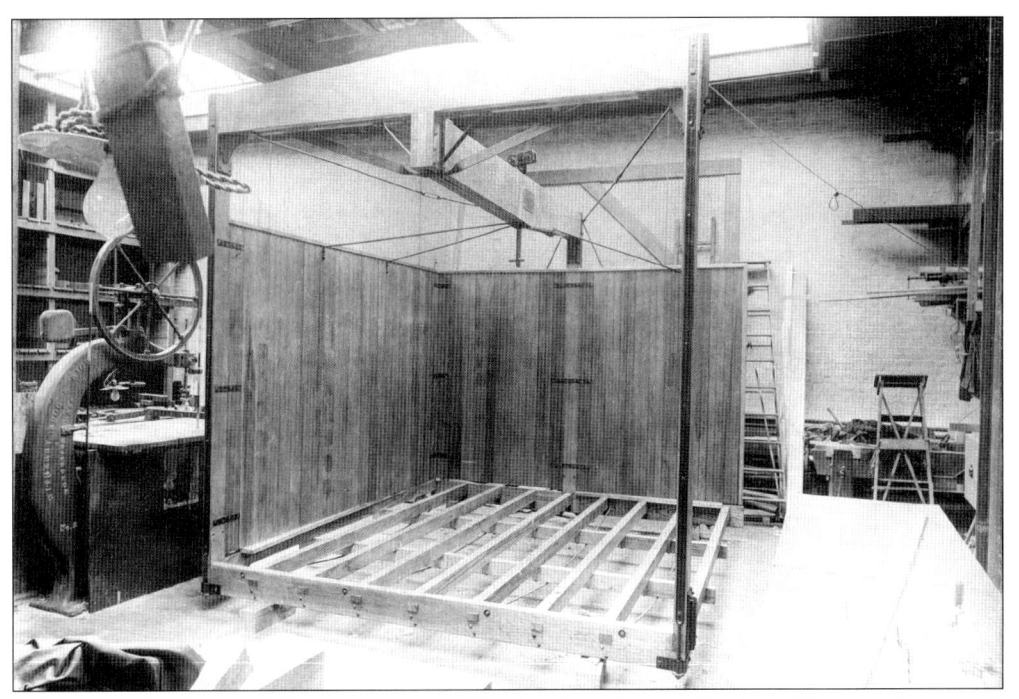

A large freight elevator is being constructed in the shops for the "Embree Elevator Company," according to the nameplate on the overhead lifting beam. Hydraulic elevators were in use before the electric ones were used.

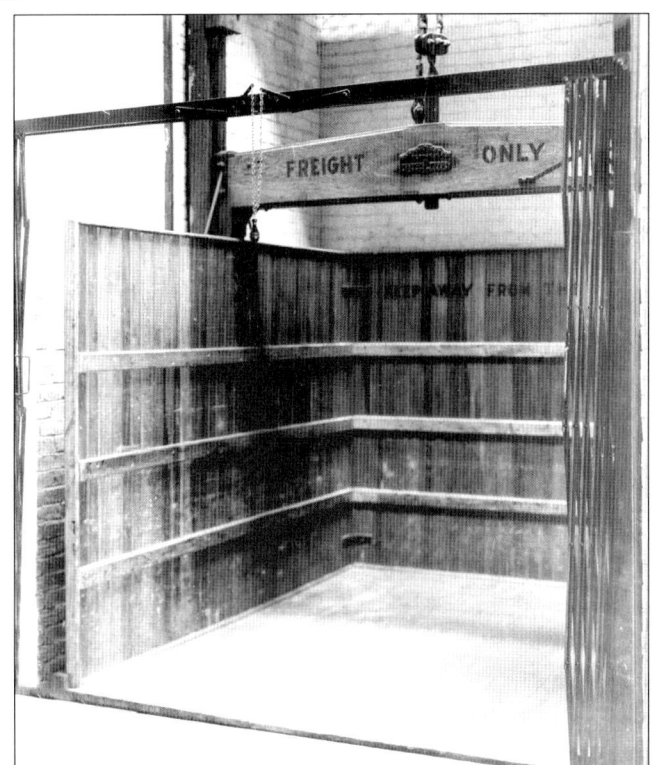

A freight elevator car is shown in use with its simple folding gate to keep people from falling down the shaft. Much of the freight elevator car was made of oak and reinforced with steel. Both freight and passenger elevators could be powered by electricity or set up for a hydraulic operating system.

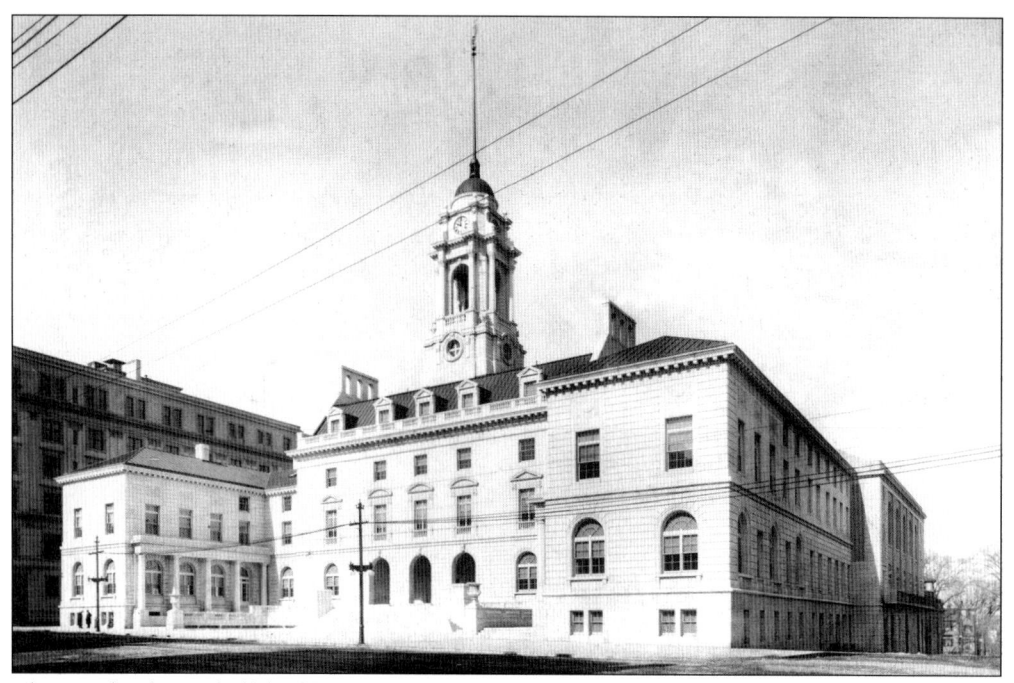

The Portland city hall building on Congress Street was equipped with Portland Company elevators. The passenger elevator was electrically operated, and the freight one was hydraulically operated. Hydraulic elevator machines were earlier than the electric ones. Also, several Portland Company streetlights adorn the area in front of the building.

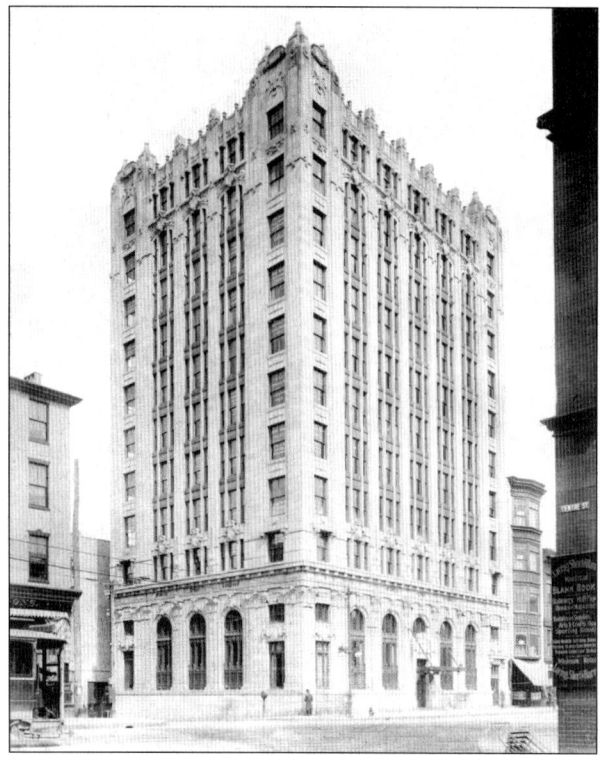

The multistory Fidelity Trust building, shown here, is on Congress Street in Portland. It was equipped with three Portland elevators. Two of the elevators were electric, and the freight elevator was a hydraulic, or "plunger," elevator. The building is now the Maine Bank & Trust Company, and one of the old Portland Company passenger elevators is still in operation there.

Six
Fire Engines

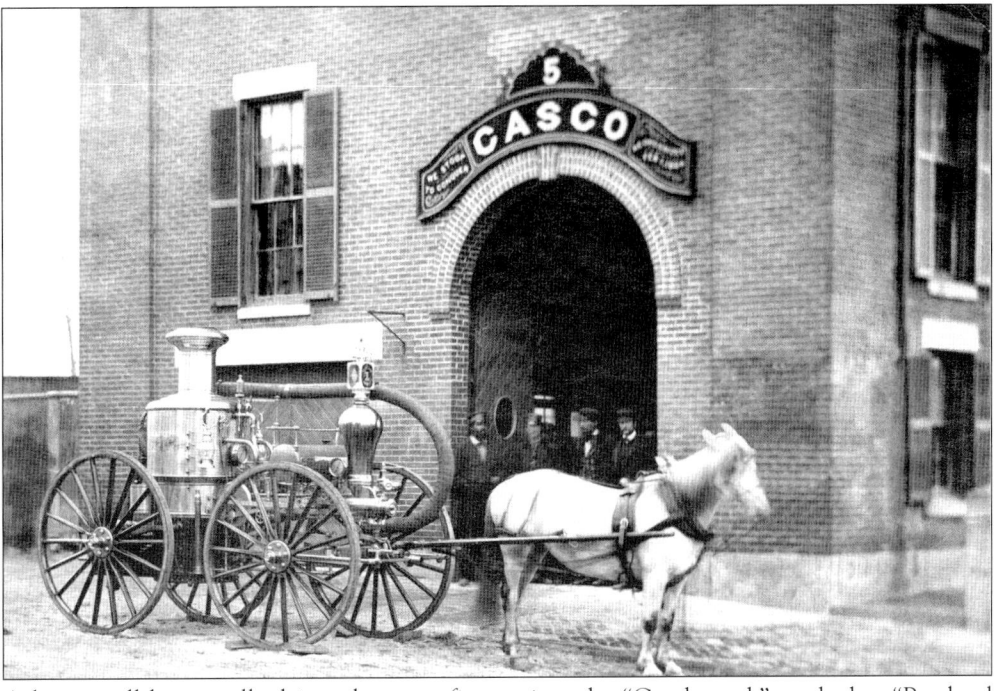

A lone small horse pulls this early steam fire engine, the "Greyhound," marked as "Portland No. 1," in Portland, Maine, in 1864. The steamer was built by the Portland Company in 1860 for its own use and the use of the Grand Trunk Railroad next door, but it was loaned to the city of Portland until its "Falmouth No. 2" was ready to be put in service. This photograph was taken on Congress Street at the head of Smith Street next to the Eastern Cemetery. The building was built as a schoolhouse, then in 1845 Ladder No. 1 and Engine No. 8 went on the first floor. In 1861, the "Falmouth No. 2" was put in service here. Later, in 1864, "Casco No. 5" made its home here, with the school continuing to be above it. Note that the pumper's wheels are chocked with firewood to help keep it in place while all of the firemen pose for the picture in the doorway of the old Casco 5 firehouse.

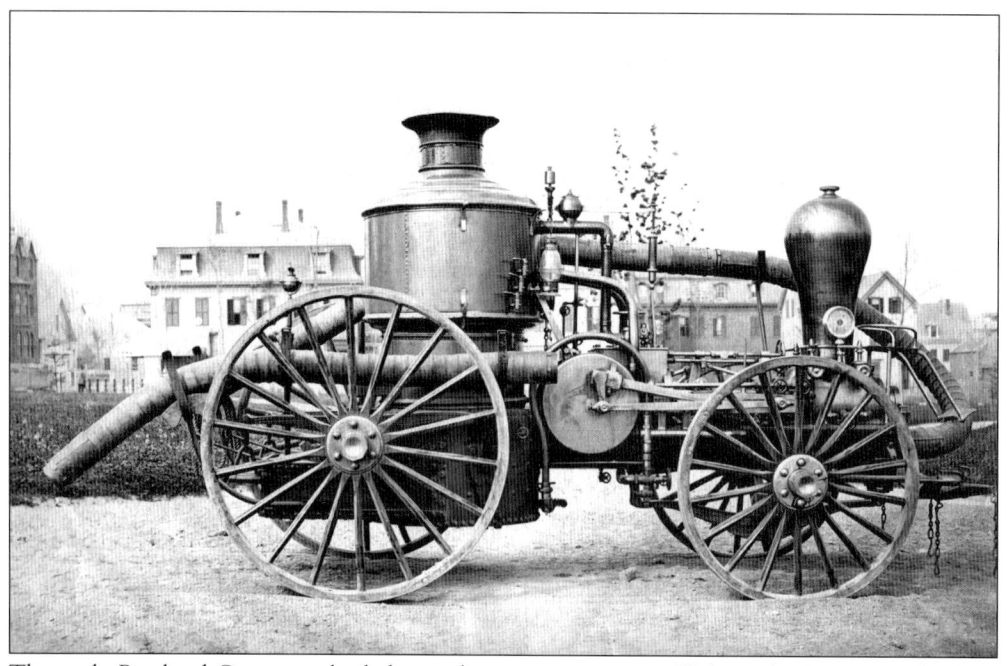

The early Portland Company–built horse-drawn steam engine "Falmouth No. 2" was built in 1861 for the city of Portland, Maine, at a cost of $3,327.78 as a first-class, or 600-gallon-per-minute, fire engine. It was the Portland Fire Department's second steam fire engine and weighed in at a very hefty 8,755 pounds. This engine later became No. 4. The Portland Fire Department's first and third steam engines were both Amoskeag engines. The first engine, built in 1859 in Manchester, New Hampshire, was named the "Machigonne 1" and cost $3,000.

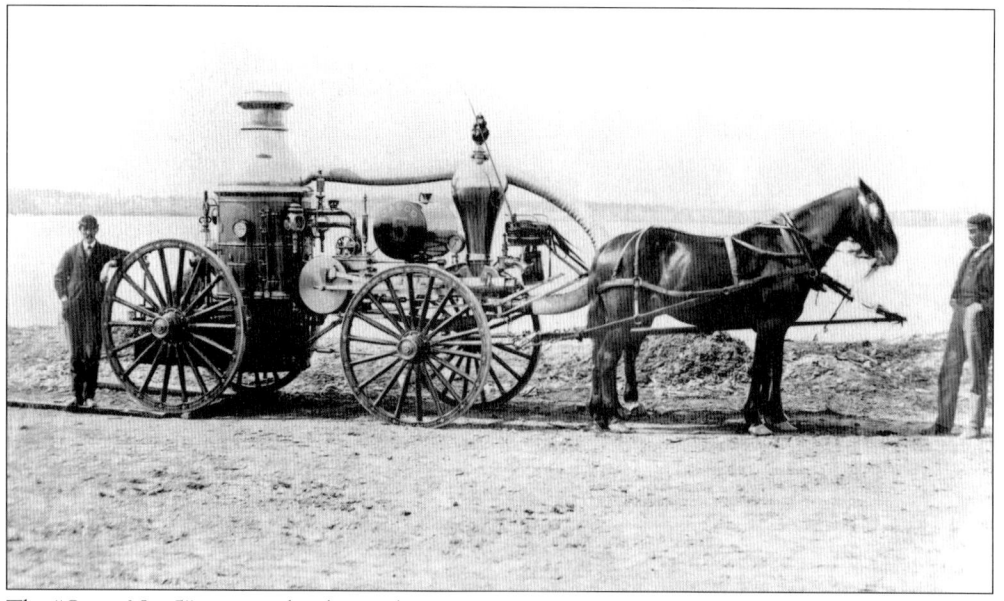

The "Casco No. 5" was another horse-drawn steam engine built by the Portland Company in 1864 as a second-class, or 400-gallon-per-minute, engine at a cost of $3,200 and weighed 5,260 pounds. It was the Portland Fire Department's fourth steam fire engine and was burned in the Great Fire in Portland on July 4, 1866. Here it is seen posed by Casco Bay for an official photograph.

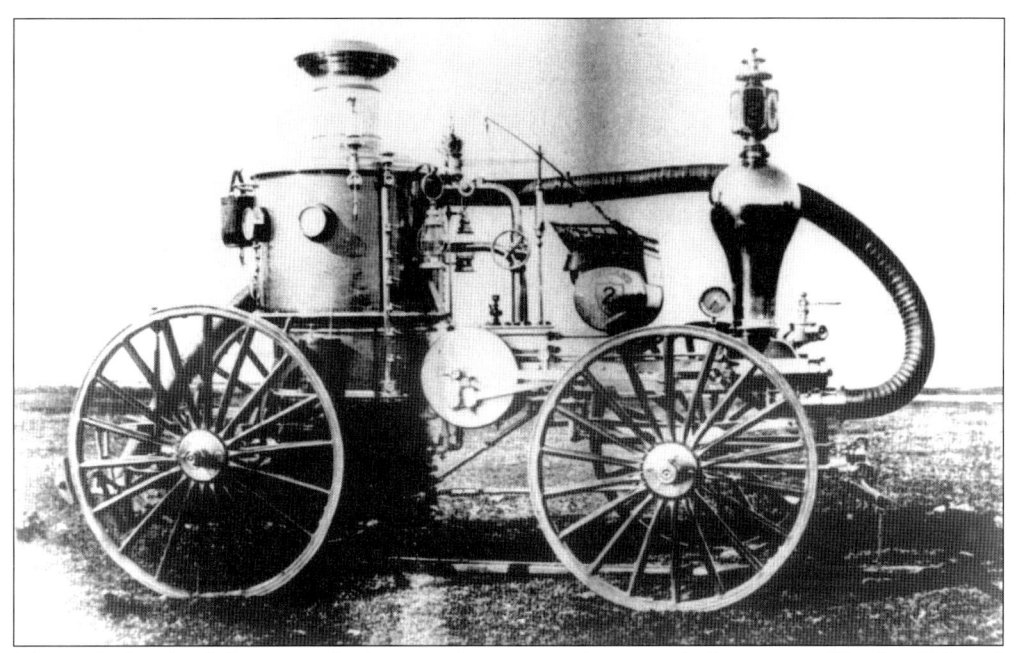

This 1864 Portland Company–built steam fire engine, the second-class engine "Portland No. 2," was put into service in January 1865 as the Portland Fire Department's fifth steam engine. It cost $4,500 and weighed 6,625 pounds.

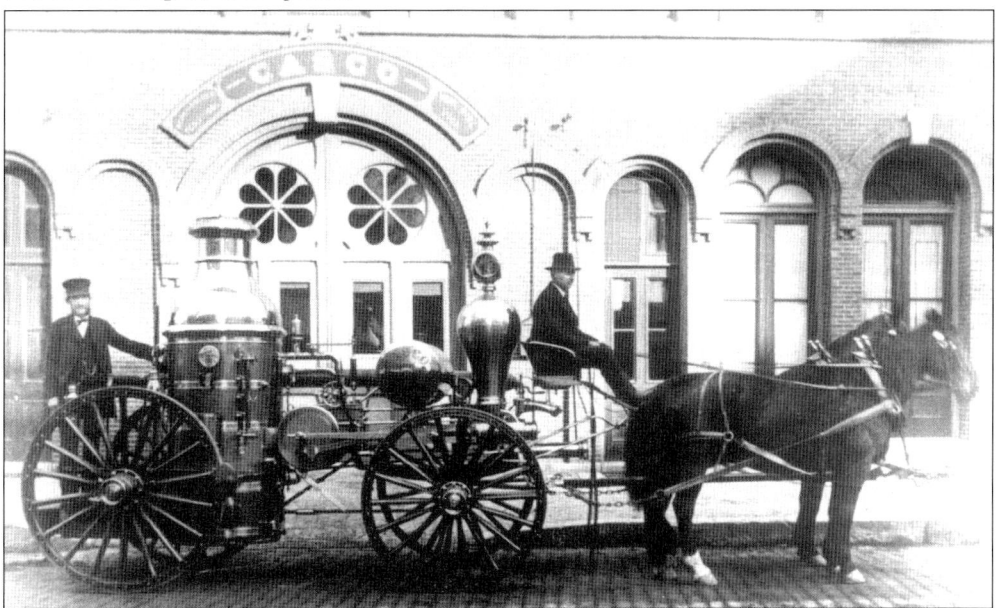

This 1866 Portland Company–built steam fire engine, the third-class engine "Casco No. 5," was put into service in September 1866 as the Portland Fire Department's sixth steam engine. It cost the taxpayers $4,500, weighed 6,800 pounds, and was the first engine to use the newly designed Portland Company boiler. The engine rests here in 1869 in front of the old central fire station, Casco 5, on the corner of Congress and Market Streets in Portland, Maine. The city fireman on the rear was the engineer, but the driver and horse were not from the fire department, as there were no department-owned horses at firehouses until later years.

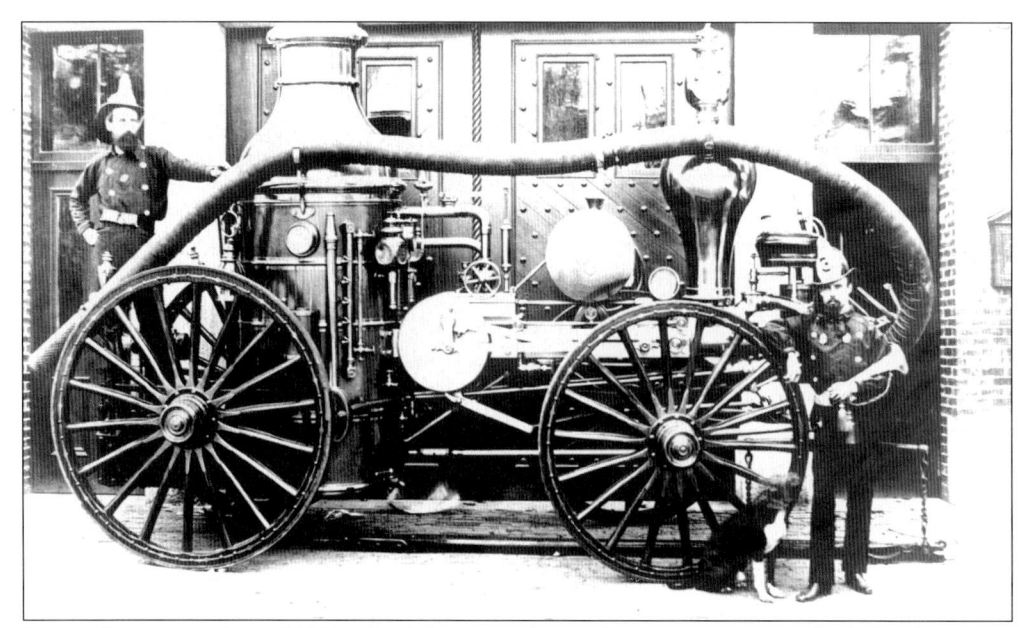

Pictured is yet another 1869 Portland Company horse-drawn steam engine built for the city of Portland, Maine. The "Cumberland No. 3" was put into service in January 1870 as the Portland Fire Department's seventh steam engine. It cost $3,618 and weighed 6,800 pounds. It was pulled by two horses instead of the commonly seen three-horse hitch used on larger steam engines in later years in other cities. This Portland second-class engine rests in front of the Brackett Street firehouse. Note the engineer at the rear and the other fireman in his dress uniform with a No. 3 fire helmet, speaking trumpet, and attentive dog.

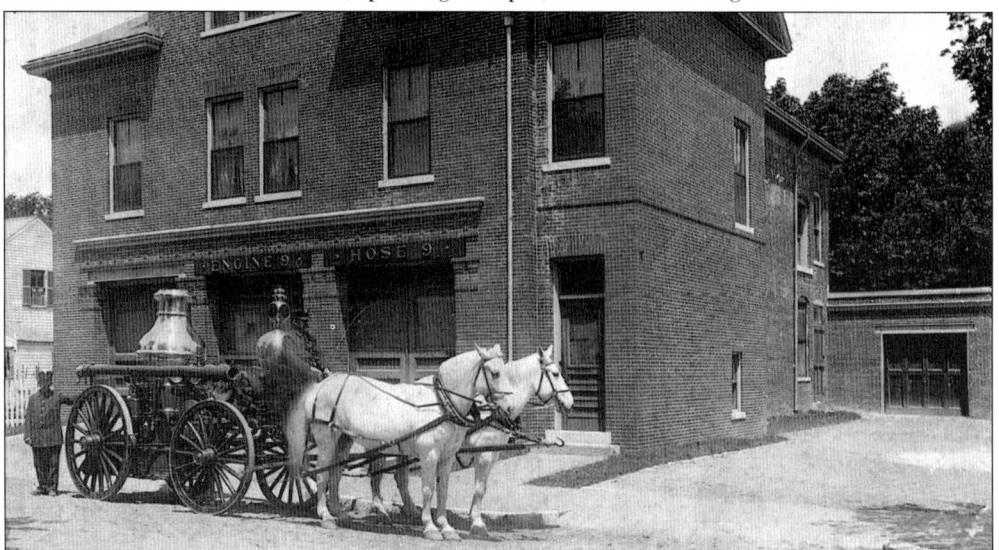

This Portland Fire Department firehouse, Engine 9, was built on Arbor Street, Morrill's Corner. In front we see the old "Cumberland No. 3" steam fire engine built by Portland in 1870 at a cost of $3,250. It was reassigned here as No. 9, but the No. 3 markings remained in the lamps for a long time afterwards. Around 1889, the fire department kept all its own horses at each firehouse and used a fireman as the driver. The size and condition of the horses were also considerably improved, as the firemen were now caring for them.

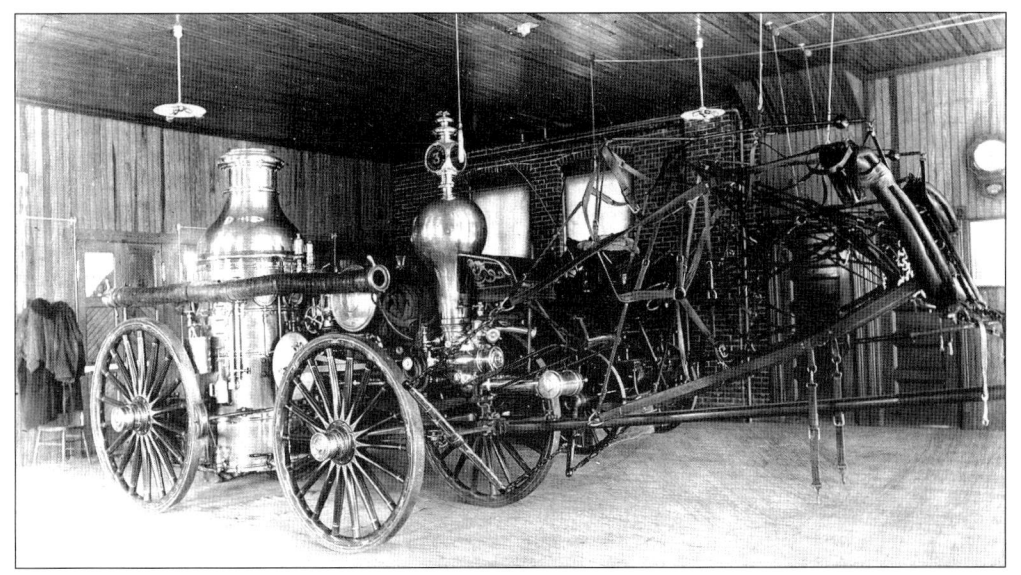

Looking inside the Portland Fire Department firehouse, Engine 9, we see the old "Cumberland No. 3" steam fire engine, built by the Portland Company in 1870, with the double horse harness suspended from the ceiling, ready for the horses to step under them. When the horses are in place, the harnesses are lowered onto them and buckled up, thus saving valuable time in getting to the fire. Behind the pumper is a hose wagon, No. 9.

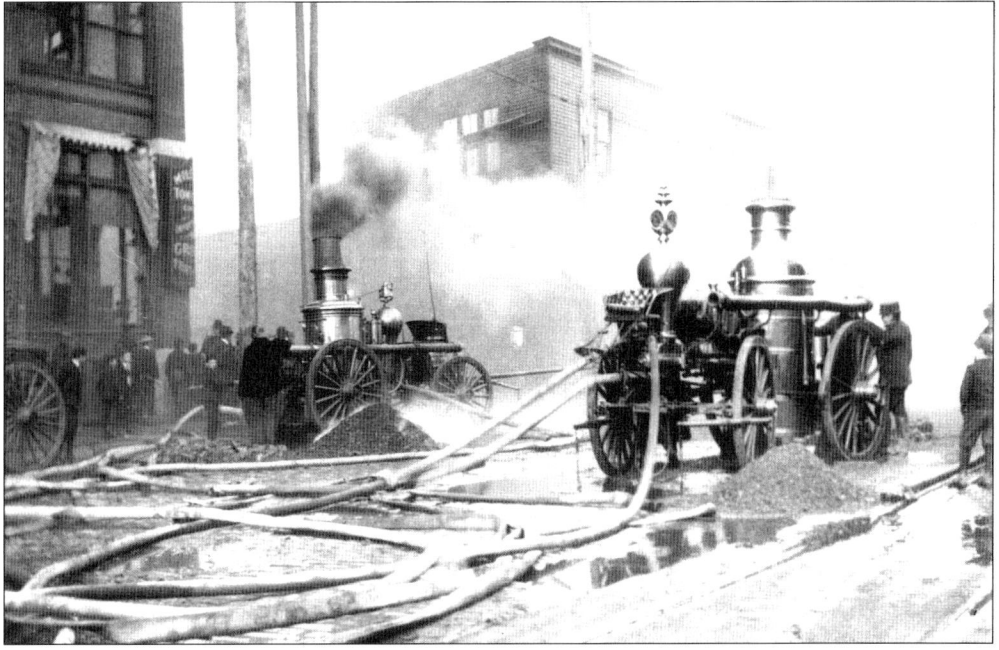

Two Portland Fire Department steam engines are working a three-alarm fire at Brown's Wharf on Commercial Street on November 9, 1903. The engine to the left is Engine No. 1, an 1871 Amoskeag engine built as "Machigonne No. 1," the fire department's eighth steamer, built by the Amoskeag Company in Manchester, New Hampshire. The second engine to the right is Engine No. 9 as reassigned, a Portland Company–built engine, formerly known as "Cumberland No. 3," built in 1870.

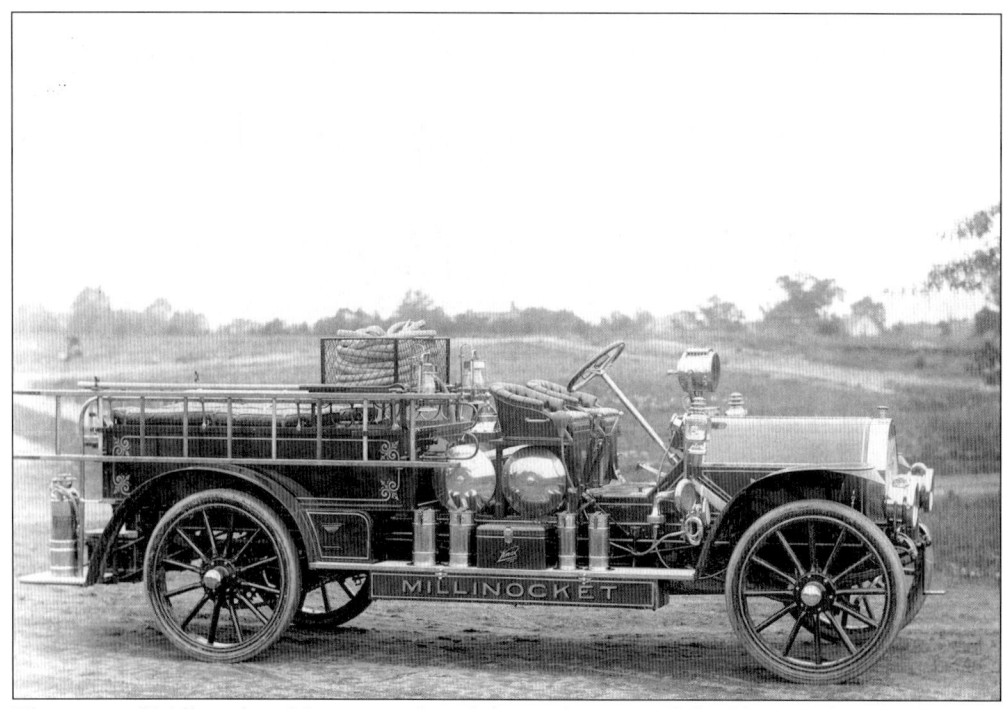

The town of Millinocket, Maine, purchased this early-1908 solid-rubber-tired Knox chemical and hose fire truck through the Portland Company. Knox was a leading name in motorized fire apparatus during the early years of the 20th century. The author's hometown of Haverhill, Massachusetts, had three Knox fire engines in its motorized fleet in 1912.

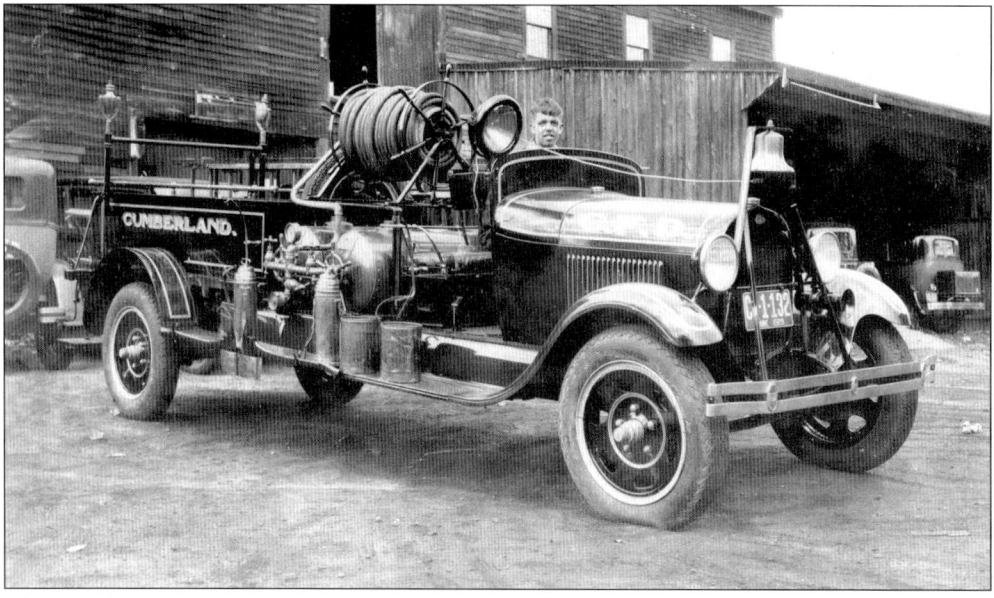

The Cumberland Fire Department sent its Ford "AA" fire truck to the Portland Company in 1929 for work to be done on it. It was equipped with a Macan fire truck body there.

Seven
Paper Mill Equipment

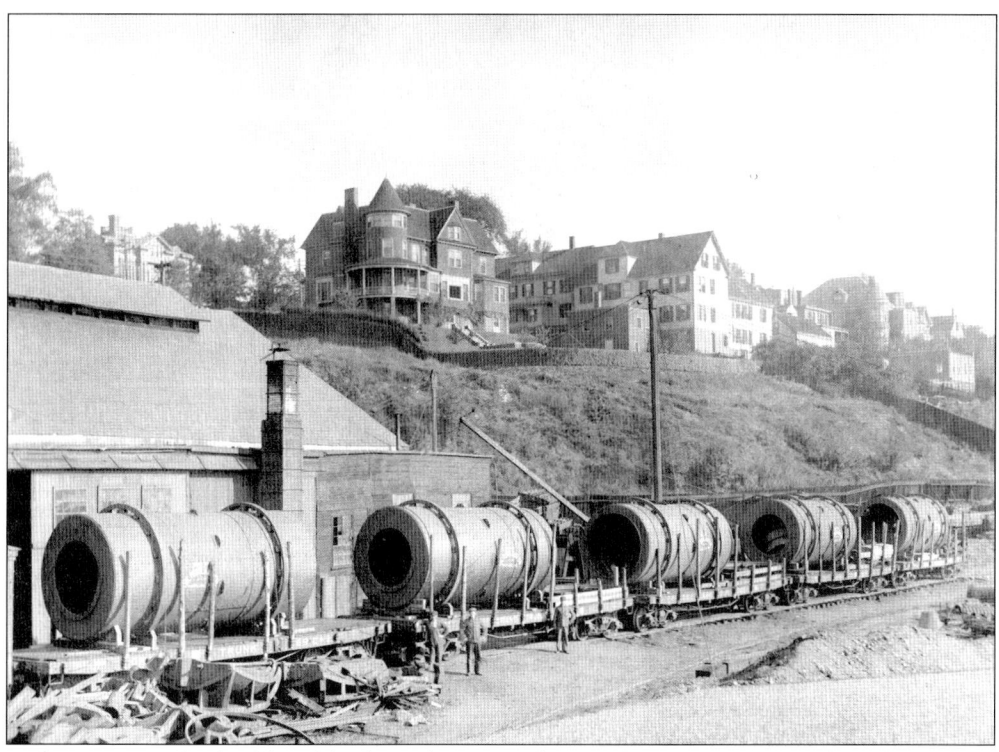

A five-car trainload of log-debarking drums in the Portland Company yard at the base of Munjoy Hill awaits shipment to distant paper mills.

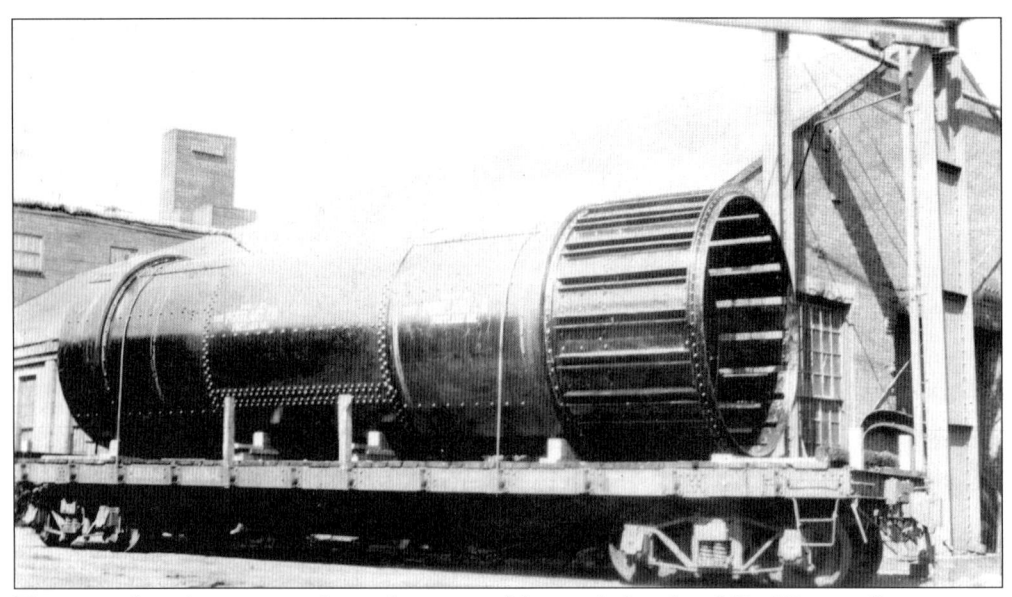

This nine-foot-diameter washing drum was fabricated for the S.D. Warren Company in Westbrook, Maine.

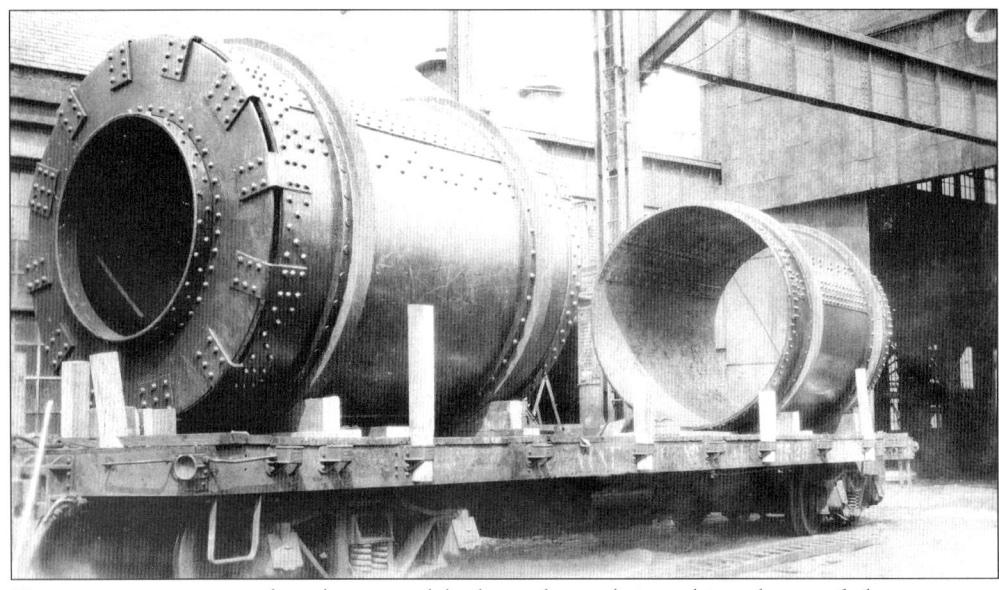

Here we see two nine-foot-diameter debarking drums being shipped out of the company complex by rail car to the Great Northern Paper & Pulp Company mill. The rail cars can be shifted right into the shop buildings to allow the huge Cleveland overhead cranes to lift and load these very large and heavy products onto them.

98

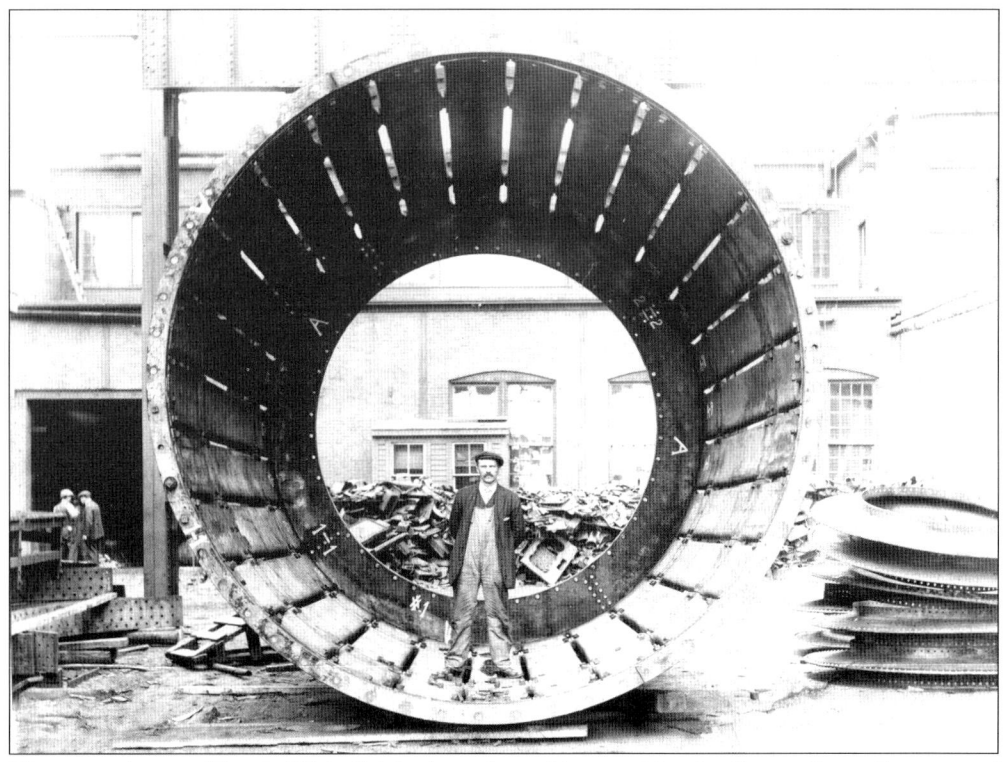

This view shows a "Busch-Widgg" debarking drum fabricated for the Brown Paper Company of Berlin, New Hampshire. The drum is about 15 feet in diameter.

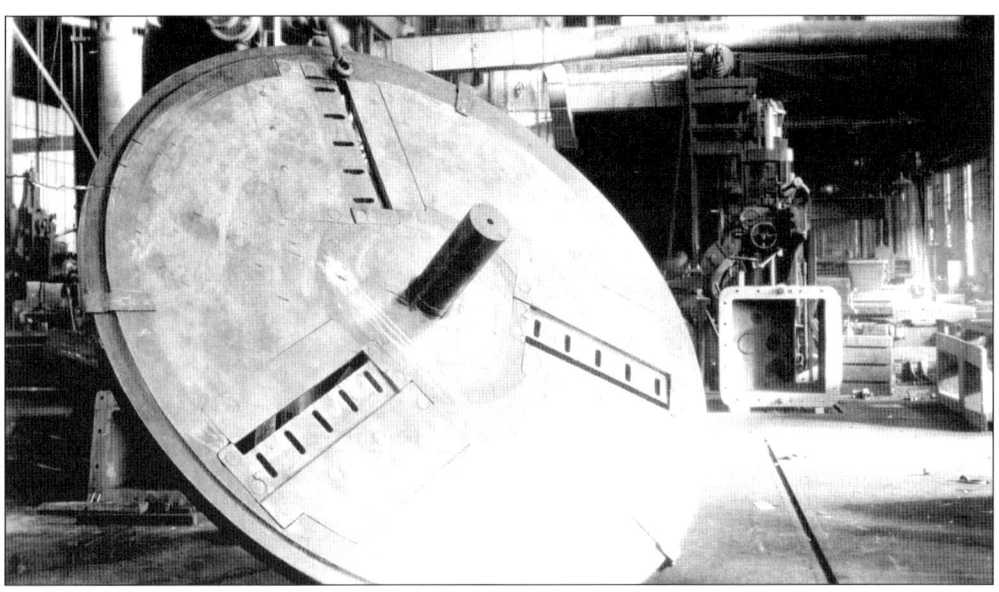

Huge chipper disks were fabricated for cutting paper pulp logs into chips for the digesters at the paper mills. This disk in the shop appears to be about 10 to 12 feet in diameter and has three cutting blades.

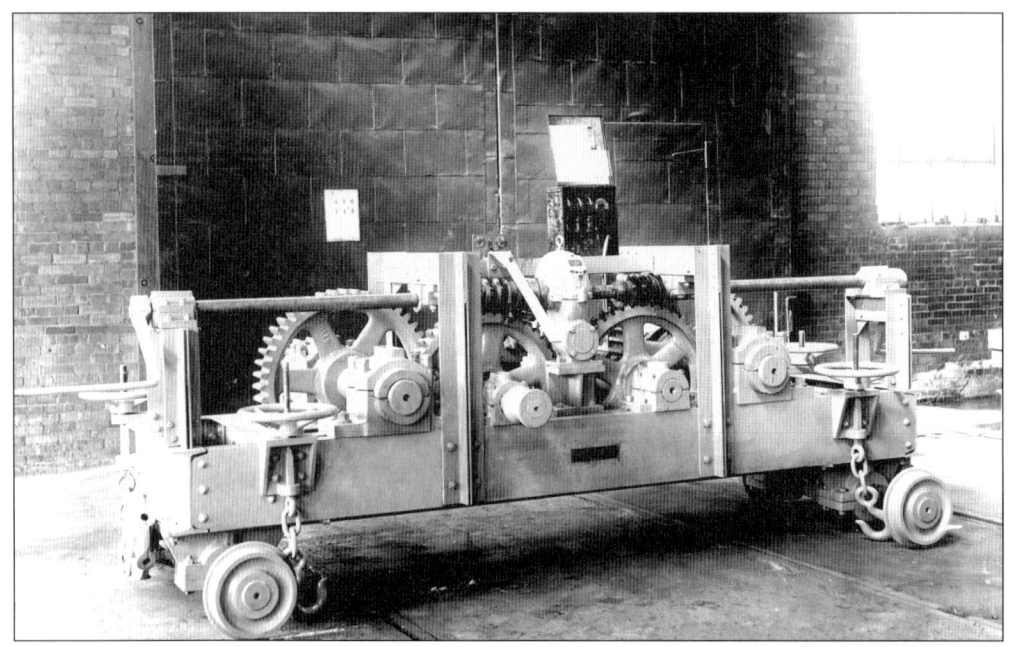

Shown here is a portable gate hoist built for the Great Northern Paper & Pulp Company. It could be moved over the gates of dams or sluices to lift the gates holding back water at the paper mills in Maine and elsewhere. The flanged wheels allowed it to be rolled along rail tracks from gate to gate at a large mill complex.

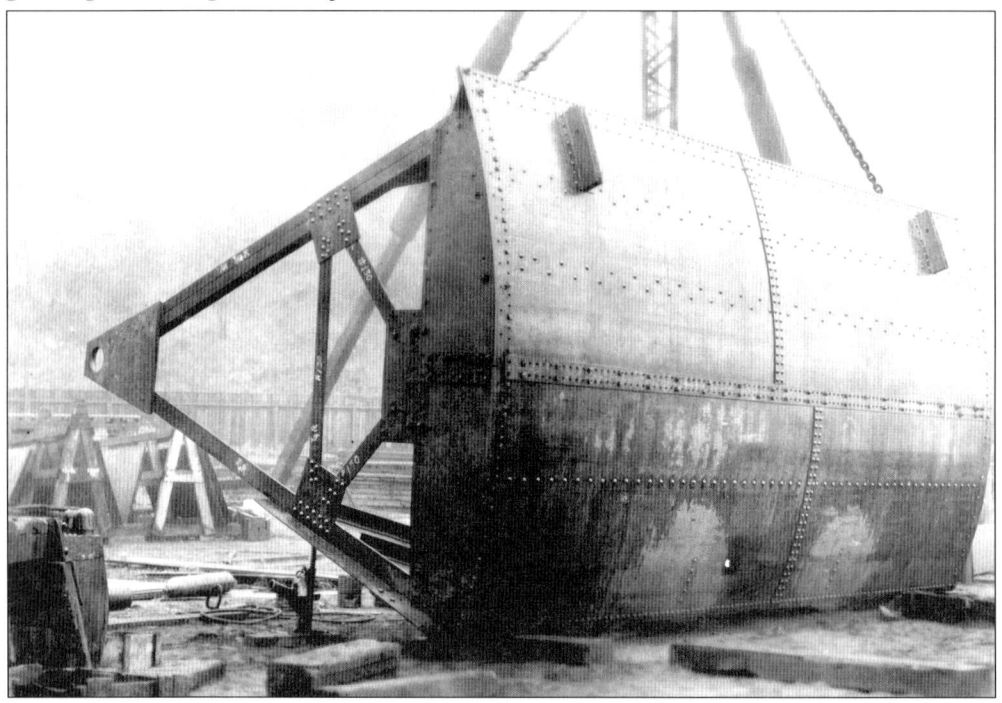

Pictured is a 12- by 24-foot radial gate for holding back the water flow at paper mills. The gates were lifted by gate winches such as the one shown in the above photograph, either fixed or portable, as water was needed.

100

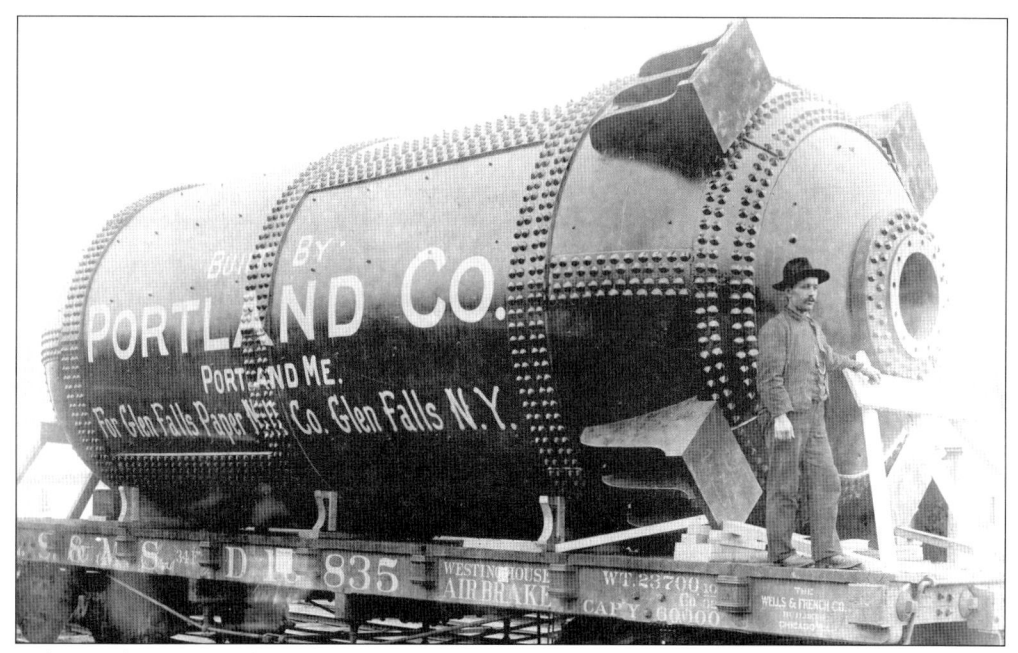

A huge "digester" is shown here loaded onto a Lake Shore & Michigan Southern Railroad flatcar for the Glen Falls Paper Company. It is used to process the wood chips into pulp for making paper. These huge vessels allow digestion to take place, creating high pressures and the familiar foul odors of digestion still prevalent in many paper mill towns even today.

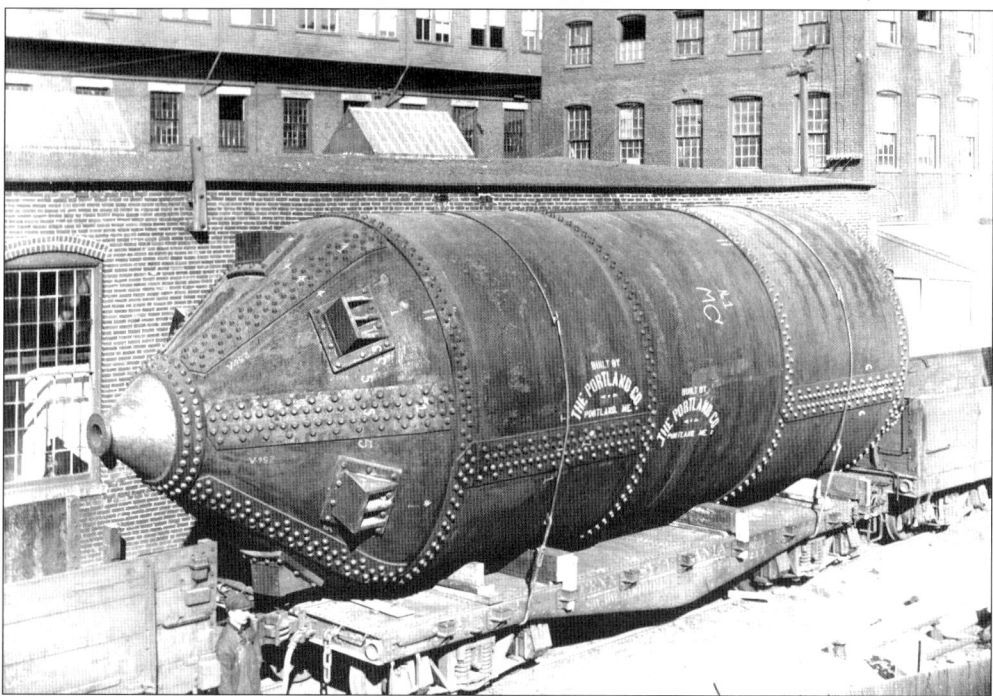

Another huge paper mill sulphite digester waits to be shipped out by rail from the Portland Company shops. The company was the largest producer of these digesters in the world at the time. All of these buildings shown here are still standing today on the Portland waterfront.

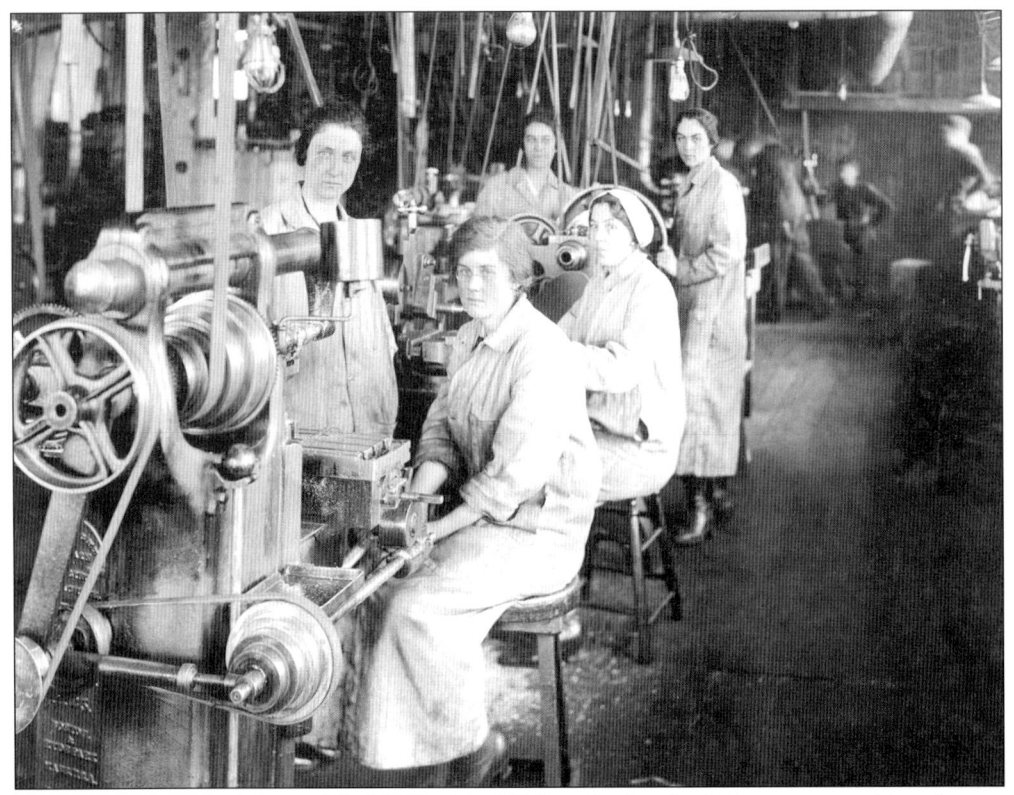

These women worked during World War I in 1917 in the Portland Company machine shop at the lathes, as most of the men were away fighting in the armed forces.

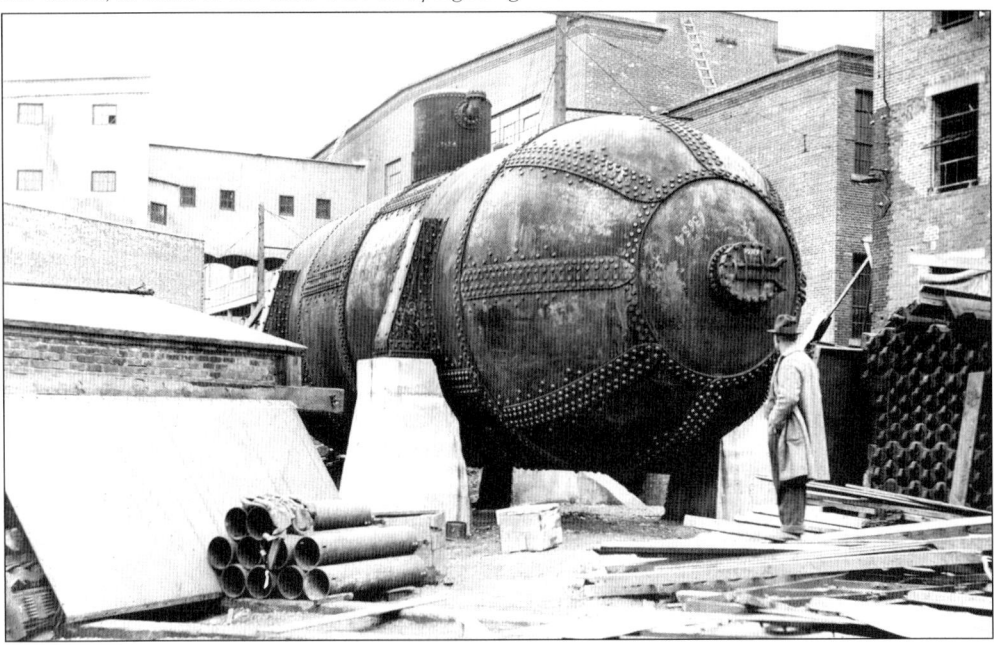

A steam accumulator from the Portland Company is being set up at a Piercefield, New York mill. Most likely, a building will be erected around this pressure vessel at a later time.

Eight
Lighthouses, Snowplows, and Other Products

The quaint Portland Breakwater Light had much of its upper section manufactured by the Portland Company. Note all the decorative architectural details on this structure made of cast iron from the company foundry. Many of the very ornate building fronts at street level in Portland, and in other cities around the United States in the late 1800s, were of cast iron from the Portland Company.

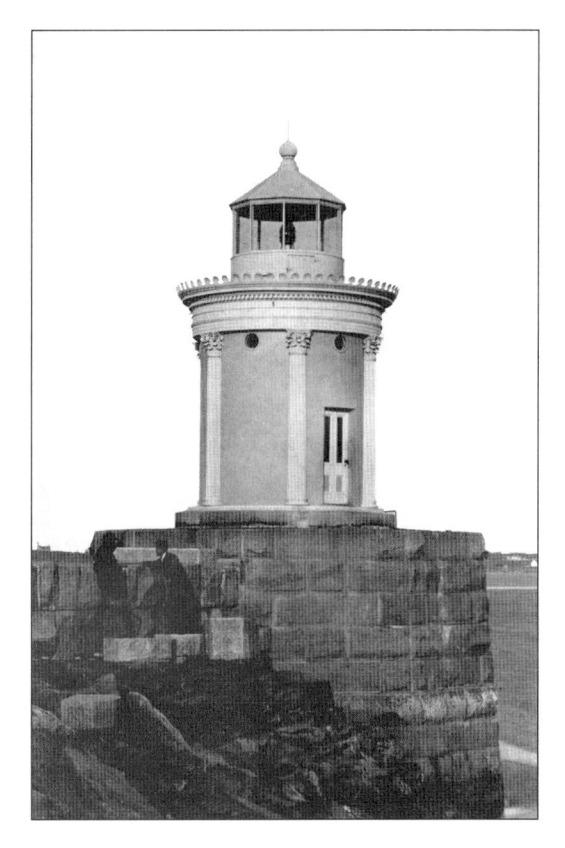

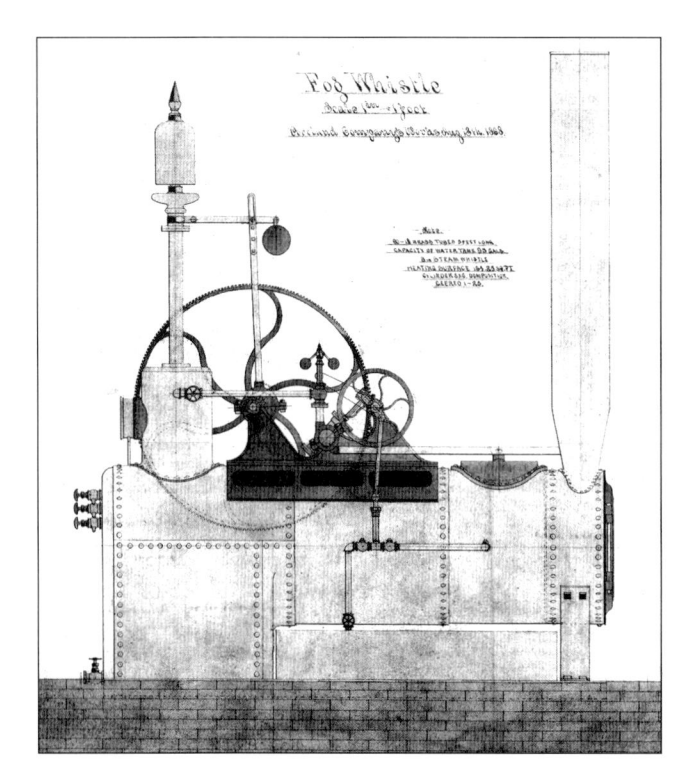

Shown here is a remarkable early original engineering drawing of a lighthouse fog whistle, boiler, and timing mechanism produced in 1868. This drawing is one of over 12,000 engineering drawings in the Portland Company Collection at the Maine Historical Society in Portland, Maine. These drawings cover a 100-year period and are of many subjects, and copies as well as photographs may be purchased from this collection.

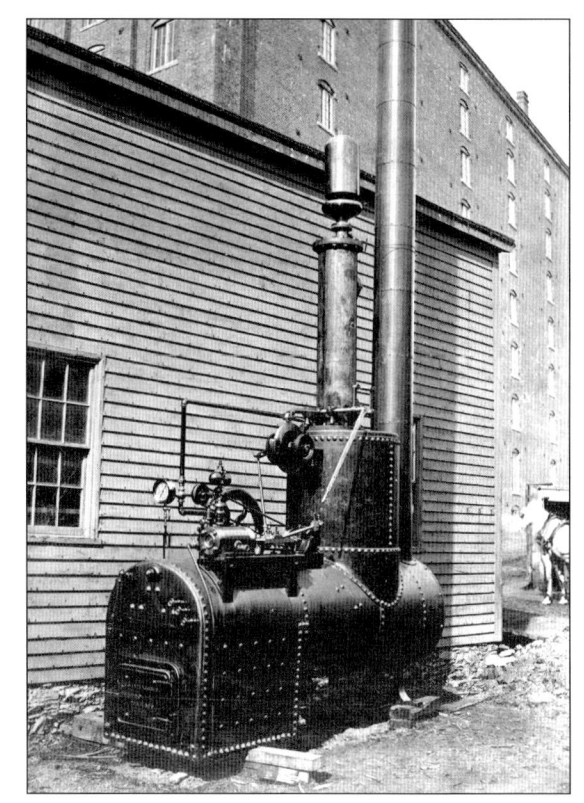

Large factory and lighthouse foghorn whistles often had their own dedicated steam boilers to provide an adequate and reliable source of steam to sound them off. Here we see one sitting outside a large mill complex, ready to be installed.

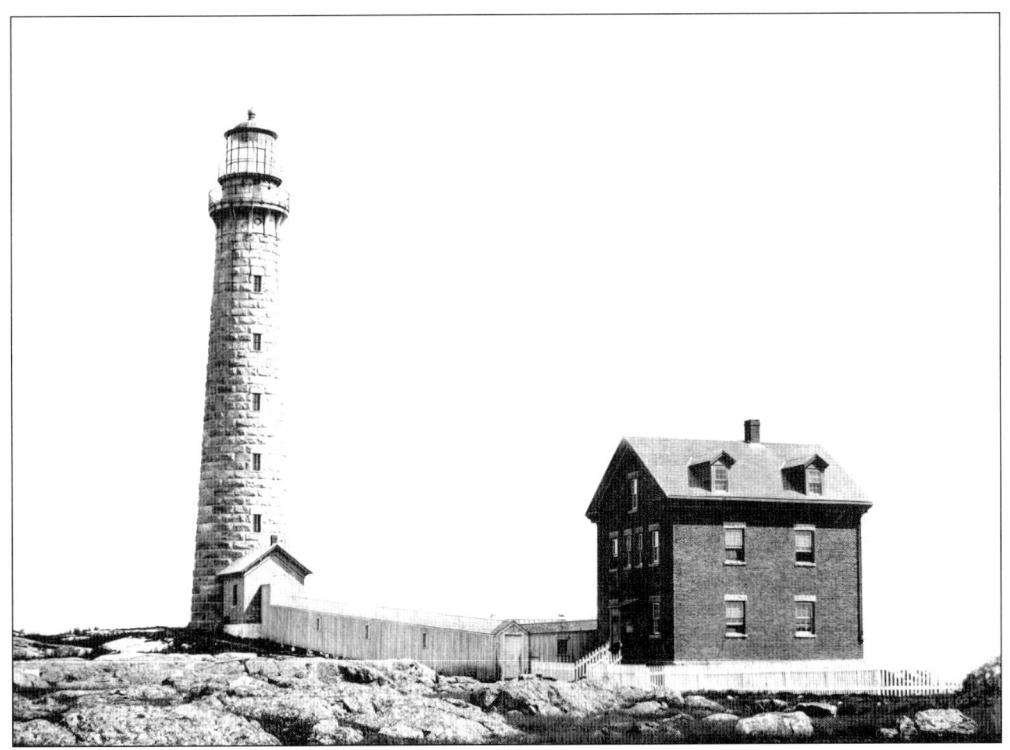

The Portland Company produced many cast parts for New England lighthouses. Thatcher's Island Lighthouse, shown here off the coast of Massachusetts, is one of them. The company made lanterns, lamp decks, spiral stairways, doors and sashes, walkways, railings, vents, spindles and markers, and even sections of the upper parts of the light tower itself.

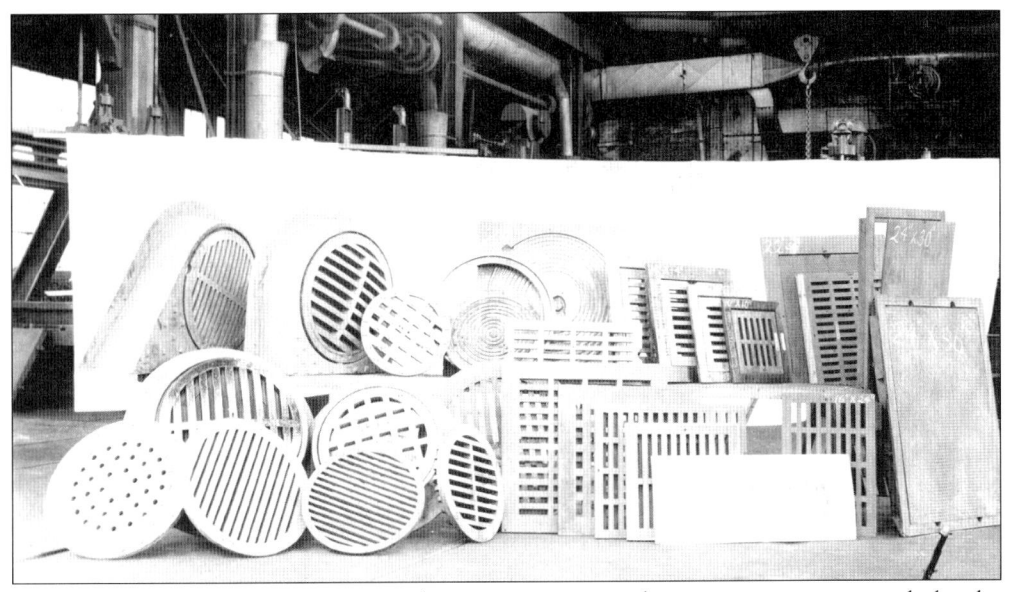

A wide variety of manhole covers and grates was among the common castings made by the Portland Company. They came in all shapes and sizes and probably can be found along many city streets even today with the company mark on them.

105

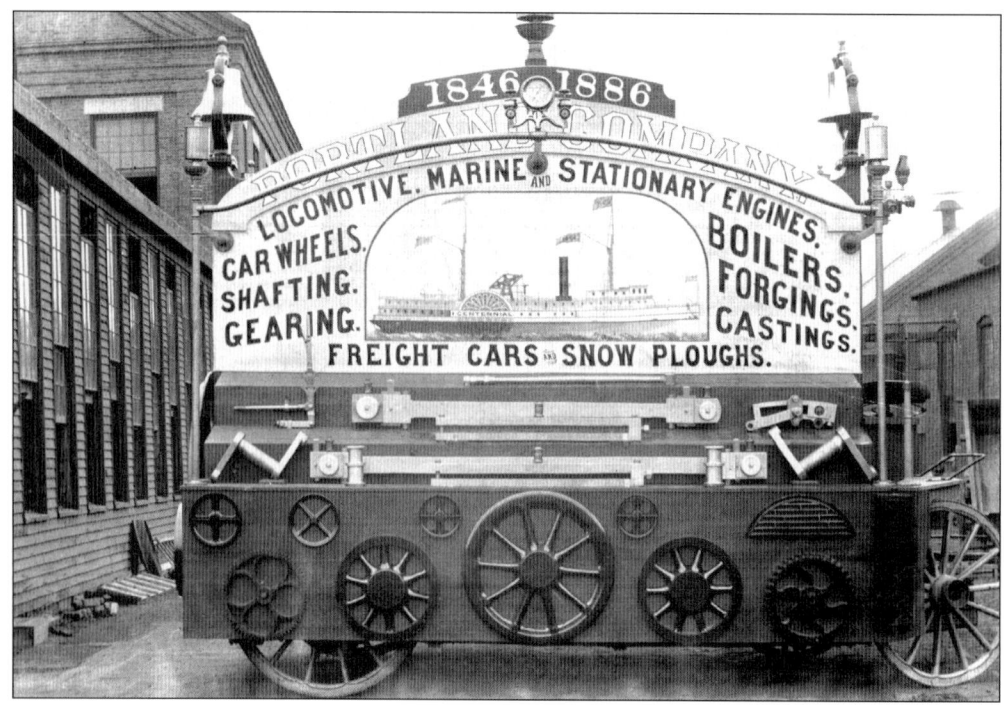

In 1846, after 40 years in business, the Portland Company constructed this horse-drawn float for the city of Portland's centennial parade and celebration. Displayed on the near side, shown here, are some of its products for railroad locomotives and steamships, such as bells, whistles, driving rods, and so on. The company equipped many steam-driven side-wheelers such as the one pictured on the float's mural.

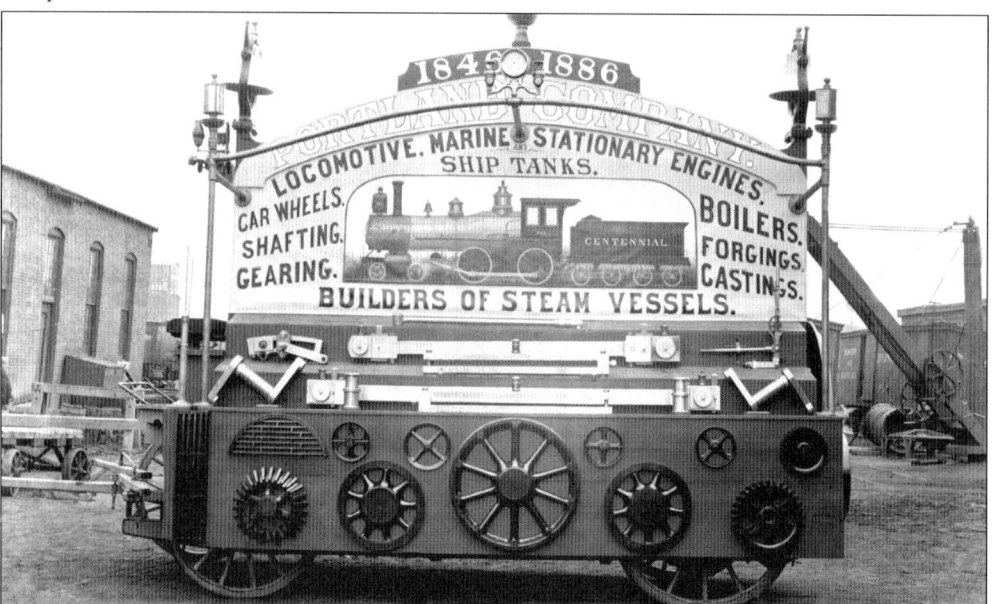

Here we see the opposite side of the horse-drawn centennial float. The view shows a 4-4-0 steam locomotive, which was the most common wheel arrangement on engines of the day. Many such locomotives were manufactured by the Portland Company.

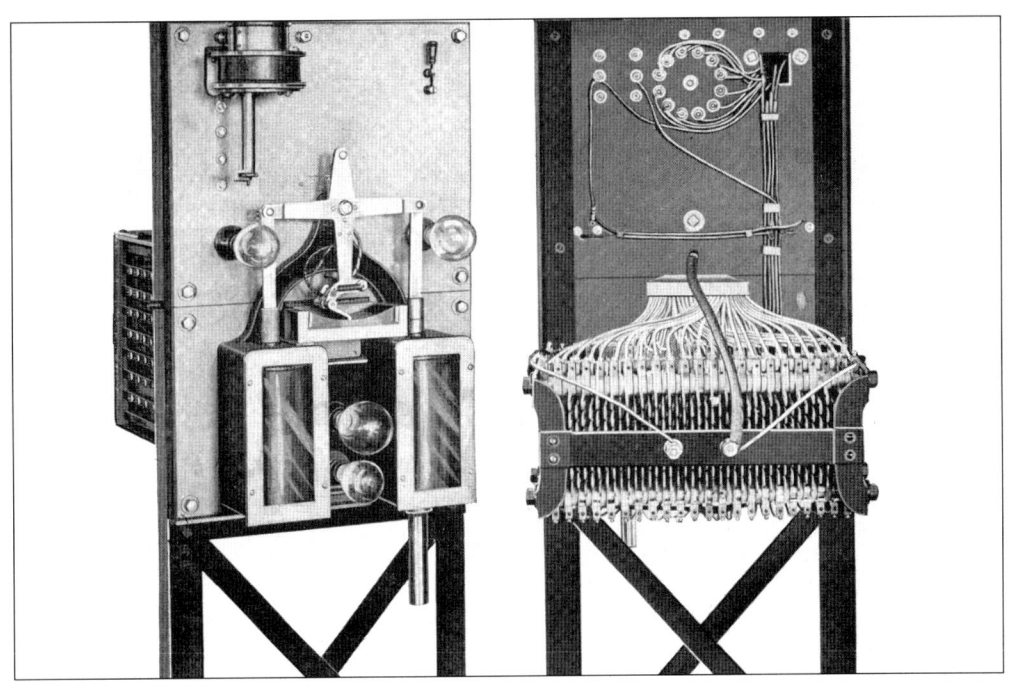

W.H.C. automatic voltage regulators were an important product of the Portland Company for the growing industrial age as more and more factories were electrified for running their machinery. These regulators were adapted to regulate both direct current and alternating current.

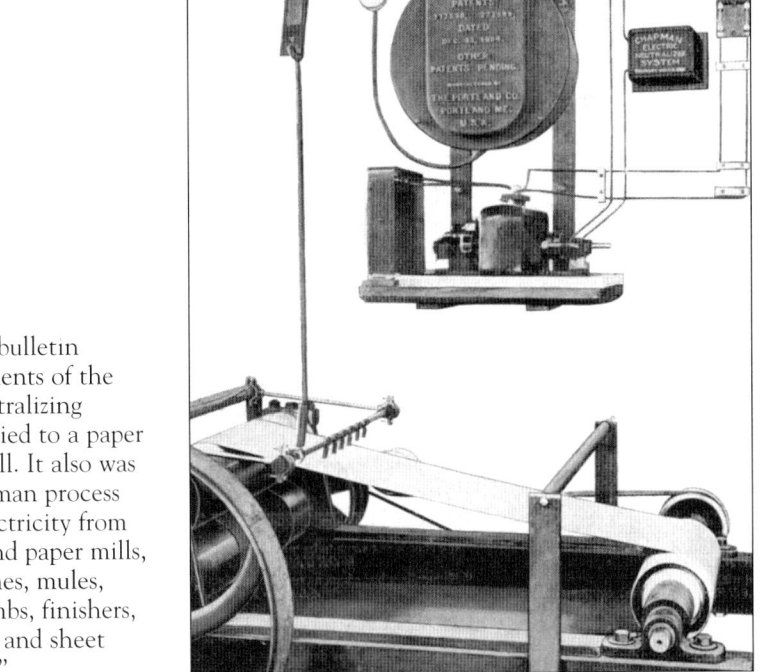

A Portland Company bulletin illustrated the components of the Chapman electric neutralizing machine as it was applied to a paper machine at a paper mill. It also was stated that "the Chapman process removed the static electricity from woolen, cotton, silk and paper mills, on cards, drawing frames, mules, unwinders, shears, combs, finishers, warpers, beamers, web and sheet calenders, cutters, etc."

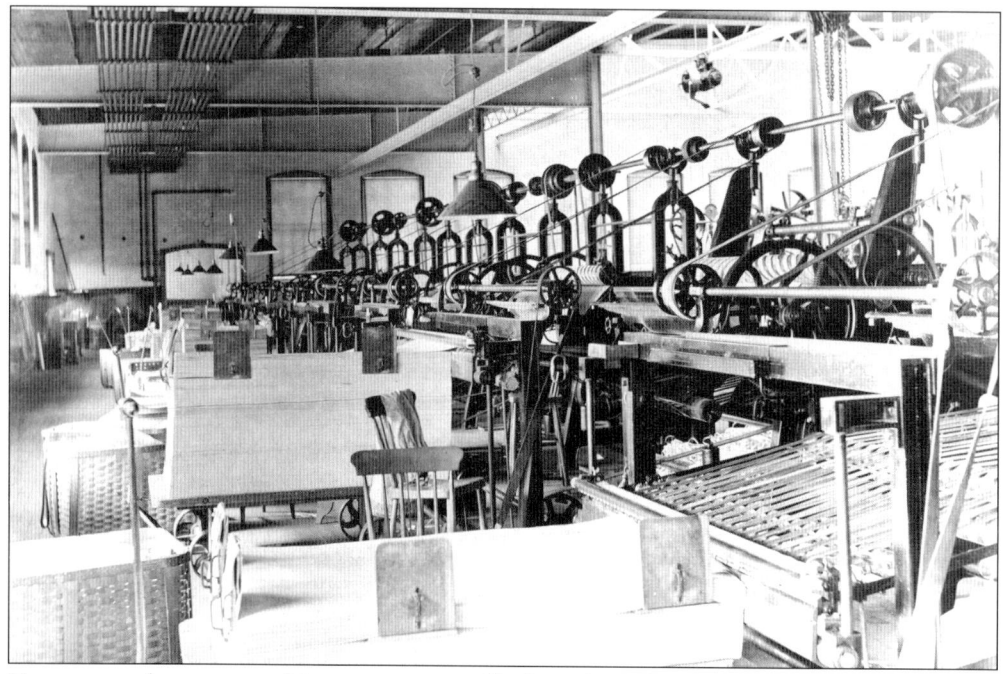

Here we see the paper machines in a paper mill where the "Chapman Electric Neutralizer" was also used to protect against the effects of static electricity.

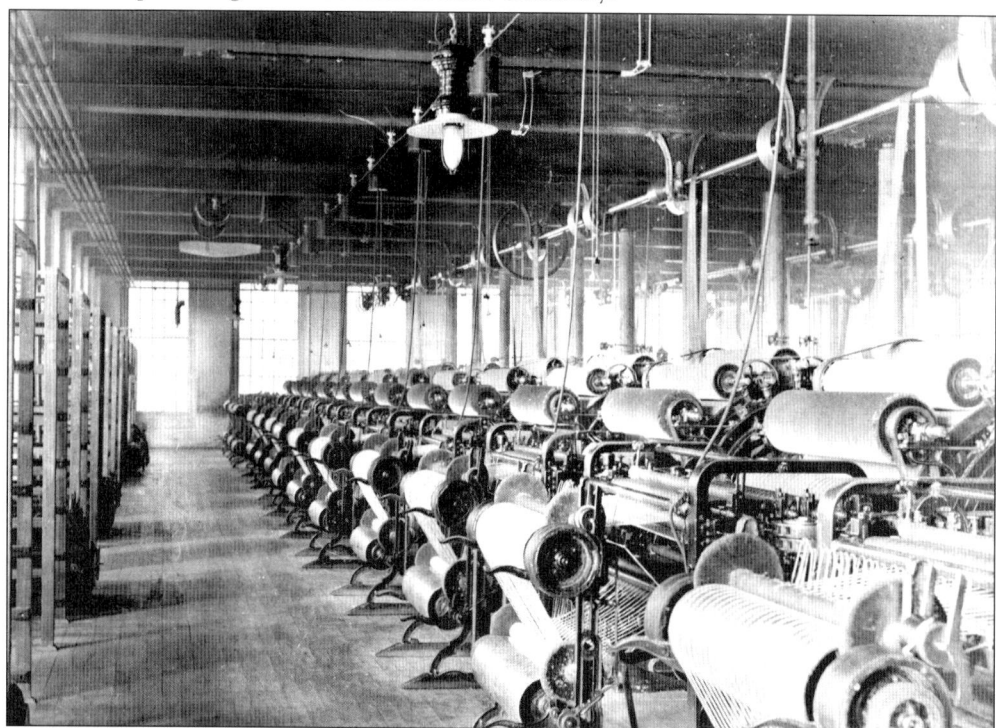

In the textile mills, such as in the carding room shown here, the Chapman electric neutralizing machine would keep the static electricity at a minimum. The machine was used in woolen, cotton, and silk textile mills.

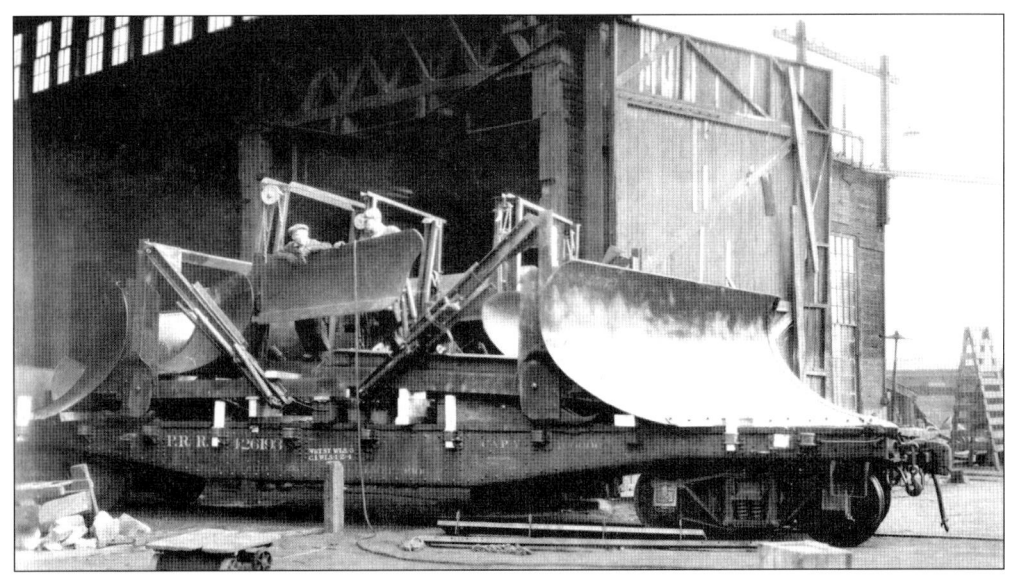

A Portland & Rochester Railroad flatcar is loaded with three M & J and two Portland Company snowplows with cable frames. These plows are being shipped to distant points to fight the heavy snows that were prevalent in New England, and particularly heavy during the 1920s and 1930s winters. Note the very high overhead to accommodate the large equipment manufactured in the erecting shops of the Portland Company.

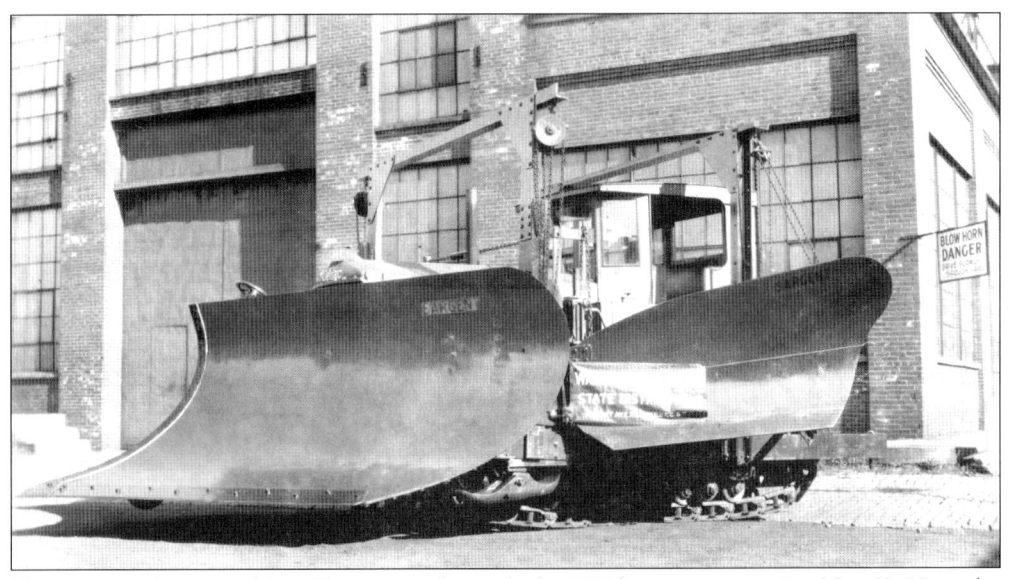

Shown is a side view of the Cletrac crawler with the 100-horsepower engine No. 62. Note the cable lift arrangement, which was used on all machines of the period. Hydraulic lifting systems were not commonly being used in 1928, when this picture was taken.

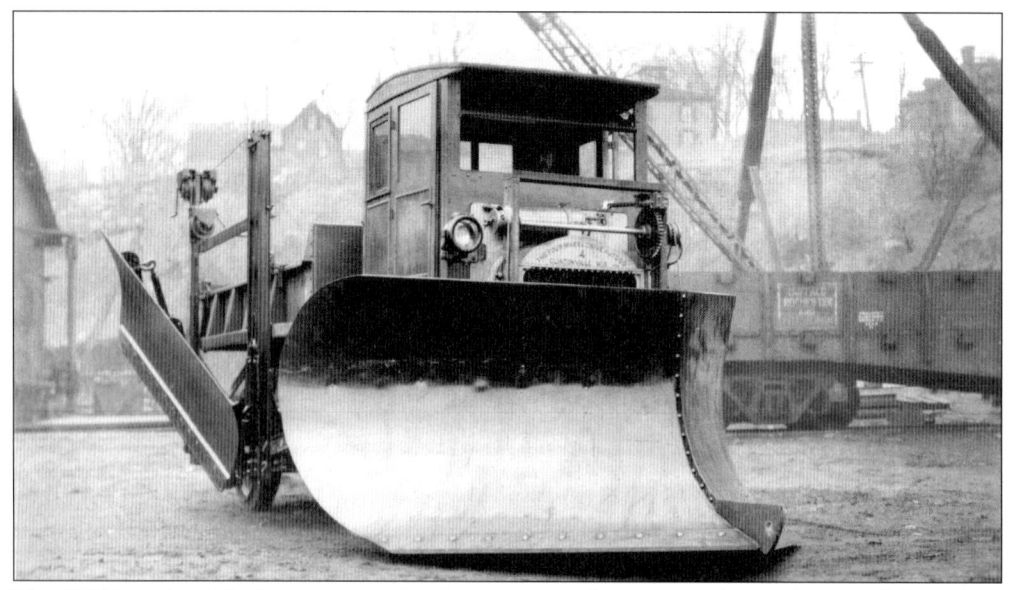

The FWD truck, with the engine under the seat, gave the operator better front visibility when plowing heavy snows. The Front Wheel Drive Auto Company (FWD) of Clintonville, Wisconsin, built these early trucks that had Sargent plows mounted on them.

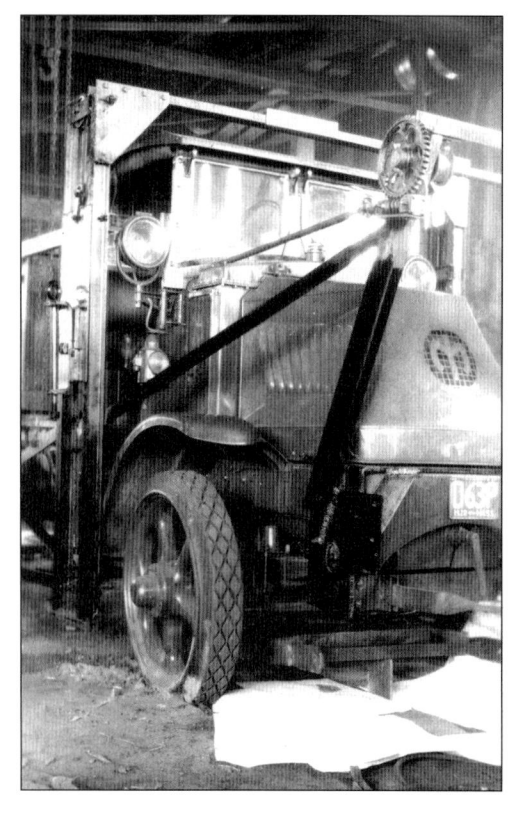

The Mack "Bulldog" truck shown here in the Portland Company shops has its plow frame on and is ready for the mounting of a Sargent snowplow. Note the 1928 Massachusetts dealer plate, denoted by the prefix "D" for dealer, on the front bumper.

110

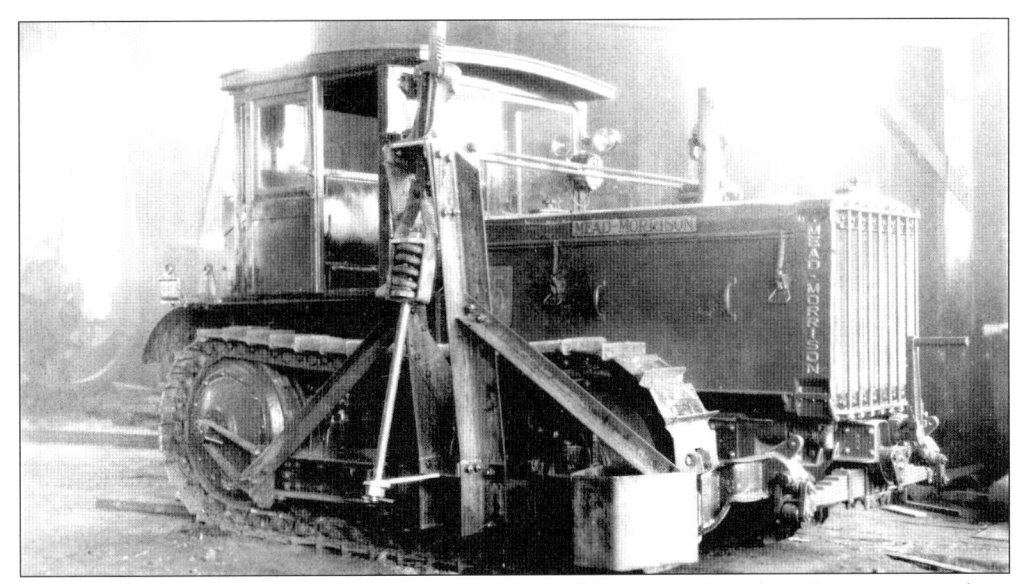

Pictured is a 75-horsepower Meade Morrison crawler equipped with a Sargent snowplow-carrying device for mounting and lifting these heavy plows.

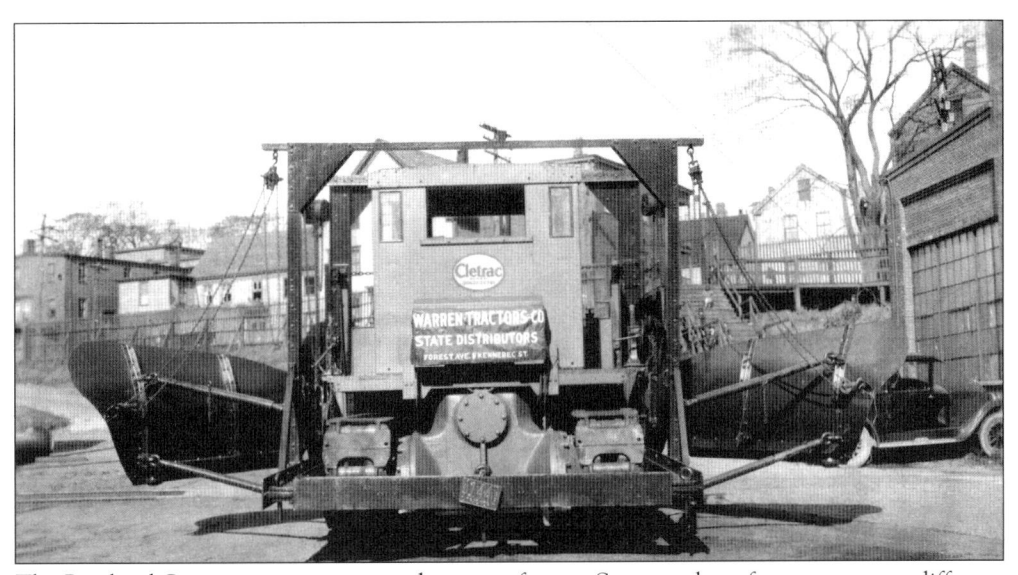

The Portland Company was contracted to manufacture Sargent plows for use on many different trucks and tracked machines. Here we see a 10-ton plow on a Cletrac crawler with 100-horsepower engine No. 62. The Warren Tractor Company of Portland sold these machines to customers all over New England.

111

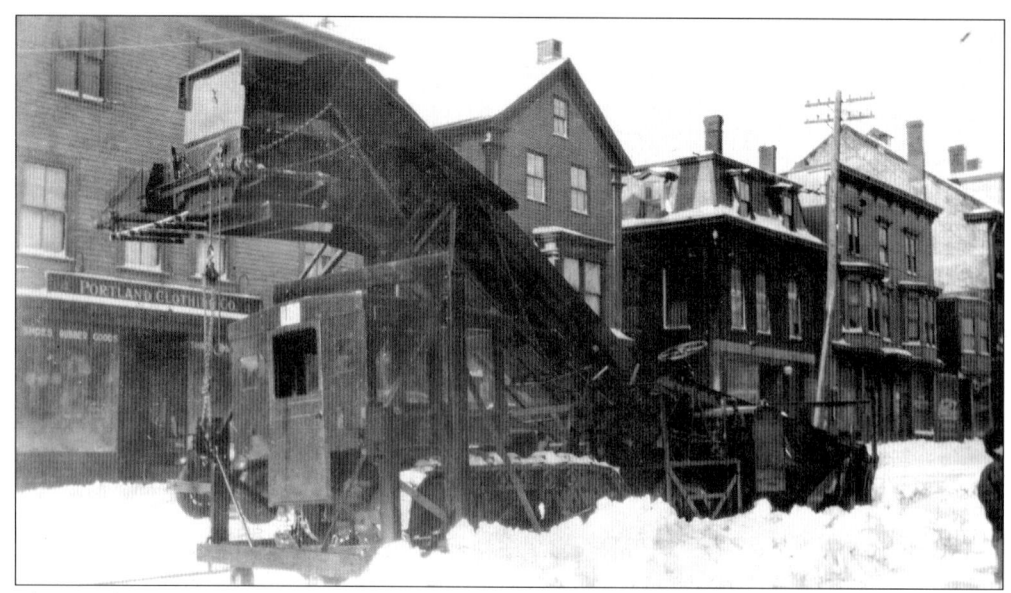

The Portland Company also manufactured Sargent snow loaders that were propelled by a tracked vehicle under them, such as a Cletrac crawler. Portland Company No. 1, shown here, is clearing the streets of snow during the winter of 1927–1928.

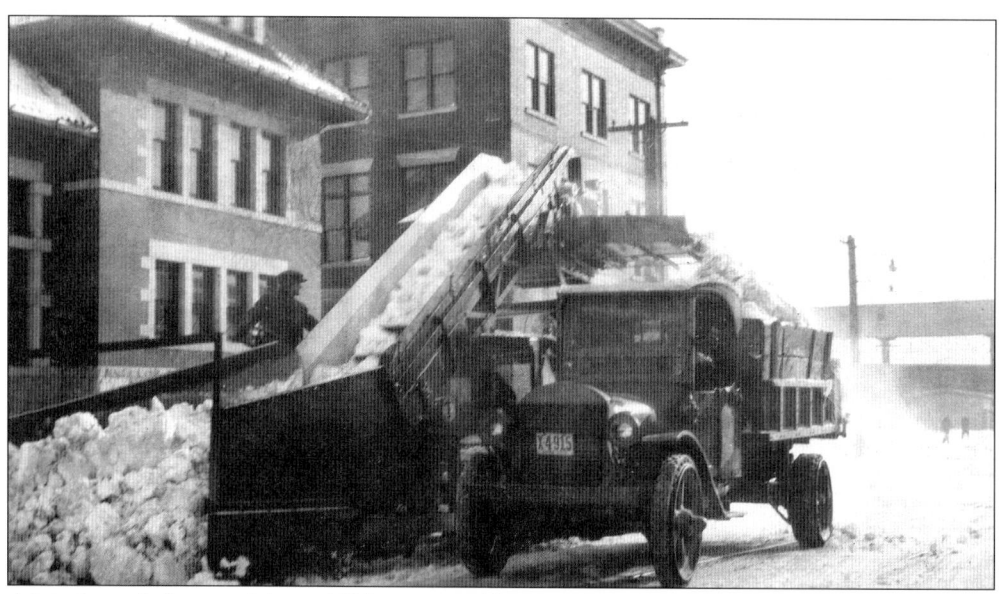

A Mack truck, bearing Maine 1927 municipal license plates, is being loaded with snow by this Sargent snow loader, Portland Company No. 1. Again we see the solid rubber tires on heavy trucks of the 1920s.

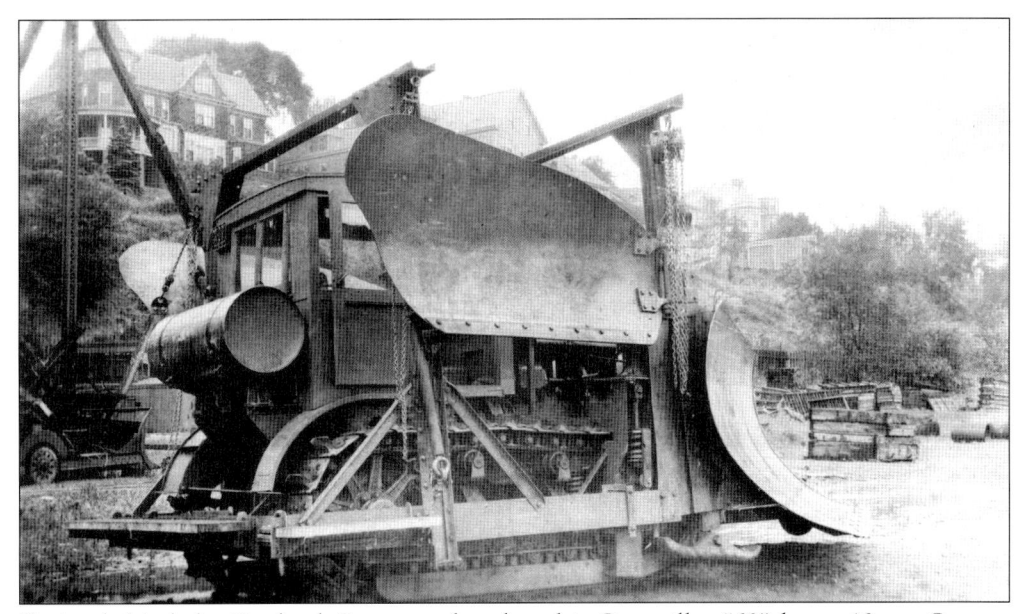

Sitting behind the Portland Company foundry, this Caterpillar "60" has a 10-ton Sargent snowplow with side wing plows on each side. Here we can see how extensive the pulley system is to raise the plows.

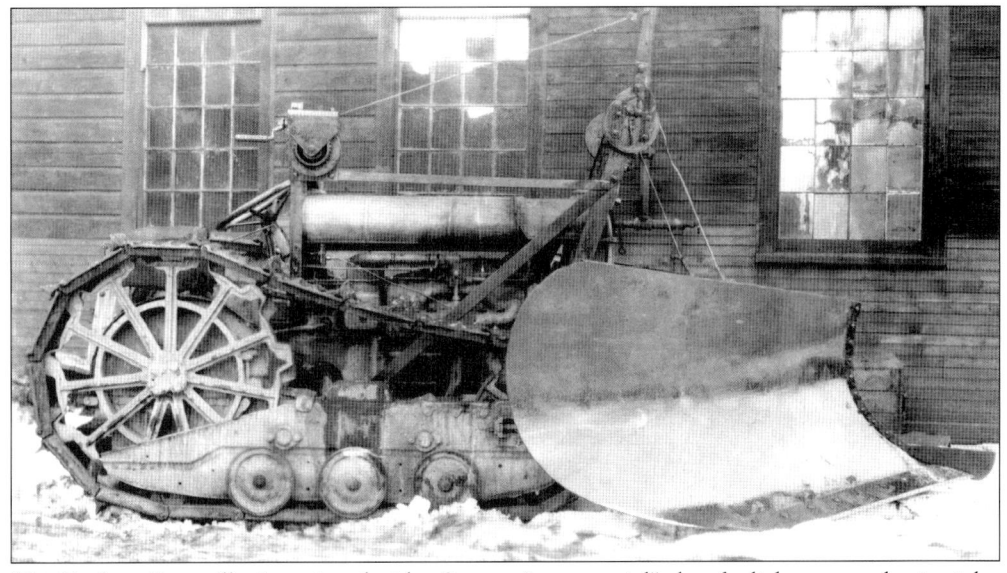

This Fordson Caterpillar is equipped with a Sargent "commercial" plow for lighter snowplowing jobs.

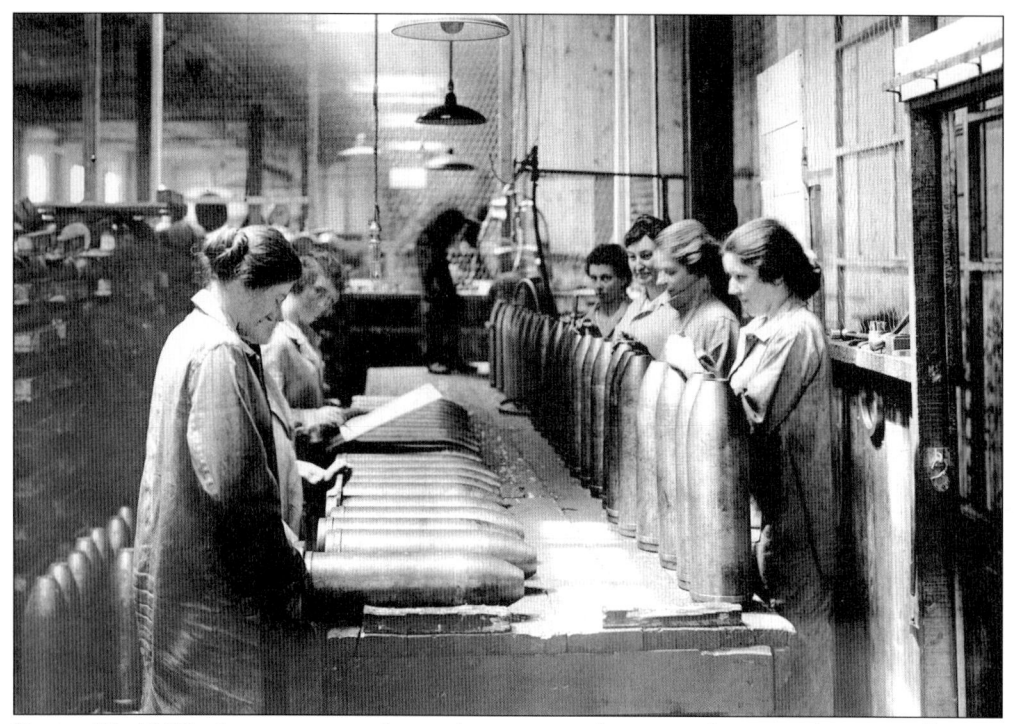

During World War I, women were the predominant workers manufacturing the 108-millimeter brass howitzer empty shell casings for the U.S. Army. These ladies appear to be finishing and perhaps inspecting the shell casings before they are packed in pairs in wooden boxes for shipment to another factory for loading.

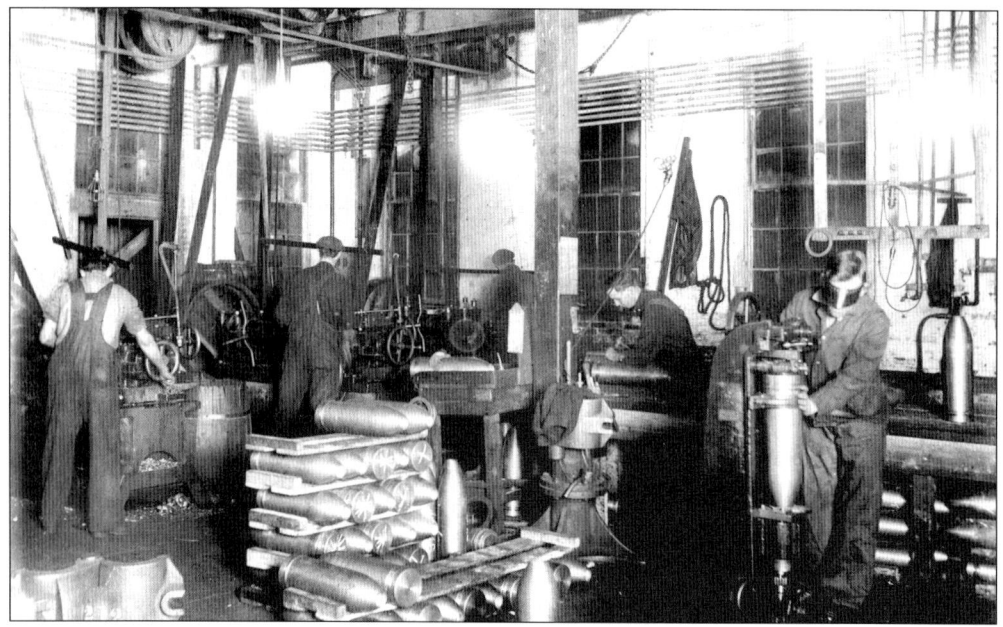

The Portland Company made tens of thousands of these brass 108-millimeter howitzer shell casings for the war effort in 1917–1918. These men are machining the casings to government specifications in the machine shop.

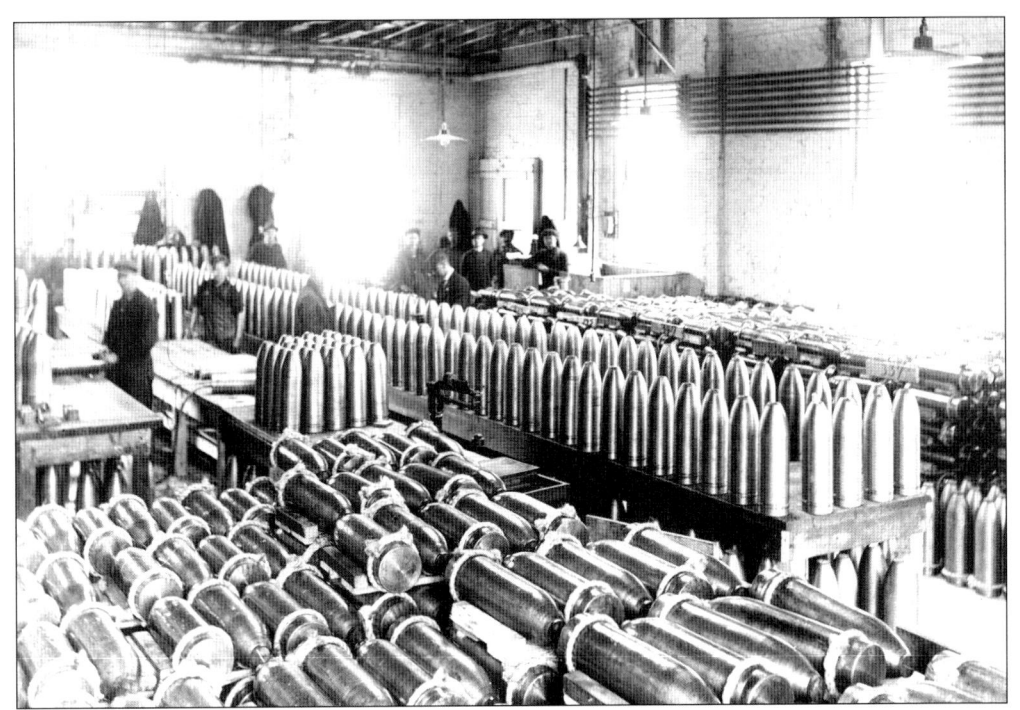

Pictured is the storage room at the Portland Company where the 108-millimeter howitzer empty brass shell casings were stacked before being crated in wooden boxes.

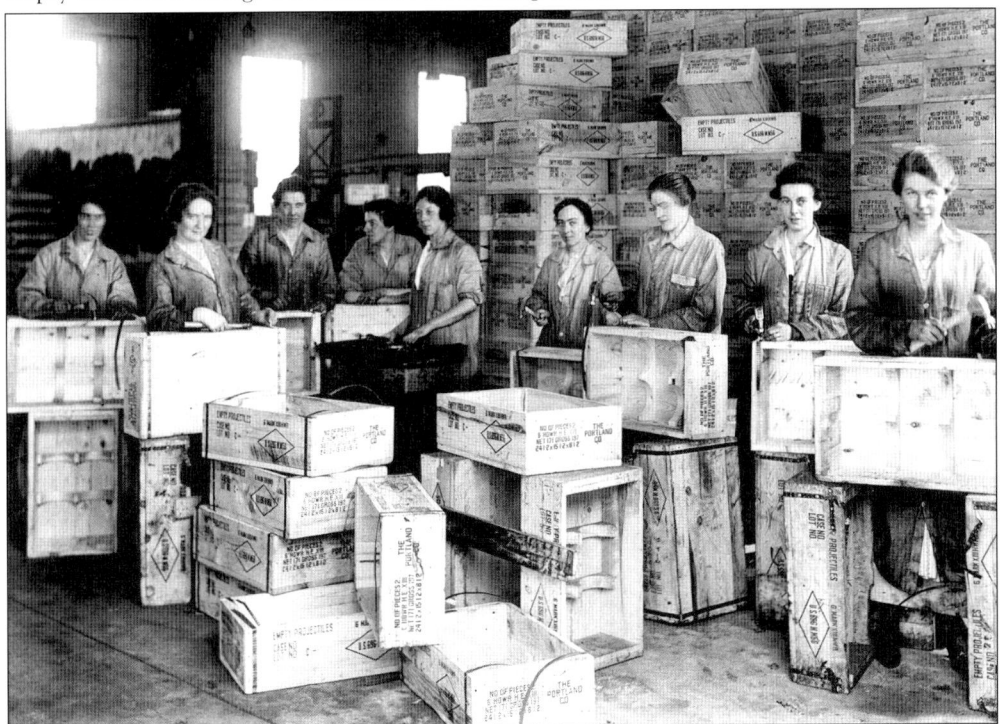

This photograph shows the packing room, with the wooden boxes for the 108-millimeter howitzer empty shell casings, where they were packed two in a box and shipped out in 1917–1918.

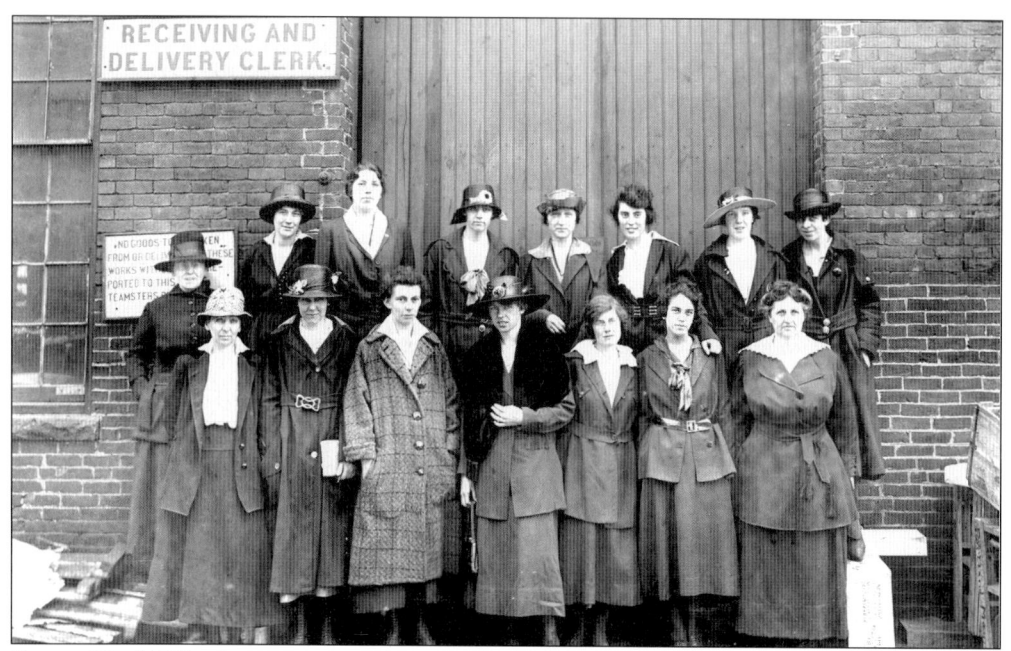

During World War I, many women were employed in the shops as the men were off to fight in Europe. Here we see ladies from the shipping and receiving department posing for a photograph in 1917. Note the wooden box beside the group, used to ship the thousands of 108-millimeter brass howitzer shells made by the Portland Company for the war effort.

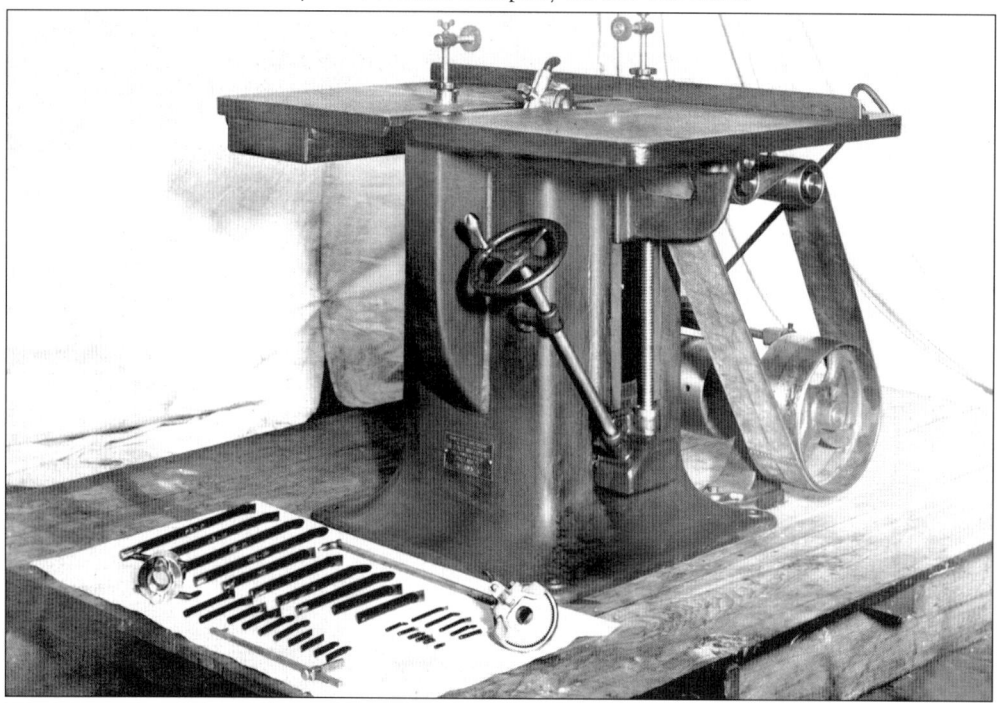

The Thomes core box machine, developed and manufactured by the Portland Company, cut the time to make core boxes and casting patterns greatly. It was a combination of a table saw and shaper. Note the tools and cutters laid out by the machine.

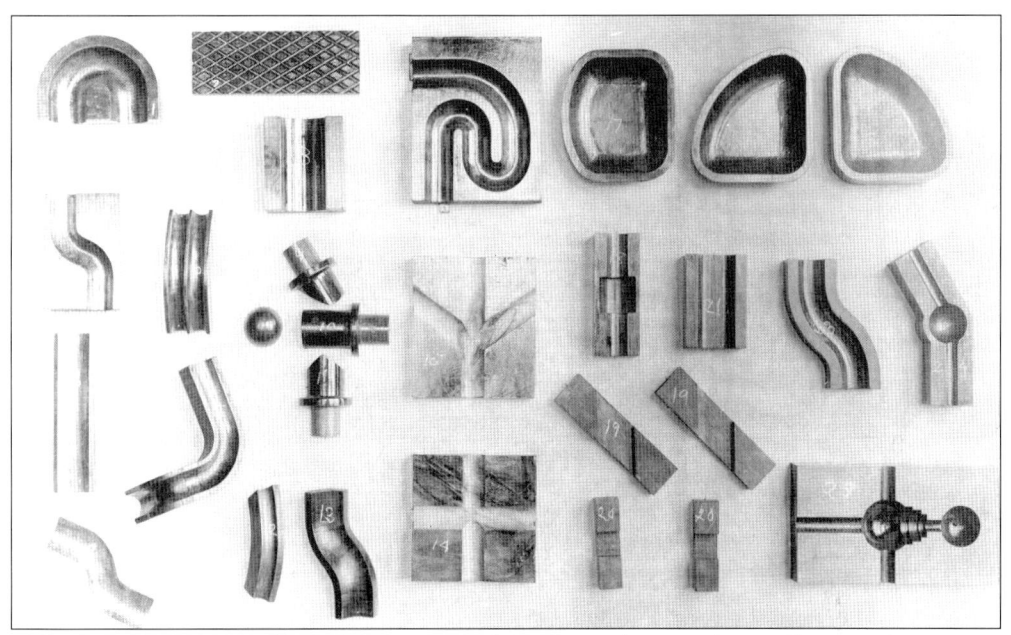

These core boxes were all made using the Thomes core box machine. The core boxes were packed with casting sand to form the cavities in cast products such as pipe fittings and other hollow parts.

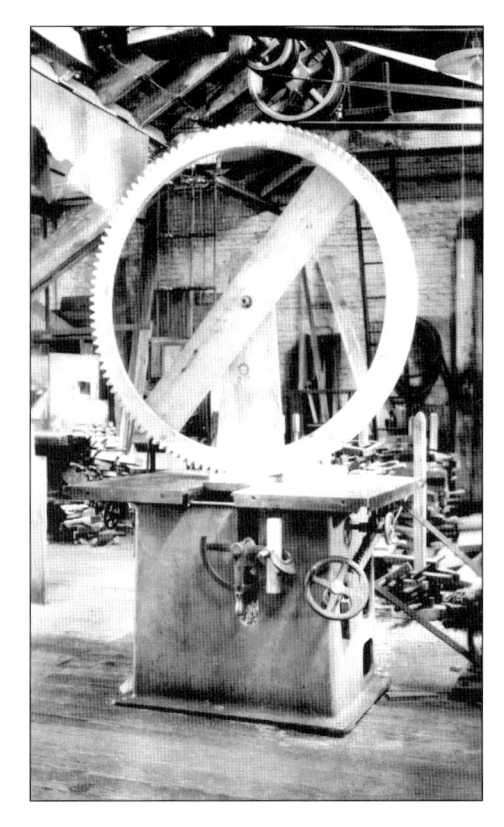

The Thomes "Universal" woodworking machine is being used here to make a large wooden gear pattern in the company woodworking or pattern shop. Gears of all sizes and in large numbers were produced by the Portland Company.

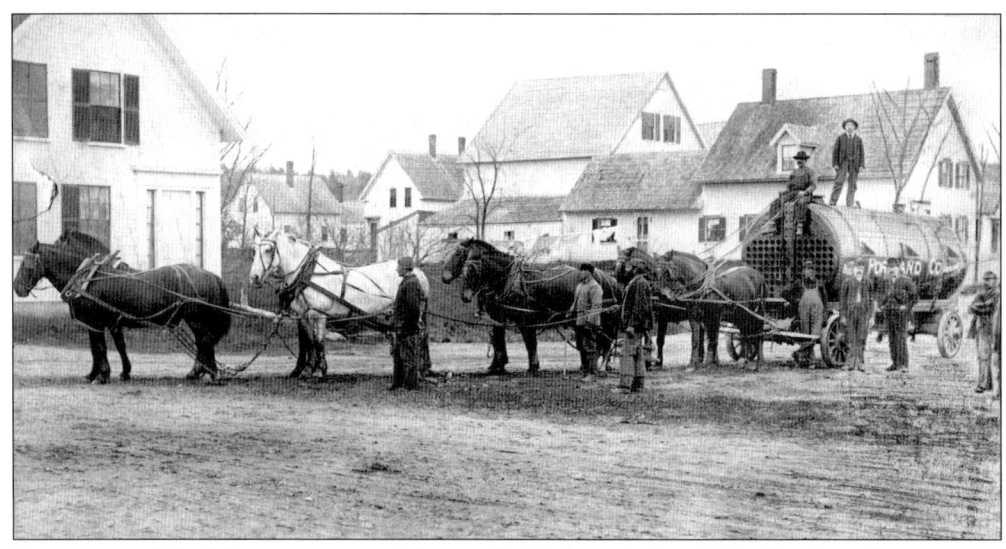

Four teams of draft horse were needed to pull this large industrial boiler from the company boiler shops to a nearby industrial complex or mill. Later, such loads were delivered by truck.

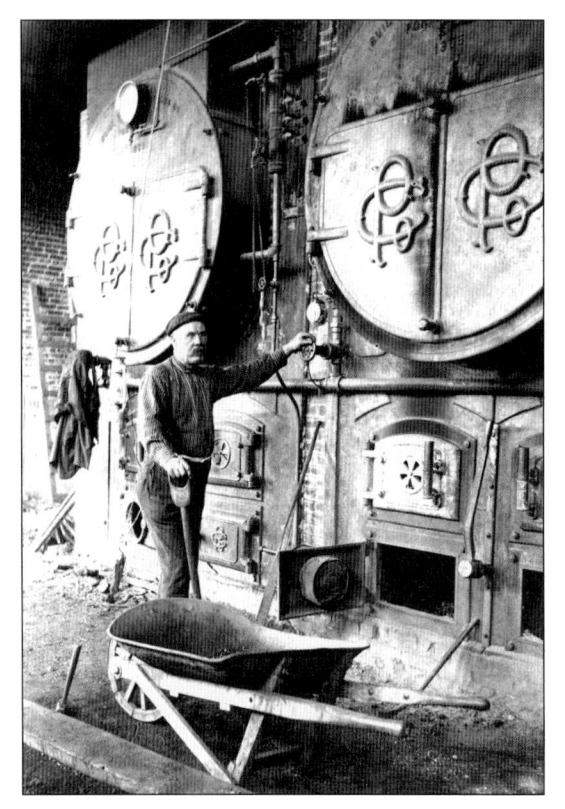

In the boiler room of the Maine Sanatorium we see these two large industrial boilers from the shops of the Portland Company. Attached to each of the double doors we see a large cast-metal "PCo." logo that was used on most boilers the company made. These boilers were built in 1905 by the company.

Another company product was this high-diving tower for one of the numerous summer youth camps in Maine.

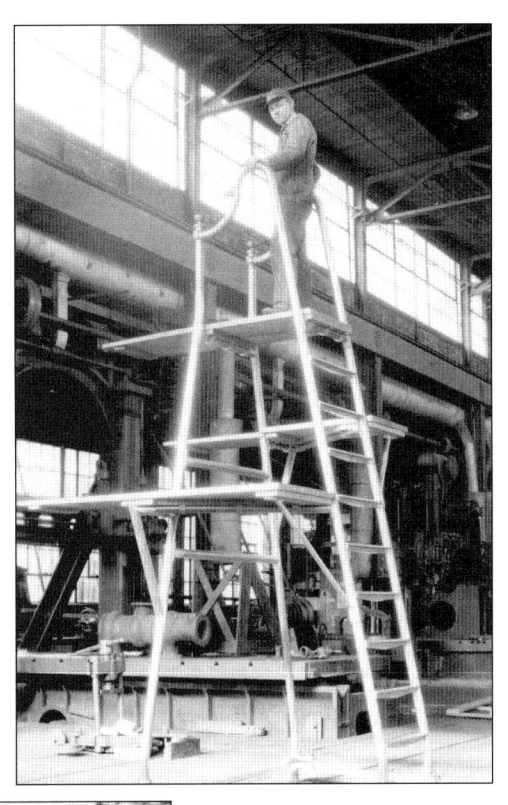

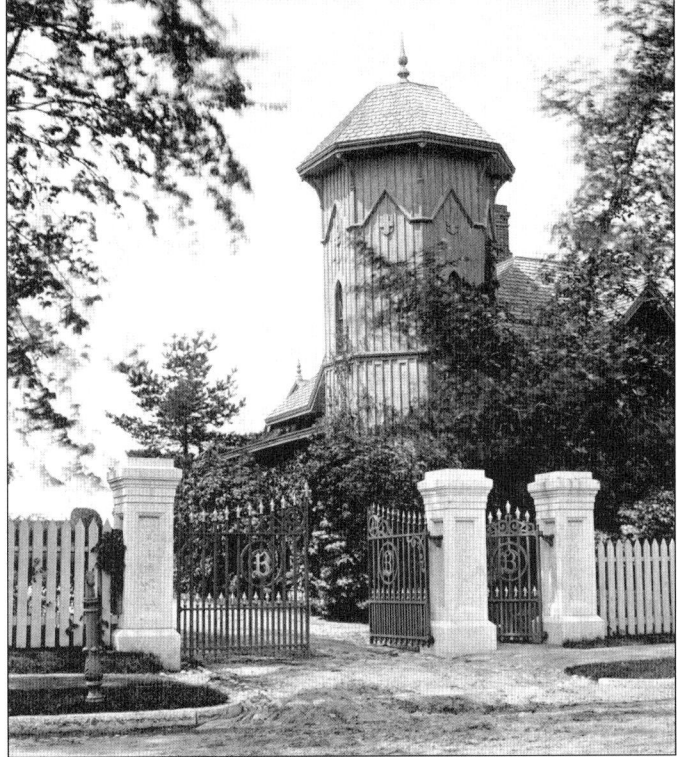

A large set of ornate entrance gates was fabricated for "Bramhall," the estate of J.B. Brown of Portland, Maine. These gates now grace the entrance to "Thornhurst" in Falmouth-Foreside.

119

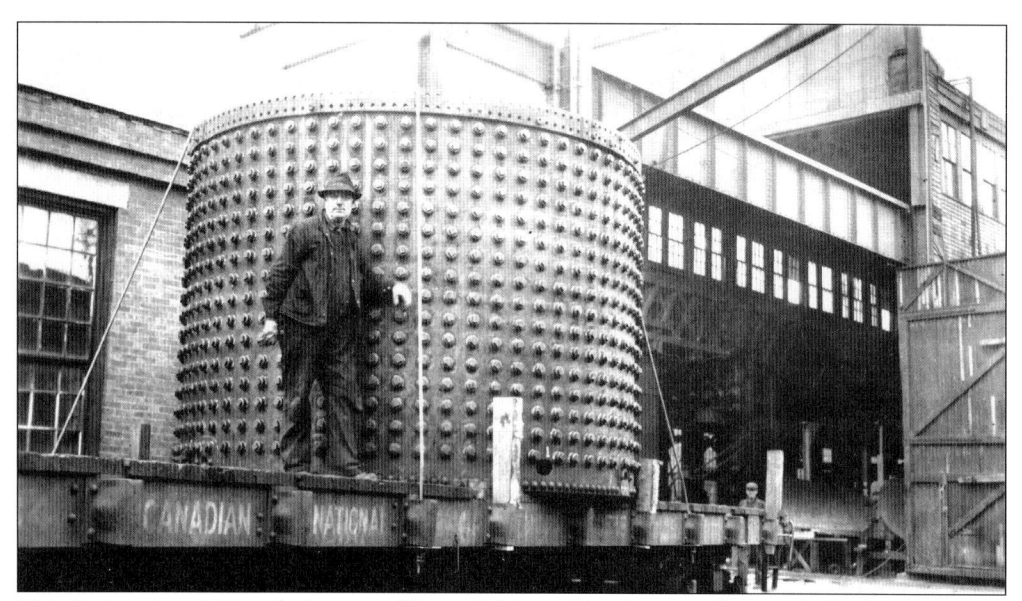

This firebox for a 120-inch-diameter "Dean & Martin" boiler was rolled in the boiler shop. Now that a crane has loaded it onto a Canadian National Railroad flatcar, it will be sent to the buyer's mill.

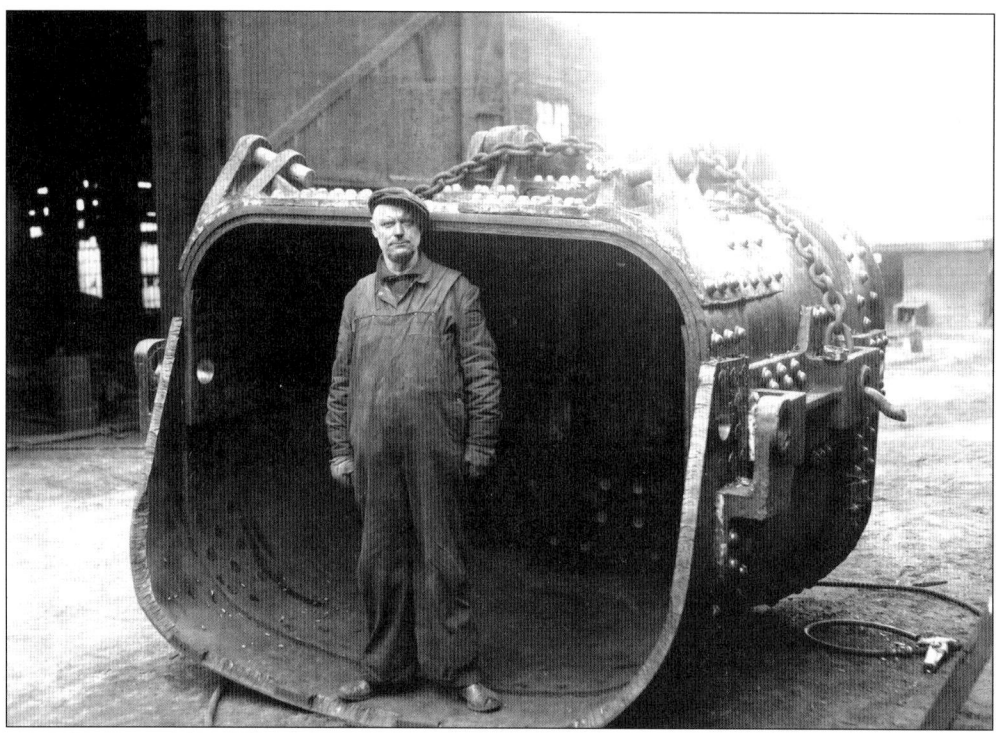

A workman stands inside the huge 10-yard mud bucket, or "dipper," just fabricated in the shop for the dipper dredge *Eugene*. The dredge was equipped with two boilers and machinery from the Portland Company and was built for George E. Breyman & Brothers of Boston, Massachusetts.

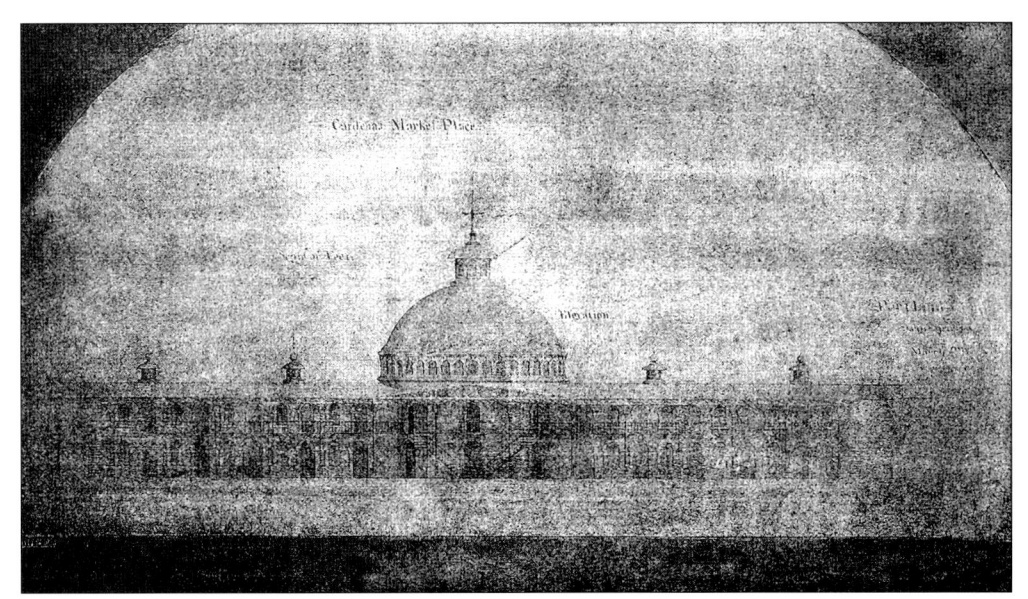

The Portland Company manufactured cast and fabricated architectural elements for building fronts usually, but here we see a complete building 200 feet long and 50 feet wide forming a cross pattern. It was built as a marketplace and shipped to Cardenas, Cuba. It was set up there as a two-story market with masonry walls and ornate cast stairs and railings. The center supported a cast dome, and it was built in 1857 at a cost of $60,000. According to local Portland newspapers, part of the structure was set up at the Portland Company yard to check the fit of the components. Incredibly, the market building still stands in Cuba, and the dome is now painted blue.

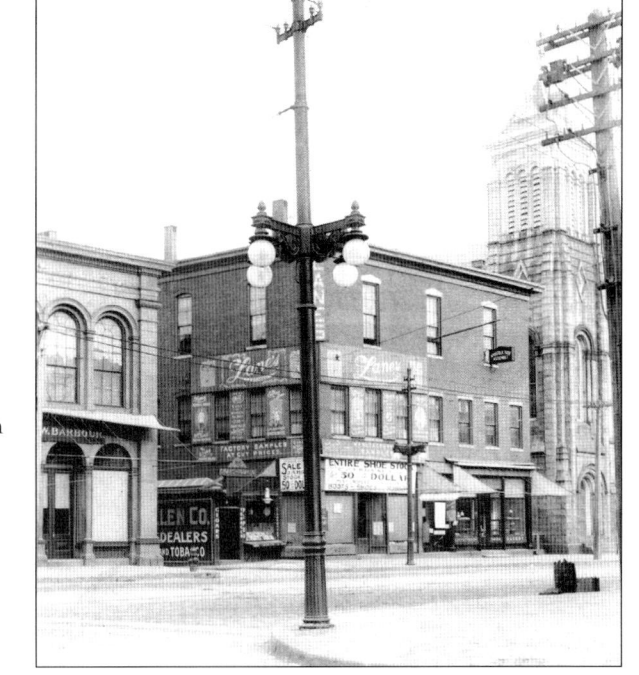

The city of Portland had cast streetlights and decorative poles on many of its urban streets. They held not only the four globe lights but also electric wires and the trolley electric catenary wires. These company-made lights are shown here in Monument Square with the former St. Steven's church to the right rear.

121

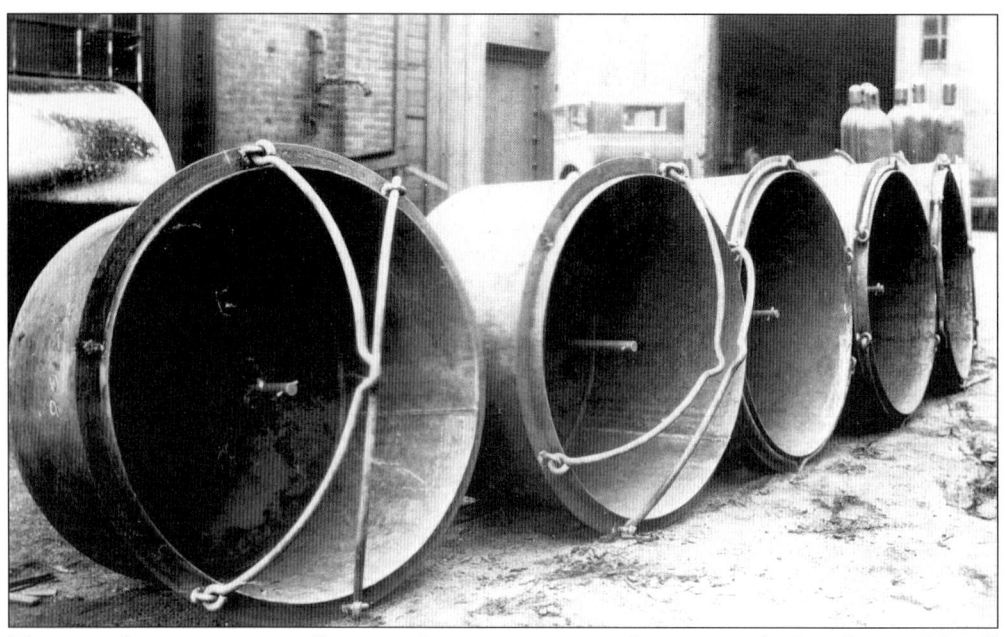

This view shows a neat row of large cast bean pots awaiting shipment to the Burnham & Morrill Company just a mile away from the Portland Company.

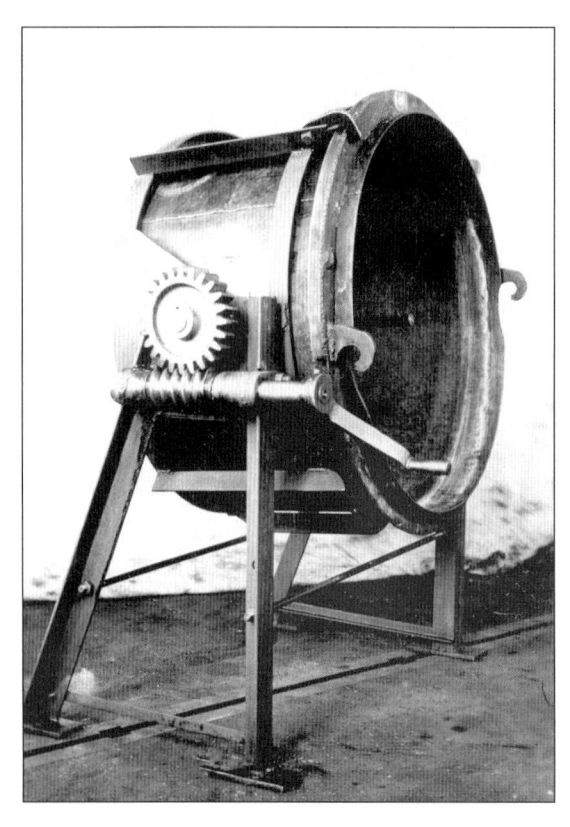

A kettle-tilting device is shown here for dumping the large bean pots at the Monmouth Canning Company.

122

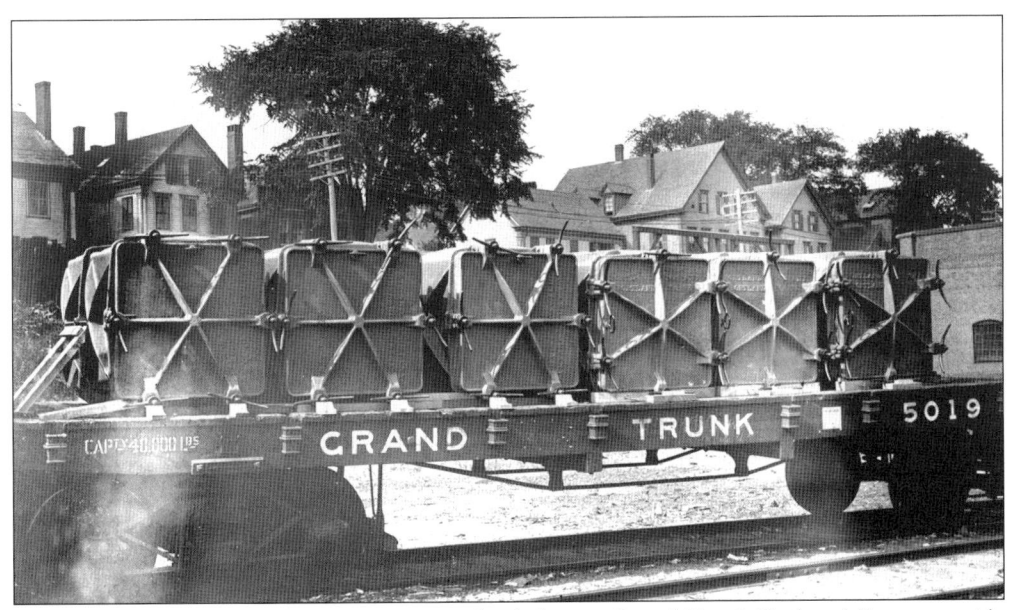

Here we can see a load of 12 steam retorts loaded on a Grand Trunk Railroad flatcar outside the Portland Company, awaiting shipment to one of the many Maine canneries. Thousands of the retorts, or pressure cookers, were used in the sardine-canning industry alone in the state.

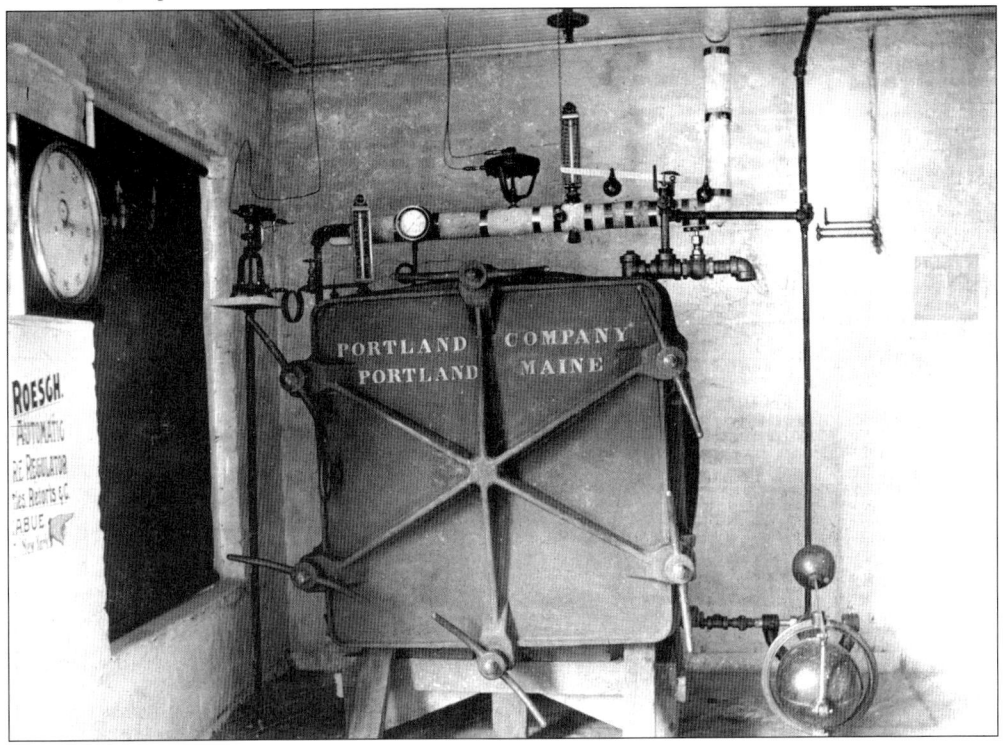

A steam retort is all installed and ready for its first batch of canned goods to cook and sterilize. One of these retorts is on display in a cannery exhibit at the Maine State Museum in Augusta, Maine, along with a large stationary industrial steam engine from the Kearsarge Peg Company in Bartlett, New Hampshire.

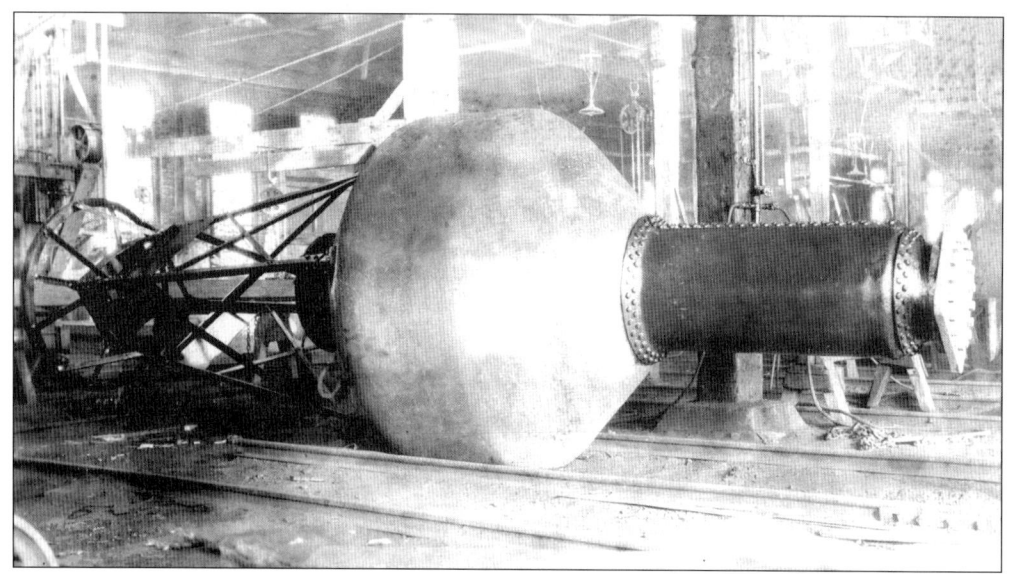

Marker buoys such as this one in the Portland Company shop were fabricated for marking the waters off the New England coast and islands.

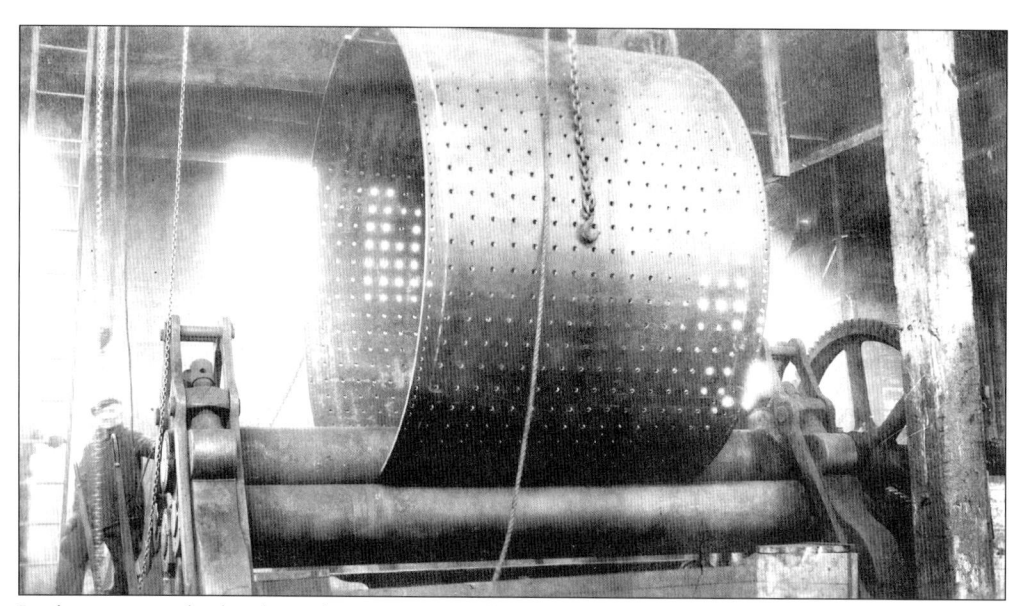

In the company boiler shop, these men are rolling a boiler plate to make the shell for 120-inch-diameter "Dean & Martin" vertical boiler. Note the very numerous rivet holes needed to make a large boiler.

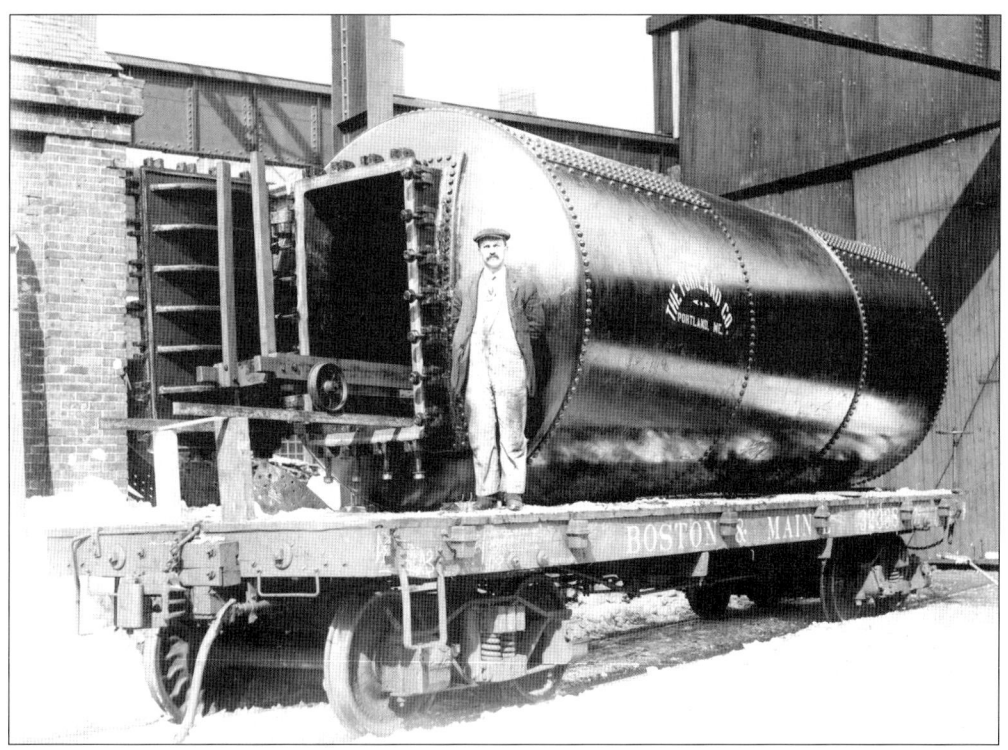

A large pressure steam box for the Sanford Mills awaits shipment on a Boston & Maine Railroad flatcar outside the company shops. Note the cart on rails to carry materials to be steamed into the pressure chamber. The Portland Company specialized in building very large pressure vessels like this as well as boilers, which are merely high-pressure vessels themselves.

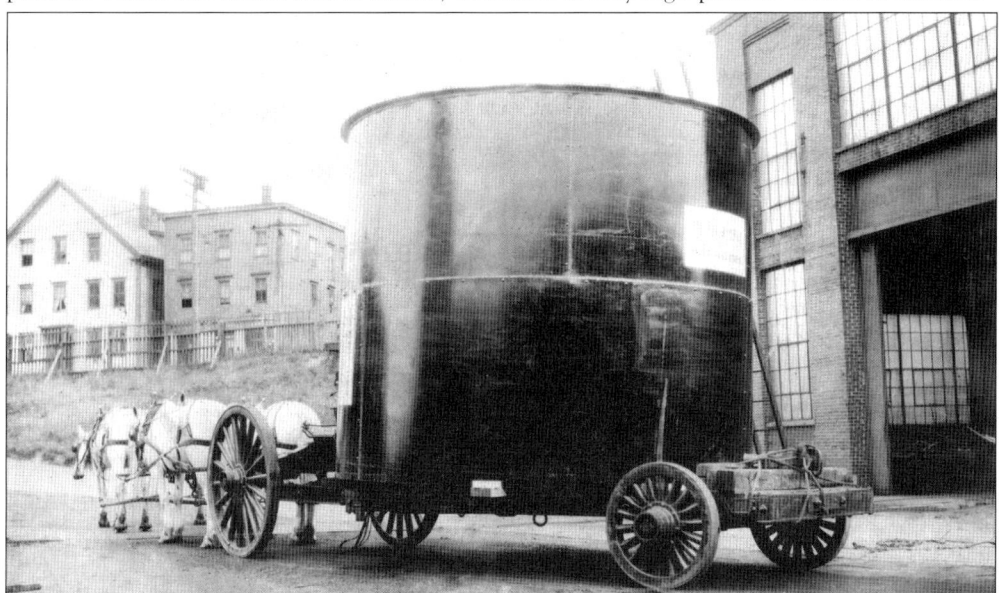

Shown is an early stock tank bound for the nearby S.D. Warren Paper Company mill in Westbrook. Horse transportation was used to move these large tanks and boilers overland to nearby destinations.

125

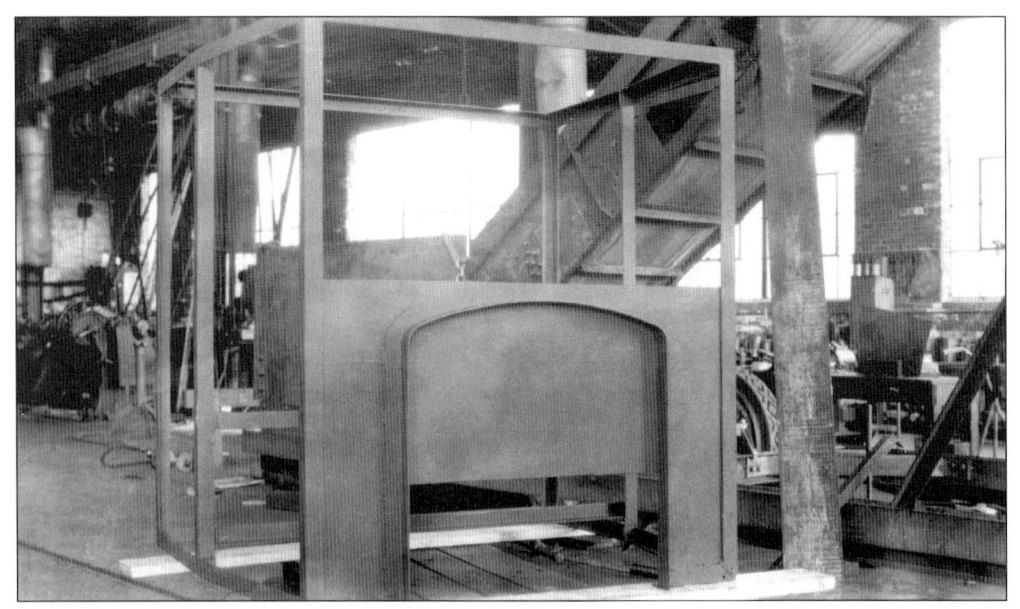

The cab frame for a Lombard Tractor & Truck Company truck is being fabricated here in the Portland Company shop.

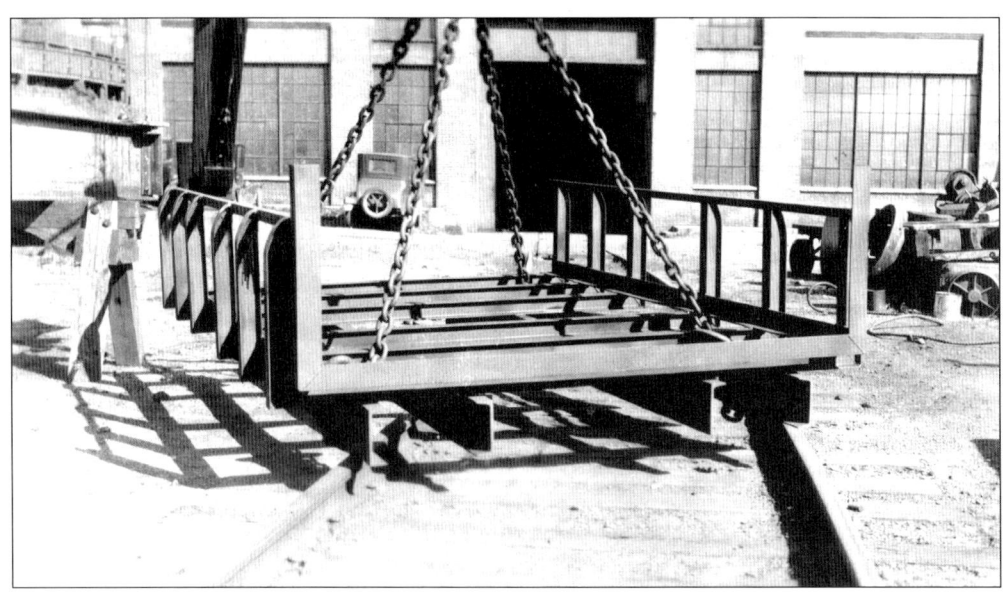

Here we see a heavy-duty truck frame being fabricated in the shops for the Lombard Tractor & Truck Company. In earlier days, Lombard was known for its steam-powered log haulers, which pulled long logs out of the woods to yards or railroad sidings.

Pictured is a wood match–making machine that the company produced for the Diamond Match Company.

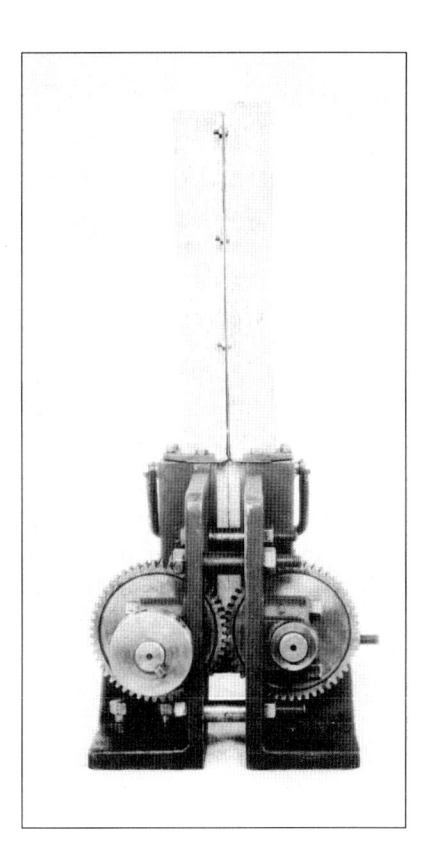

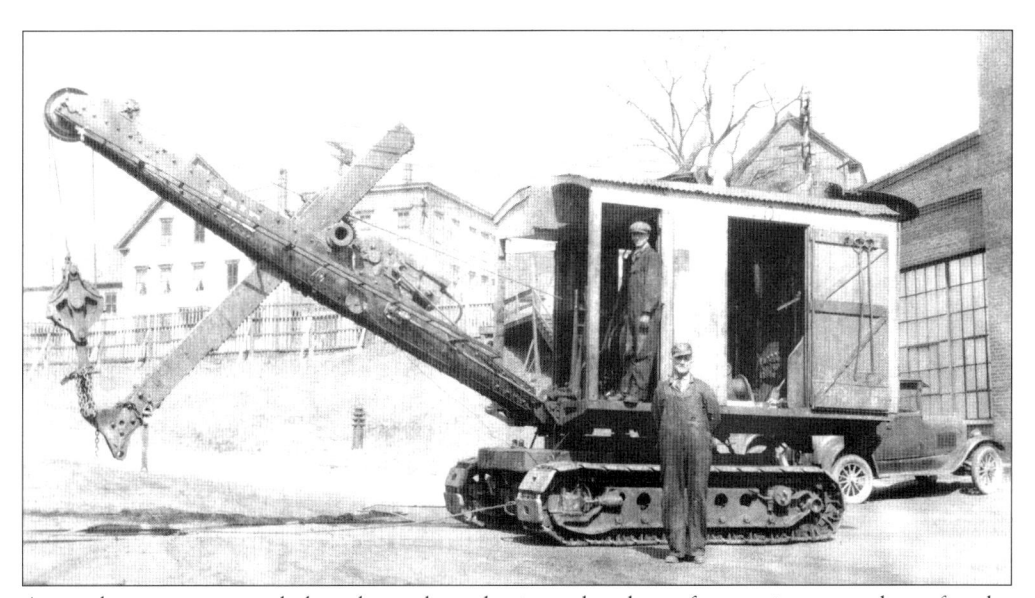

An early steam-powered shovel was brought into the shops for repairs, or perhaps for the fabrication of a new boiler or shovel bucket.

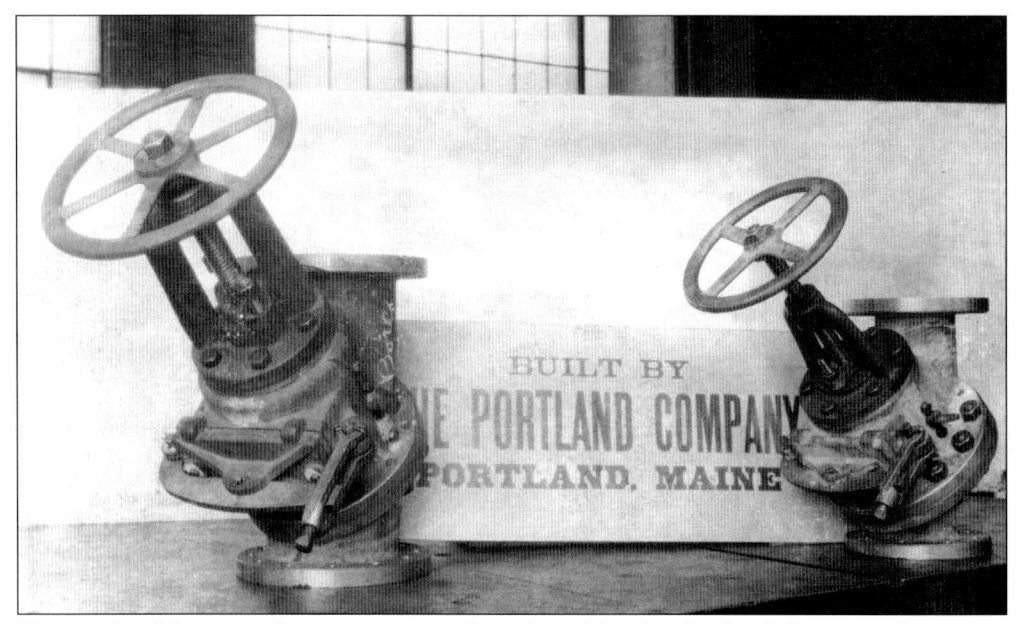

Thousands of bronze valves were cast and machined by the Portland Company for use on marine vessels and machinery. The company had, in addition to the iron foundry, a large brass and bronze foundry.

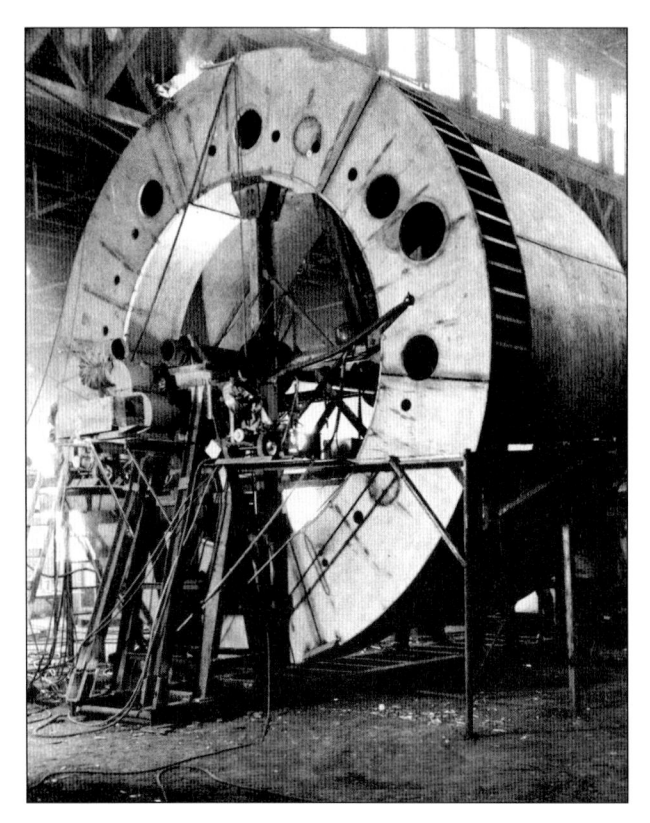

In later years, the Portland Company made parts for rotary-welding the insides of pipes for the nuclear power plants along with neutron reactor shells, such as the one shown here. The company also made many types of plastic-forming and extruding machinery for bottles and other plastic products.